THE DOWNFALL OF CAPITALISM AND COMMUNISM:
Can Capitalism Be Saved?

BOOKS BY RAVI BATRA

Studies in The Pure Theory of International Trade

Theory of International Trade Under Uncertainty

The Great Depression of 1990

Surviving the Great Depression of 1990

The Downfall of CAPITALISM & COMMUNISM

Can Capitalism Be Saved?

DR. RAVI BATRA

First Edition published in 1978
by MacMillan Press, London

Second Edition published in 1990 by

VENUS BOOKS
5518 Dyer Street, Suite 3
Dallas, Texas 75206

Published by Venus Books
             5518 Dyer Street, Suite 3
             Dallas, Texas 75206

Distributed by Taylor Publishing Company
               1550 West Mockingbird Lane
               Dallas, Texas 75235

This is a revised edition of the work originally published by Macmillan Press Ltd., London in 1978 under the title: The Downfall of Capitalism and Communism: A New Study of History

Library of Congress Cataloging-in-Publication Data

Batra, Raveendra N.
    The downfall of capitalism and communism : can capitalism be saved? / by Ravi Batra, — Rev. ed.
        p.   cm.
    Includes bibliographical references, index.
    ISBN 0-939352-09-5 : $19.95
    1. Civilization—Philosophy. 2. Capitalism.
3. Communism and culture. I. Title.
CB19.B294   1990
901—dc20   90-30562
                                                CIP

Printed in the United States of America

10 9 8 7 6 5 4 3 2

THE BIGGER THE GOAL, THE BIGGER THE OBSTACLE
THE BIGGER THE OBSTACLE, THE BIGGER THE ACHIEVEMENT
SO BLAME THE FAILURE NOT ON OBSTACLES
BUT ON THE ABSENCE OF RELENTLESS EFFORT

To Sujata

Contents

Preface

Few questions have fascinated the modern historian more than the mystique of the rise and fall of civilizations. Within a span of one hundred years three path-breaking studies—by Marx, Spengler, and Toynbee—have appeared, made their mark on the academic profession, but are now considered incomplete or seriously deficient. Their dogmas, which once caused much intellectual ferment, have undergone careful scrutiny by critics, and have now fallen into disfavor. It is not that they have been forgotten, for in their thought there is much that will endure forever, only that few today concede their claims of universal validity. Their method of analysis, namely the method of historical determinism wherein the scholar attempts to detect a pattern in the quagmire of historical events, is now regarded by some as an idea buried so deep in the grave that it can never come to life again.

It is this dead idea that I am trying to revive. What converts me from a student of economics to one of history is a fascinating new theory by an Indian scholar, P. R. Sarkar, who synthesizes many of the available theories of civilizations into one ecumenical law of social cycle. His analysis not only expounds the dynamics of past history, but also abounds in predictive content. Unfortunately, this prodigious work, written in Bengali a little after Toynbee completed his monumental *Study of History* in 1954, has not yet been transmitted to the world at large. Sarkar's philosophy of history, to my mind, is more general than any the world has yet seen; it is an answer to all the pointed darts that the critics, for good reason, have hurled at popular dogmas of historical determinism.

The purpose of this book is threefold: first, to introduce

13

Sarkar's doctrine to the world; second, to subject it to the empirical testing from past human experience embodied in three variegated civilizations—Western, Russian, and Hindu—which are selected for their diversity and uniqueness of expression; third, to draw inferences for the future of India, Russia, and the Western world. Despite the fact that these civilizations have evolved along very different tracks, I find that Sarkar's theory fully explains their evolution. That is what lends credence to my predictions concerning capitalism, communism, and democracy. I raise and answer the following questions that matter today:

1. What is the future of capitalism and communism?
2. Are they going to dissolve—if so, when and why?
3. What will be the philosophy of life guiding the world in the next generation?

The questions I raise have been raised by others before, but the answers I give are completely different, somewhat unsettling, but also reassuring. In the world we inhabit today, in the tensions in which we live and breathe, in the complex international problems which we must solve to survive, it is important that such epochal questions be raised and answered. The world today is polarized into a loose tripartite alliance of capitalist, communist, and under-developed nations. All systems are facing internal fissures and external traumas. There is brutal inequity in the distribution of wealth within and among all nations, while millions of people go undernourished and even starve to death year after year.

The world today suffers from a potentially crippling energy crisis, environmental pollution, population explosion, and a host of other tumors. The basic cause of all these ills, I find, is the ultra-selfish materialism of the ruling cliques in all, not just a few, countries: the philosophy of life guiding the world today is rooted in pure self-interest. This is a malaise that cannot last long, and Sarkar's thesis tells us why. It tells us where we are headed. It tells us that if the present ruling classes fail to curb their egocentricity and materialism, soon many countries will be caught in the throes of revolutionary and violent turmoil. This is the submission of this book to the world, and I sincerely hope that it will not go unheeded.

The organization of the book is as follows: the first three chapters deal with introductory remarks and Sarkar's law of social cycle. The next three chapters are devoted to testing Sarkar's theory in terms of the three societies mentioned above. The final three chapters take up the question of the future of capitalism, communism, and democracy. Whenever a source is cited in any chapter, it is first indicated by a numeral in a square-bracket in the main text, and then listed at the end of the chapter.

A work of the kind I have attempted has creditors of many hues and disciplines, and the present volume is no exception. I owe my greatest intellectual debt to P. R. Sarkar whose monumental work lies at the heart of my investigation. It is my good fortune that I have been among the first to come across his contribution of which there are numerous tributaries. For Sarkar has ventured not just into the mysteries of history but also into the arena of psychology, sociology, criminology, economics, and social philosophy, among many others. The present book only makes use of his contribution to the philosophy of history, for it is beyond my ability to do justice to his genius in one volume.

Among others who have been contributory to this work, I am grateful to Prasanta Pattanaik, Satish Kohli and Thomas Fomby for reading the manuscript in entirety and offering useful suggestions; to Glenn Linden, Daniel Orlovsky, Dhangoo Ghista, Rajendra Gupta, William Russell, Jagdish Upadhyay and Aman Ullah for going through earlier drafts of various chapters. Needless to say, their generous help does not implicate them in any of my errors.

I am also indebted to Southern Methodist University for providing me a tranquil workplace and a University Fellowship that enabled me to devote many working hours to my writing. Speedy and accurate typing by Gloria Jones, Carolyn Simmons, Elaine Brack, and Jessie Smith must get credit for easing my burden in checking various chapters.

Dallas, Texas   RAVI BATRA
July 1977

1

Introduction

I wrote *The Downfall of Capitalism and Communism* in 1977 to stir the public conscience against cruelties of the two economic systems prevailing today, and Macmillan Press published it in England the following year. The cruelties of communism were obvious to an objective eye, but those of capitalism had long been masked behind a veil of affluence and glitter of the wealthy few.

Throughout its history communism had repressed its people, feeding them false hopes, lies, and propaganda that the state existed and worked only for their well-being. In reality the state had existed behind an iron curtain that insulated its subjects from truth about other nations. Basic freedoms such as the freedom of speech, of the press, of assembly, taken for granted in other societies, were lacking in the Marxist countries. Although most were provided the basic necessities of life, the general living standard under communism paled before that of advanced capitalist nations. No wonder that many communist citizens had tried to escape to the West, risking their lives.

While the tyrannies of communism were glaring to the free people, those of capitalism were generally swept under the rug, especially in the United States. America had long enjoyed one of the highest living standards in the world, yet within its borders there was (and is) plenty of inequality and deprivation. Millions of Americans subsisted below the official poverty line, while millions more were unemployed and suffered from the ravages of inflation. Even among the employed, there were millions without

17

health insurance in a country that had seen the fastest growth in health costs in recent years.

It is true that communism was and is far more oppressive than capitalism. But tell that to a jobless American or one without any health insurance at all; tell that to the afflicted elderly thrown out of a hospital because they cannot afford to pay their doctor's bill. The hungry and the dying couldn't care less about which system is less cruel.

I had written this book to give hope to the downtrodden. From a careful analysis of history I had come to conclude that both systems were going to fade away by the year 2010, give or take a decade.

First published in England in 1978, the book attracted some attention from the British media and critics, but in the United States it was completely ignored. The American distributor of the book sent review copies to many newspapers, radio and television media, but none cared to even mention my unorthodox work.

What an irony. In 1989, the same media that had summarily discounted my work vied with each other for eloquence and immediacy to describe the collapse of the Berlin Wall and Marxist regimes. The U.S. intelligentsia overwhelmingly declared the communist turmoil as not only the top story of the year but of the 80s' decade as well. Yet when my work had reached their desks in 1978, they had regarded my prophecy of communism's downfall as mere fantasy, and brusquely brushed it aside.

I had argued that the contradictions of Marxism would force it to crumble under its own weight around the year 2000, a forecast that I repeated in *The Great Depression of 1990*. But blinded by years of communist lies and propaganda and unwilling to shed their jaundiced views, the American intellectuals totally ignored my pleas. To be sure, some American and European writers such as Karl Marx, Arnold Toynbee, and Robert Heilbroner had indeed foreseen the doom of capitalism, but hardly anyone was ready to write communism off. My words fell on deaf ears. Few believed me in 1978 and few believed me until November 9, 1989—the day the Berlin Wall came tumbling down.

The American intellectuals, as with most intellectuals in general, were unwilling to accept or even explore new ideas. How myopic were they, though? What a huge price this country has paid by heeding their mistaken and misinformed beliefs. In the 1980s, America spent an extra trillion dollars on defense to fight communism, amassing a huge debt in the process, only to belatedly discover that the foe had been perched upon a shaky foundation all this time. In hindsight, the defense buildup turned out to be a colossal blunder, and the government's policymakers and their supporters at least owe an explanation to the public for the monumental waste of resources.

I had done my duty, informing the public and the government about the inevitable collapse of communism, but no one listened, and now the country is sinking in a vast ocean of debt that was at least partially avoidable.

At the time of this writing, January 1990, one half of my prophecy—the downfall of communism—is already beginning to unfold. The other half, the downfall of capitalism, is yet to begin. But it is not too far off. Capitalism will begin to collapse in 1992 or 1993 and both systems will disappear in the next 15 years.

The time is now ripe for a second edition of this book that few have heard about. Even though it is tempting to make some editorial changes to the text, I have made very few alterations to the first edition. This is because I hate to be accused of rewriting my predictions, though the changes would be slight. All I have done is added a new chapter at the end; translated the Sanskrit terms in the previous edition to English in this one; eliminated a chapter on ancient Egyptian history, and relegated a largely technical and difficult chapter into an appendix.

Any change in my views since 1977 is indicated in the new chapter, where I also examine the question: can capitalism be salvaged? My answer is yes: it can be saved if we eliminate the influence of money from politics, but not otherwise. I also describe the mental and spiritual preparation that everyone must undergo to face the social, economic, and political turbulence of the 1990s. While reading the chapters on prophecies, remember that they were written in 1977. Many things have changed since then, but you will find that most of them were predicted in this book.

Time and again I have been accused of making far-fetched predictions. My dear readers, yes my forecasts are indeed far-fetched, but that does not mean they are wrong. At any rate, what's the point in forecasting the obvious?—something many of my critics love to do. So read with heart and don't ignore my warning that capitalism, like communism, is soon going to die. From the ashes of the two systems will arise a new compassionate and wonderful system, the likes of which our planet has never seen.[1]

NOTES

1. Although a summary of some ideas in this book appeared in my subsequent work, *The Great Depression of 1990,* I have left them intact here so that you may get a complete picture of the philosophy that enabled me to make a variety of bold forecasts, in 1977, about the world's future.

2

Sarkar's Theory of Social Cycle

Prabhat Ranjan Sarkar is a man of profound learning, and a leading Indian philosopher. Since 1955 he has written numerous books and articles providing penetrating insights into spiritual philosophy, historical change, and pressing economic and social issues which have engaged prominent minds of all ages.[1] The bulk of his prodigious work has been in Bengali, and although it has recently been translated into English, outside India it is largely unknown. Let us first examine his theory of social cycle, which expounds a civilization in terms of a sequence of certain eras.

In generality and breadth, Sarkar's theory surpasses all others espoused before, including the contributions by such celebrities as Marx, Toynbee, and Spengler. In a short, simple and yet decisive discourse, it sets to rest, once and for all, the paroxysm of heated criticism that has previously greeted the hypotheses of historical determinism.

CHARACTERISTICS OF THE HUMAN MIND

Every author with a new and deep message to convey introduces his own terms, concepts, and definitions. In this respect, Sarkar is no exception. Even where he borrows a bit from the stock of already known ideas, especially those of Marx and Toynbee, his exposition is novel and original.

Sarkar's thought is based on a simple and yet deep perception. It begins with the fact that society is basically composed of four types of people, each with a different frame of mind. Some by nature are warriors, some intellectuals; some are capitalists and some laborers. This way there are four broad groups or classes in a community. Thus Sarkar differs sharply from Marx and other socialists who define classes on economic grounds—on the basis of income and wealth. Sarkar, of course, does not neglect the economic aspect, but to him it is only one of the four aspects that describe the totality of society. Class divisions, in his view, exist, and have existed ever since the genesis of Civilization, because of inherent differences in human nature.

The four types of people mentioned above do not, of course, cover the full range of society. There are many gradations among the stated groups. Among laborers, for instance, some are highly skilled and some unskilled. Similarly, capitalists did not exist in the past in several societies. In order to provide class definitions independent of time and space, Sarkar goes deep into human behavior and commences with the fundamentals—with characteristics of the mind which he classifies into four distinct categories. That is why every society basically comprises only four types of people, whom he groups into laborers, warriors, intellectuals, and acquisitors.

To a scholar of Hindu civilization, these groups relate either to the caste system still lingering in India or, as in ancient times, to one's occupation. But to Sarkar they convey an altogether different meaning and significance: they simply reflect four types of mind, each manifesting itself in nothing else but one's deeds, thinking, and outlook towards life. Of course, given the freedom of choice, the mental makeup is also reflected in one's occupation. Therefore in the case of society's privileged classes, which are usually free to make such a choice, the profession is a true gauge of their mentality.

By a laborer, Sarkar means a physical worker whose mind is dominated by the environment surrounding it. A laborer's mind is not as intelligent as the other types. The laborer fails to do anything subtle or intellectual, for it is ruled by materialistic thoughts which run parallel to the waves of matter. Sarkar believes that every entity in this universe emits certain waves and vibrations which the naked eye cannot perceive. The waves of laborers are similar to those of matter, and therefore a physical worker cannot subjugate material forces or the physical environment in which he or she resides.

Unskilled workers, peasants, and serfs generally belong, or have in the past belonged, to the laborer class. Exceptions, of course, may be discerned in all these occupations. Some peasants or farm-workers may be persons of keen intelligence, or there may be other physical workers who perform hard labor not by choice but under social oppression. Such persons are not, of course, laborers.

Similarly, in virtually all societies in the past, slavery was a common institution and slaves were forced to do the servile, physical work. But in no way does it mean that the slaves were laborers. A laborer is simply one who performs physical labor either by choice, or because he or she is unable to acquire technical skills. Even though imbued with physical strength, laborers lack the initiative, ambition and drive to subdue matter or to succeed in the world.

The mind that is moved by the spirit of subduing matter is the warrior mind. "To make a slave of matter," says Sarkar, "is the wont of a warrior" [1, p. 14]. Thus, a warrior is one who loves adventure, is full of courage and high-spiritedness, has natural curiosity to learn new ways, and applies his physical strength and skills to solve his problems. Since the warrior's intellect is subtler (more intelligent) than the laborer's intellect, the warrior makes the worker do a considerable amount of his work.

Of the three divisions of time—past, present and future—a laborer abides only in the present, whereas the martial mind abides in the past as well as the present. A warrior does not just live; he wants to live with dignity and self-esteem. Those endowed with superlative martial qualities want to leave their mark on history, to seek eternity through their exploits. The warrior class is usually composed of army officers, skilled workers, adventurers, professional athletes, etc.—anyone who struggles to solve the problems through a direct fight or through physical prowess.

An intellectual's mind is one that is more prone to scholarly pursuits than the warrior mind. Like the warrior, the intellectual too wants to subjugate matter, he too strives to make the environment conducive to his living, but, unlike the warrior who wrestles material forces with heroism and physical skills, the intellectual uses his intellectual forte to attain the comforts of life. The scholarly mind is subtler than the martial mind; hence in social interactions as well as in politics, the intellectual eventually comes to sway the warrior. Thus the ambitious intellectuals, lacking in the martial endowments of virility and fearlessness, endeavor to dominate society by controlling the warrior mind and through it the laborer.

In Sarkar's words, "the warrior wants to bring matter under his subjection by a direct fight and the intellectual wants to keep the warrior, the conqueror of matter, under his own subjection through the battle of wits" [1, p. 36]. Thus, a warrior's behavior is straight and simple, not difficult to read, but the intellectuals usually approach a problem in a roundabout way. They devise theories, cults, and dogmas to confuse the warrior and take advantage of his straightforwardness.

Priests, scribes, poets, scientists, lawyers, physicians, teachers and the like constitute this group. Most intellectuals keep aloof from politics and earn a living by dint of their intellectual caliber; but those seeking high social status and political power attain them by prevailing upon the martial mind. Thus, whenever the intellectuals rule, they rule by winning over the warriors, who alone are physically and mentally equipped to maintain order in society.

Finally, we come to an acquisitor's mind. Most people want enjoyment from material things, but the acquisitive mind also has a penchant for their accumulation. In fact, acquisitors, according to Sarkar, "are more partial to possession than to the enjoyment from material objects—want to feel peace in the mind thinking of them or feasting upon them with their eyes" [1, p. 101]. Of the three intervals of time, the acquisitive mind frets constantly about the future and seeks to amass wealth for a rainy day. At some point in time, the affluent acquisitor comes to dominate the other three groups by purchasing their services with his opulence. In other words, accumulation of wealth is the lever through which the acquisitor seeks not only the comforts of life and the security of the future, but also prestige and dominion in society.

Money-lenders, merchants, feudal lords, and capitalists belong to the acquisitive class. Not all the rich people engage in politics, but those interested in it usually rise in society by hiring the intellectuals. However, since warriors can be controlled by intellectuals and laborers by warriors, so at some point in time all non-acquisitive classes readily submit to men of fortune—to those abounding in acquisitive mentality.

Let me illustrate the difference in the four mental types through a simple example. If a problem crops up, a laborer may ignore it or postpone the solution as long as possible. A warrior, by contrast, faces it head on, uses his physical prowess, and does not rest until the resolution is in sight. An intellectual applies his intellect, but, if that does not work, either requests help from a warrior, or attempts to win him over through persuasive arguments. Finally, an acquisitor tackles the problem by pouring down his money to hire intellectuals, warriors, and laborers. This illustration does not cover all cases, but gives a pretty good idea of the different attitudes with which men and women in general lead their lives.[2]

Wherever civilization developed, in Africa, Asia, Europe, or anywhere else, a careful examination of history reveals this four-pronged division of society. Sarkar calls it the "quadri-divisional social system." His categories of mind are broad enough to cover the full range of a mature society. Thus every civilization, which is what we call a mature society, is composed of four sections, each comprising people reflecting the predominance of a certain type of mind. Ordinarily, individual behavior displays two, or even all, of the four attitudes, but, for the most part and especially under duress, only one mentality betrays its true colors.

There is a bit of acquisitive instinct in each and every one of us, but only a few constantly long for money and make it the *summum bonum* of life. We are all after a comfortable living standard and social prestige, but some of us attempt to attain them through physical strength and skills, some through intellectual pursuits and excellence, and some by ceaselessly saving money or making more money with money already at hand. In this order, we are warriors, intellectuals, and acquisitors. Those of us imbued with little ambition or drive, wanting in basic education and skills of the time are the laborers.

It is worth noting that Sarkar's division of society into four different groups is very flexible. Social mobility among the groups may occur if an individual's mental characteristics change over time. Through concerted effort or through prolonged contact with others, a person may move into the realm of the other class. For example, a laborer, under the command of a warrior, may become a genuine soldier, or through vigorous education he or she may become an intellectual, and so on. Similarly an intellectual, through contact with money, may turn into an acquisitor, or an acquisitor into a laborer. Thus even though class distinctions in society, according to Sarkar, derive from differences in human nature, they may or may not be hereditary.

THE THEORY OF SOCIAL CYCLE

Having described the four types of people in society, I am now in a position to state Sarkar's theory of social cycle. In accordance with his quadri-divisional social system, he argues that a society evolves over time in terms of four distinct eras. Sometimes warriors, sometimes intellectuals, and sometimes acquisitors dominate the social and political system. Laborers never hold the reins, but at times the ruling class becomes so self-centered and decadent that for a while society may have to languish through disorder which, as he contends, marks the laboring times. Thus no single group can exercise social supremacy and power forever.

What is more interesting, as well as intriguing, is that the movement of society from one epoch to another follows a clear-cut pattern. Specifically, in the development of every civilization, ancient or modern, oriental or occidental,

the laborer era is to be followed by the warrior era, the warrior era
by the intellectual era and the intellectual era by the acquisitive era,
culminating in a social revolution—such a social evolution is the
infallible Law of Nature. [1, p. 40]

This is Sarkar's law of social cycle. Note the word "evolution."
This law of nature is "infallible" because it is based on evolutionary principle. Just as human evolution from animal life is indisputable, just as the onward march of humanity up the evolutionary
ladder cannot be arrested, so is this movement of social cycle an
inevitable natural phenomenon, whereby social hegemony shifts
from one section of society to another, from the collectivity of one
type of mind to another. Thus underneath the seemingly haphaz-
ard change in society lies the invisible but unmistakable imprint of
certain laws of nature: social evolution goes hand in hand with
human evolution.

It is in such apocalyptic terms that Sarkar conveys his message. To him society is a dynamic entity, and perpetual change is
its essence. A civilization emerges with the advent of the martial
era, and, after considerable ups and downs through intellectual,
acquisitive and laborer eras, it goes back to the martial age, only to
resume its evolutionary march in step with the same old rhythm.
This, in short, is Sarkar's social cycle.

Why must society go through these changes? Why must it
move in cycles and not in a straight line? Sarkar argues that the
dynamics of every mundane entity—singular, or collective such as
society—is systaltic; that is to say, just like the heart-motion its
movement is characterized by alternate flow of systole and dias-
tole—ups and downs. The systolic aspect of every movement is
simply an expression of its progressive state, at the culmination of
which it reverts to its retrogressive or diastolic phase.

The reason why every relative movement is systaltic is that
its source of inspiration is the state of motionlessness, which to
Sarkar defines not a static state but a state of equilibrium and
poise: it is from motionlessness that every activity springs, and it is
back towards motionlessness that every activity proceeds. For instance, suppose that the equilibrium of an entity is disturbed by
some extraneous force. Then this deviation from equilibrium and

the corresponding agitation of that entity constitutes its diastolic phase. If during that phase it still has some vitality left, there begins its systolic phase marked by a reverse movement. The entity, which may have been transfigured in the process, then goes back towards equilibrium or towards what may be called a steady state. Depending on its momentum, it may evolve during the systolic phase with a far greater inspiration than ever before. However, if during the disequilibrium or diastolic phase, no reverse movement occurs, the entity meets its death.

Thus all relative movements are pulsatory. They may perish before or after the completion of a full cycle or, depending upon the innate strength, may indefinitely move along a cyclical path marked by alternate currents of diastoles and systoles. Uninterrupted, unidirectional flow of any entity is impossible.

A civilization also is a relative movement. It also like every action has a certain velocity along which society evolves at a much faster rate than a primitive community—one that according to Toynbee [2] fails to offer adequate response to the challenges of life. Being relative movements, civilizations are also systaltic; they too are subject to the phenomenon of cyclical variations that Sarkar's social eras represent.

What then is the laborer era? The society of laborers is one that suffers from complete lack of guidance, leadership, and authority; one where the so-called leaders become so egocentric that the majority of people, following in their footsteps, display laboring mentality, a mentality ruled by instinctive behavior and pure self-concern. The laborer era is then characterized by anarchy, by a lack of social order. There the family ties are not binding; people scoff at higher values and finer things of life; religious behavior, if any, is born out of fear of the unknown; morals are extremely loose, crime is rampant, and materialism permeates society to the core.

People of laboring propensities exist at all places and in all civilizations, but it is only when society lacks all purpose and the ruling class oppresses the masses to the maximum that the laborer era begins. The state or government may exist in the laborer era, but its dominion is not respected. And in any case the laborers, despite their majority, do not control the government. The important point is that the laborer era arises because of the self-conceit of dominant groups who care nothing for how their actions affect others.

The martial era, in terms of the political and social structure, is diametrically opposite to the laborer era where, as stated above, laborers are in the majority but the government, if any, is controlled by a different group of people. In the martial age, the warriors, though not necessarily in the majority, dominate society as well as the government. There the political authority is extremely centralized, people are highly disciplined, family ties are morally binding, social prestige through physical prowess and feats is earnestly sought, the religious behavior of people reflects the common warrior desire for victory over crude matter, and so on. Intellectuals and acquisitors enjoy some respect in the warrior era, although they have little say in governance. But laborers perform physical labor for the warrior, and in the closing stage of this period, as in that of every other era, they are mercilessly exploited. However, at the dawn of the martial era, the ruler respects their contribution and treats them with care and compassion.

The intellectual era is marked by the rise of priests and secular intellectuals, though here again the ruling class does not have to have a numerical superiority. Many new theories dealing with various aspects of life are then born. Although most scholars are interested mainly in pursuing their worldly careers, a few, through earnest yearning, come to attain a beatific experience transcending the mind. It is through them that the ideal of prayer to God for love alone was born. Whereas in the beginning of the warrior era strong, benign leadership comes from persons of physical might, in the intellectual era it comes from selfless intellectuals and a few rare, enlightened beings. Unscrupulous intellectuals, however, exploit warriors and laborers in the name of these sages who themselves had tamed all infirmities. Near the end of the intellectual age this exploitation becomes oppressive.

The acquisitive era bears close resemblance with the final stages of the intellectual era where, as mentioned above, warriors and laborers are heavily exploited. The scholars, however, are no longer at the helm of the polity; rather they work for the affluent class which foists a highly decentralized regime on the community. It is in the acquisitive era that the inherent or practical value of things is reduced literally to zero. Everything is valued in terms of dollars and pennies. Human values begin to recede. Art, music, religion, sports, everything is commercialized. Crime flourishes, family ties again become loose, and gradually the acquisitive age heads toward the lawlessness of the laborer age. At the end of the acquisitive era, all non-acquisitive groups are remorselessly exploited by the acquisitors. Society then passes through a period, which may be very brief, of the laborer age, only to be engulfed in a social revolution, following which it resumes its march in terms of another martial era, and so on.

THE DYNAMICS OF SOCIAL CHANGE

Sarkar's law of social cycle states that power and influence shift from one group to another in accordance with the phenomenon of systaltic motion. Several questions naturally come to mind. First, is the transition from one era to another smooth and peaceful or is it violent and marked by convulsions? Second, how do stages of progress and decline behave within each era? Is the rise or fall during an era unimpeded, or is it subject to cyclical oscillations as well?

Let me consider the second question first, for my response to it will determine the answer to the broader question of transition from one age to another. If the movement of every entity is pulsatory, then within each era also the steady ascent or descent of a group's fortune is impossible. Each action or each movement has a certain wavelength that some may call life. For instance, the social cycle has a vastly greater wavelength or life than the social dynamics within a certain age, but all relative movements, whether short or long, even the tiniest ones, are systaltic. That is why one discovers so often that all activities, social, political, cultural, and economic, are subject to cycles. Therefore even within a particular era of civilization, both the rise and fall of a group are marked by cyclical variations. It is for this reason that some historical events appear to be repetitive. Even each person's life, with a far shorter wavelength than a social era, is subject to ups and downs.

In order to explain the vicissitudes in any era, Sarkar introduces his concepts of social evolution and revolution. He defines them in terms of the rate of change or the momentum that ushers in a new epoch in society.

Social evolution occurs when, through gradual changes over a long period of time, society moves from one era to the succeeding era; that is, from the warrior era to the intellectual era and so on. Here the social system evolves sluggishly and the change from one system to the other does not deeply touch the masses; it benefits a privileged few who come to dominate the new government, while, in comparison, the common people benefit only slightly.

The reverse of social evolution is "counter-evolution" which takes place when, in contradiction to the law of social cycle, one era reverts to the preceding era; that is, the acquisitive era recedes to the intellectual era, and the intellectual era to the warrior era. Being in violation of the evolutionary principle of the social cycle, "counter-evolution" has a relatively short span of life.[3]

Sometimes the transfer of power between sections is abrupt, swift, and tumultuous. If it conforms with the social cycle, there occurs a social revolution; if it conflicts with it, the event is called "counter-revolution." Social revolution is usually accompanied by a totally new way of life for those in power as well as for the masses. It may or may not be beneficial to everyone in society, and need not be productive of violence and bloodshed; but it culminates in the replacement of old ideas by ideas that meet imperatives of the time.

In fact, Sarkar's social revolution is synonymous with a sudden introduction of new ideas even if no parallel change occurs in the governing body. Thus any event, violent or not, that shocks the polity into some drastic surgery of age-old traditions and institutions may be called revolutionary. For example, the diminution of the King's powers and prerogatives by the British parliament in 1688, even though peaceful, was a momentous event that can be easily hailed as a social revolution. On the other hand, countless revolts and uprisings that occurred in the past but left no visible imprints on the future cannot be called social revolutions even though they were violent, and, at times, accompanied by changes in government.

The converse of social revolution is "counter-revolution," which usually involves a violent reversal of the social cycle and has a shorter life than even "counter-evolution." Both counter-evolution and counter-revolution usually occur as an era nears its end.

The transformations in society through partial episodes of social and counter-evolutions (or revolutions) may occur numerous times before a particular era gives way to the succeeding era. Society grows at a faster pace when a benevolent ruler leads the masses, who usually emulate their leaders. A careful study of the rise and fall of civilizations reveals that this is what generally happens at the outset of each era, especially the warrior age. The rate of evolution in society is accelerated by what Toynbee [2] calls "social mimesis" of creative personalities, whereby the great bulk of uncreative people follow in the footsteps of the creative few. But the prerequisite for what we may call positive social mimesis is that the ruler either patronizes the creative minority or is a creative person himself. Whatever the reason, the first half of every social era, except the laborer age, is usually distinguished by impressive social, economic, artistic, and humanitarian achievements.

In time, however, the reigning class loses its benevolence and degenerates into what Toynbee calls a "dominating minority," which no longer commands the natural allegiance of its people, culminating in a social reaction against the official oppression. Why this degradation occurs, why the once effulgent flower of humanity withers into decay need not bother us at this point. What matters here is the universally observed phenomenon that such is the fate of all mundane entities, of all relative movements, of all facets of a civilization.

The oppression of the domineering class—which fails to abdicate the supremacy it once merited but has now ceased to deserve—creates a powerful clash in the minds of the oppressed, the victims of the dominant minority. As a result, those enduring persecution evolve at a faster rate than the ruling clique. Their children, living with memories of the tyranny which their fathers had to suffer, turn into inveterate foes of the ruling class. As tyranny grows, so does their resolve to fight, until one day, equipped with superior character and mind, they wrest power from their rulers. If such transformation occurs abruptly, and gets firmly established, then the event in Sarkar's terms is a social revolution. If it occurs gradually and after a long time of oppression, then it is social evolution.

Those who proclaim the new era, the new leaders, having been raised in suffering and deprivation, are once again magnanimous of heart. Under their guidance, society resumes its forward march of evolution at accelerated speed. This is the systolic phase that springs from the benevolence of leaders, from the creativeness of the creative minority. On the other hand, the diastolic phase of society arises from the depravity of the ruling faction.

This is the process that manifests itself time and again in the course of societal evolution from the martial era to the intellectual era and then to the acquisitive era. Whereas in all phases of civilization society consists of four broad sections, at the end of the acquisitive era only two remain: acquisitors and laborers— warriors and intellectuals having been reduced to laborer's poverty by acquisitors' rapacity. In the initial stages of the acquisitive era, warriors and intellectuals fail to see through the acquisitor's exploitation, and willingly provide services to make a living. For a while, the entire social order works to prop the acquisitive dominance. The acquisitors, however, return this loyalty not with gratitude but with a crescendo of exploitation. Under their acquisitive impulse, they keep on amassing wealth. But material resources available to society are limited, with the result that the wealthy acquisitors grow richer and richer only at the expense of other classes.

The acquisitive mind is averse to sharing wealth with others unless, of course, that sharing appears profitable. As more and more wealth ends up in the acquisitive coffers, the living standard of the other three classes progressively declines, and there comes a time when society degenerates into two classes—the haves and the have-nots. So strong is the power of want and hunger that the distinctive features of the warrior and intellectual mind succumb to the compulsions of survival. It is during such dark days of high exploitation that the laborer era is born. The boundless acquisitive greed eventually invites the revolt of the masses who are led by the very warriors and intellectuals—now diminished to the laborer's level of poverty—who had once received the acquisitive system with open arms.

Sarkar calls this revolution the laborer revolution, one that occurs in the terminal phase of the acquisitive era, contributes towards its demise and is brought about by disgruntled warriors and intellectuals.[4] The label laborer revolution reflects not the fact that it is engineered by laborers, who are generally unable to lead, but the fact that it is masterminded by those reduced, under the incubus of acquisitors' avarice, to the laborer level of living. The terminal phase of the acquisitive age may be called the laborer age or the acquisitive-cum-laborer age, because laborers are then in stark majority with acquisitors still at the helm. Few warriors and intellectuals then remain, for, forced by the acquisitor's rapacity to devote all their time to make a living, they are unable to pursue activities of adventure and art, activities that interest warrior and intellectual minds.

It is at such times that the laborer revolution occurs, and acquisitors are swept aside: the limitless acquisitor's greed ultimately becomes its own nemesis. In the ensuing polity, which may arise immediately or after a brief interlude of adjustment, power reverts to the warriors and social evolution starts all over again. In this manner, one era will always be followed by another.

Note that in every age other than the acquisitive era, the transfer of power may occur through social evolution or revolution, but the acquisitive era positively ends up in a social revolution of the laborers. This rotation of societal dominance round the hub of warriors, intellectuals, and acquisitors culminating in the laborer revolution is Sarkar's law of social cycle. In his view some countries today are in the decadent phase of the warrior age; at places the intellectual era is about to be established, whereas in many democratic countries the acquisitive period is in vogue.[5]

There remains the question of whether a civilization can perish before going through the full range of the social cycle. The answer is yes. If during the diastolic phase of any era, no new leaders emerge, no dynamic personalities appear, that societal era may die under the weight of the dominant minority. Civilization may then revert to the laborer anarchy perpetuated either by dominant natives or by the emergence of what Toynbee calls *Volkerwanderung,* which is a German word for "barbarian invasions." Thus the period of transition from one era to another is perilous for the fate of civilization. It can mean the difference between prolonged life or death, between civilized or primitive existence. Once having reverted to the laborer era—which can last for several centuries—if that decadent society wakes up again, temporarily or permanently, it will start anew its course of evolution through the martial era to the intellectual era, and so on.

NOTES

1. All the English translations of Sarkar's work are available from Proutist Universal, 1354 Montague Street, NW, Washington, D.C. 20011.

2. The categories of mind presented above have been defined for men, but they apply equally to women. Unfortunately, the English grammar as well as most other languages have so evolved that no author can write anything doing justice to both men and women. The neutral pronouns describing man are automatically taken to hold for woman as well. This attitude, this male superiority complex is not a part of the natural order as most believe, but a relic of the past intellectual dominion over disparate societies. As the present work slowly unfolds to the reader, the truth of this statement will become manifestly clear.

3. In Chapter 4, which deals with Western civilization, some events of counter-evolution are pointed out.

4. On this definition, few of the well-known revolutions—such as the Glorious Revolution in England, the French Revolution of 1789, and the Bolshevik Revolution in Russia—qualify as the laborer revolution, for, as argued in subsequent chapters, they did not occur at the end of acquisitive eras. On the other hand, the rise of Henry VII in England, Chandragupta Maury's revolt against the Greeks and Dhana Nanda in India, etc., turn out to be those events that helped terminate various acquisitive periods.

5. In terms of the theory of social cycle, Russia and China today are prime examples of the warrior age, whereas Western and Indian (Hindu-Muslim) societies are passing through their acquisitive phase. Even though India and the West have little cultural and economic affinity, both are under the sway of the acquisitive mentality.

REFERENCES

[1] Sarkar, P. R., *The Human Society, Part II* (Denver: Ananda Marga Press, 1967).

[2] Toynbee, A. J., *A Study of History, Vol. I* (London: Oxford Economic Press, 1948).

3

Class Attitudes and Human Exploitation

By now I have introduced the reader to Sarkar's theory of social cycle and the four social classes upon which it is based. The theory simply states that of the four groups—warriors, intellectuals, acquisitors, and laborers—the first three take turns in exercising political power and social supremacy in any civilization, the fourth being uninterested in attaining prominence. I have also examined some features distinguishing the rule of one class from that of the other.

Let us now explore some intriguing corollaries that follow from Sarkar's main hypothesis explaining the change in society, including questions ranging from women's rights and human exploitation to the evolution of institutions. For instance, Sarkar explains how social attitudes towards feminism vary from one era to another, how the intellectuals play their tricks in all eras, how they connive with the acquisitors to perpetrate an unprecedented social exploitation during the acquisitive age, how they have been responsible for women's plight all over the world, and so on. What is interesting about these corollaries is that one way or another they all relate to the mental frame of the ruling class.

THE LABORER ERA

We already know that a person of laborer mentality lacks initiative and is not as intelligent as persons belonging to other groups.

Laborers do not take the lead in society. For these reasons, all laborer societies in ancient times were primitive, and remained primitive until some warriors emerged and wrested leadership into their own hands.

What distinguishes a civilization from a primitive community has for some time been a matter of controversy among historians. Sarkar's division of society into four classes in accordance with their mental characteristics, however, suggests a straightforward definition. Using his concepts, a primitive society is one where all its members display laboring characteristics, so that it has little chance of growing out of the chasm of illiterate, ignorant, and savage existence. The rise of civilizations may then be ascribed to the rise of persons with non-laboring disposition, especially those endowed with martial qualities.

One way to differentiate between laborers and other groups is to look at their levels of literacy. In general, literary attainment is highest among intellectuals and lowest among laborers, with warriors and acquisitors standing somewhere in the middle. In many societies in the past, only churchmen, who were intellectuals, had the ability to read and write. The access to education was then considered a privilege of which the laboring peasants, serfs, and unskilled workers were totally deprived. Today educational facilities are available to all, yet the physical laborers are relatively the least educated. The schooling of warriors and acquisitors is difficult to compare, but the intellectuals clearly excel other groups in this regard.

Of one issue there is little doubt. The early history of humankind, the prehistoric or the Paleolithic period—covering the times of *Homo habilis* to the Java man, to the Neanderthal man and finally to our immediate ancestor, the Cro-Magnon man—belongs to the laborer era. Sarkar describes this epoch with great acumen:

> At the embryonic stage of the human race, when human bearing or Man-ness had first moulded itself out of animality, the then people also, like the people of today, had found only two paths open to them—the path of a laborer, and the path of triumphing over matter and mind through the thought of subtlety, i.e., the path of a warrior. In those days they had to be so preoccupied with material thoughts

due to their being in the midst of hostile environments of nature that they all had to remain involved with the laborer's thoughts. [3, p. 10]

The genesis of the laborer era may be traced back to 1,750,000 B.C. when the Paleolithic men are supposed to have evolved enough from apes to perform what archaeologists and historians call astonishing feats. There is some evidence that the Neanderthal and Cro-Magnon men, who lived in caves, had begun to cook their food and bury their dead. Group life, which is traceable to the lower Paleolithic culture, had become more regular and organized with the advent of Cro-Magnon men. Their supreme achievement, however, is in art (especially painting), which throws ample light on what is known as the upper Paleolithic culture.

Although group life had been established during the Paleolithic age, the essentials of an organized society were still absent. The institution of marriage and family life was yet to evolve. Men and women lived together not in a morally and legally binding relationship, but purely because of biological attraction to each other. They felt little love for their own children, much less for their fellow beings. Each powerful man had several concubines: being feebler than men, women had to accept an inferior status. Since there was no government, there was no law and order; there was anarchy, with everyone preoccupied with self-preservation.

Today, over the aeons, we have all evolved to an extent that our relapse to the prehistoric culture, to that savage existence is inconceivable. Can we then say that humanity cannot now degenerate into the laborer era? The answer is no.

Everything in this world is relative, changing with respect to time and place. A laborer society today would be similar in some respects to its counterpart in ancient times, but it cannot be exactly the same; that would be negating the fruits of millions of years of natural evolution. The laborer mind is now much more intelligent than it was at the birth of human consciousness; no longer need it be passive in the absolute sense. A laborer today is one with low initiative and drive relative to the other types of people. And for this reason, in all countries the laborer class is exploited as much today as in the past. Its toil is still indispensable to the survival of any society, but ruling classes are taking advantage of it everywhere in the world.

The distinctive feature of a laborer society today would be the flagrant disregard of governmental authority and law by its dominant members. Thus, unlike the Paleolithic age, government may exist in contemporary laborer society, but its command would not be respected; violent crime would become rampant, with people living in fear. In ancient times there were no family ties worth the name. Today, by the same token, the lack of family bonds would be reflected in the indiscipline of children or their disrespect for parental authority, in frequent divorces and other intrafamily feuds, in the heartless abandonment of the elderly. Women had a lowly status in the distant past; in today's laborer society, such inferiority would be manifested in ubiquitous prostitution as well as in the general subservience of women to men.

In short, if all, or most, of these characteristics permeate a society, it is unmistakably languishing through the laborer age. A close scrutiny of history reveals that all civilizations, including those now alive, occasionally had to pass through the pangs of laborer periods. There were times when they were shaken by internal fissures or external assaults. Actually the difference between the extinct and existing civilizations is simply that some societies were crushed by the laboring times, whereas others came out of them to resume their forward march of evolution. In subsequent chapters that examine some extant civilizations, I will point to those tumultuous years when the laborer era briefly prevailed, but was overcome by the spirited people.

THE WARRIOR ERA

In most respects the martial age, where persons of warrior disposition rule, stands out in sharp contrast to the laborer age; and for this the acute difference between the laborer and warrior mentality is chiefly responsible. Laborers, though physically strong, lack the enterprising and adventurous spirit of the warriors, who use their physical prowess to advance in life, to excel within their circle. It is the warrior spirit that enabled Columbus to discover

America, Robert Peary to reach the North Pole, Edmund Hilary, and Tenzing to climb Mount Everest. Propelled by the same spirit, the Russians launched a Sputnik and the Americans set their footprints on the moon.

A warrior believes in physical discipline, in firm authority over his family. However, when a warrior comes to power, his family extends to the entire people living in his domain. Therefore a warrior ruler believes in authoritarian government, in absolutism. That is why martial eras have always been characterized by political centralization, by the unimpeachable divine right of kings, monarchs, and dictators.

Going back to ancient times, it may be seen that the warrior era began with the Neolithic period or the New Stone Age, which seems to have been established by 3000 B.C., although in Egypt it had arrived as early as 5000 B.C. The Neolithic age is marked by the beginning of agriculture and by the domestication of animals. This is the period when men and women began to live out of caves to attain a better mastery over environment than their forefathers. What else but a warrior spirit could have inspired them to go out without fear and look for dependable sources of food? In the words of Burns and Ralph, "whereas all the men who had lived heretofore were mere food-gatherers, Neolithic man was a *food-producer*" [1, p. 13].

Another distinct feature of this period is the rise of institutions, for which a highly organized group and social life is essential. The origin of state may also be ascribed to this period, in which the discovery of agriculture and the subsequent population explosion made social organization indispensable to survival.

Political scientists commonly cite various reasons to account for statehood. It could have derived from war activities undertaken for conquest or defense against foreign invasion; from the natural expansion and clash of group life; or from early religion, involving witchcraft whereby the magicians and witch doctors, though lacking in physical force, came to rule their people.

According to Sarkar, however, the sovereign state can be traced mainly to the rise of some powerful men, endowed with warrior disposition and superior physical force, who chose not to be cowed by nature. Those who fought their environment with some success must have inspired laborers with awe and admiration. In the laborer epoch of yore, there were no institutions of family, state, and property. Warriors emerged from what Sarkar calls "the socio-psychic transmutation" of laborers under the stress of physical and mental clash generated by the hostility of natural surroundings.

When the laborers organized under the emblem of a warrior, social evolution, in Sarkar's view, occurred in human history for the first time. In this way, several groups and tribes, each led and commanded by a warrior, came into being. A few clans might have been established under the suzerainty of the intellectual magicians and medicine men, but they were soon engulfed by tribes led by the high-spirited warriors.

Although traces of Neolithic culture can be observed in places even today, it is supposed to have ended when metal was discovered. In Egypt it terminated as early as 4000 B.C., and in Europe by 2000 B.C. [1]. In most other parts of the world, where primitive societies were replaced by ancient civilizations, the Neolithic epoch came to an end around 3000 B.C. However, the warrior era seems to have continued with few interruptions, although, in accordance with the general human evolution, its anatomy underwent drastic surgery. In order to distinguish the earliest warrior epoch of a society from the later ones, a distinction important to ancient civilizations, the Neolithic period may be called the rudimentary warrior age.

In the immediate post-Neolithic age, the warrior era is represented by the supremacy of royalties—kings, emperors, monarchs, dictators. The ancient Egypt, the Rig-Vedic age in India, ancient Greece, ancient Rome, the centralized national monarchies, and many communist and underdeveloped countries today (1977) are prime examples of societies belonging to the warrior era.

In the martial age, the sense of discipline, first in the family and then in society, is extremely strong and for this reason women enjoy a high social status, at least relative to the way they are treated by society in other eras. In the Neolithic period, many different tribes were led by muscular warriors. Being constantly at war with each other, they soon discovered the importance of numerical strength. Fast growth of population thus became their common objective, an objective in which women were at least equal partners. On this account, and to maintain the purity of blood, brave and daring women were honored as Group Mothers in Neolithic times. Thus early warrior society was governed by a matriarch who provided lineal identity to every man and woman belonging to a particular clan.

The institution of marriage first emerged in the rudimentary warrior age. In the laborer era there was hardly any marital life. Once the laborers united under the banner of warriors, and woman's contribution towards procreation received recognition, men and women began to feel a certain sense of bond in their conjugal relations. At the same time, the father came to have a sense of duty and responsibility towards his offspring. Consequently, woman's burden in raising children declined to an extent, and with this began the decline in her social status as well.

Gradually families began to be dominated by men who were also the bread-winners. In time, Matriarchy gave way to Patriarchy wherein the tribal head was a man, and in which descent was reckoned in his name. How long the Group Mothers dominated society cannot be easily ascertained, but it appears that the patriarchy had emerged before the end of the Neolithic times. As women's influence declined, men began to have many wives toward the close of the rudimentary warrior age.

The warrior art also reflected a certain type of mind. A warrior by nature is courageous and fearless. This mentality found expression in the deification of lions and elephants, animals that are masters of jungles, and embody fearlessness and might. The lion and elephant heads that one finds on human torsos of stone belonging to ancient Egypt and India are simply manifestations of manliness and valor. Phallus-worship that prevailed in many warrior societies of yore also reflects their need for growth of population, a need arising from incessant tribal warfare.

In martial societies, the contribution of laborers was by no means insignificant. Laborers themselves were incapable of subjugating matter; but once inspired by the warriors, they too plunged into the task of subjecting the natural environment. In return, the warriors provided them with patronage and protection. The early martial societies thus benefited a great deal from the ruler's benevolence. In fact, we will later find that in every civilization the benevolent phase of a new warrior age exceeded all that society had achieved during the preceding intellectual and acquisitive eras: most, if not all, Golden Ages in the past occurred during warrior periods.

During Paleolithic times also, there were frequent fights among the laborers, but they were actuated solely by self-preservation. In the warrior era, however, warriors, and their soldiers recruited from the ranks of the laborers, warred for their own survival as well as that of others. Whereas laborers had fought for food and shelter, the army officers fought for dignity and self-esteem as well. In due time, however, the warrior rulers became more authoritarian; they lost much of their early benevolence, and as a result the laboring soldiers and laborers were mercilessly exploited. The warrior domains also expanded manifold; many tribes were unified after protracted warfare into vast kingdoms headed by monarchs and emperors. In the holocausts that the warriors unleashed on each other, laborers were the helpless participants. And for what? For the momentary ego-gratification of the megalomaniac warrior who craved supremacy over the entire world.

In most warrior societies, sanguinary wars of conquest portended the end of warrior domination and the birth of intellectual influence. As we shall see in subsequent chapters, at the end of the warrior era, intellectuals in the guise of the priest or the prime minister came to power in every civilization.[1]

THE INTELLECTUAL ERA

Despotic governments of the warriors were fundamentally unstable, for nothing based on fire and sword can command obedience from the people forever. The absolute rulers had felt the need for theories that could pander to higher sensibilities of their subjects; they had needed dogmas that could minister to passions and prejudices of their people. In this they were ably assisted by those endowed with superior intellect—the intellectuals. To pursue their own careers, the intellectuals volunteered theories that justified the ruler's absolute authority over his people. Thus were born such concepts as the infallibility of monarchs and the divine right of kings. Poets and playwrights came forward to sing panegyrics about the ruler's performance in battles and wars—even in romance.

That is why, in the heyday of the martial age the intellectuals enjoyed a social status second only to the warriors. Therefore when the martial influence waned as a result of their myriad wars, the power and leadership vacuum could be filled only by the intellectuals who alone commanded enough esteem and authority at the time. Everywhere do we find that the intellectuals came to power in the aftermath of the carnage that the warrior warfare had so copiously handed down to posterity. In the West, for instance, the Catholic Church rose to primacy after the fall of the warrior Roman Empire.

The intellectual mind has been defined as one that lacks the gallantry of the warriors but abounds in foresight and keenness of intellect. In general an intellectual is cautious and pragmatic; he or she relishes comfort but not the physical labor that it requires. Actually his or her constitution is not built for this purpose. Consequently, the intellectuals attain dominion only by vanquishing the warriors in the intellectual arena. They rule indirectly— through their control over the apparent warrior ruler who alone has the physical and mental prowess to keep order in society.

Whenever, and wherever, the intellectuals perceived that the time for their rule had come, they devised new cults and dogmas rationalizing their hold on the people. First they managed to convince the warrior of the possibility of his perdition after death, and then concocted rituals so complex that the bewildered warrior earnestly sought their religious service. This the intellectuals were more than glad to provide in exchange, of course, for political sway and creature comforts.

After outwitting the warriors, the intellectuals set out to inject baseless fears and prejudices in other sections as well. Once the apparent warrior ruler was won over, it was just a matter of time before the rest of society yielded to their self-serving doctrines. Thus we find that in every civilization all nonintellectual groups were once caught in the stranglehold of religious tenets and practices.

One of the most remarkable features of the intellectual age, as mentioned earlier, is the indirect rule of the intellectual ruler. The apparent or direct ruler is a mere puppet in the hands of advisers who pull all the strings. For this reason, the intellectual groups enjoy the best of all worlds: in case of victory, the glory is theirs; in case of defeat, the blemish falls on the warriors. The structure of government and administrative machinery in the intellectual era changes little from that prevailing in the warrior age, except that now, because of the weakness of the apparent ruler, the real authority is exercised by someone behind the scenes. Yet the intellectuals need the warriors to maintain their dominion over the general public, and, therefore, the intellectual polity is somewhat decentralized in comparison to the warrior regime: the apparent ruler is no longer absolute, nor is the indirect ruler.

Digging deep into the pages of history, one discovers that at times the intellectuals ruled as priests, at others as elected representatives of the people. In any case their rule was indirect, in the name of a figurehead—the king. At times the intellectual primacy can be ascribed to their control over the church, at others to their gifts of oratory and erudition. During the Middle Ages, for instance, many kings and princes were overshadowed by the Pope, heading the Catholic Church. Similarly, in England, following the Glorious Revolution of 1688, the king had to play second fiddle to his prime minister. History abounds in such examples. Thus, according to Sarkar, whenever the intellectual assets of a group enable it to dominate society, usually in the name of an apparent ruler, the intellectual era prevails.

Because of their intellect, the intellectuals in general contribute greatly to the finer aspects of life. The intellectual epoch, especially that run by the prime minister rather than the priest, is distinguished by its outstanding achievements in music, art, dance, and literature—anything that derives from subtler intellect rather than crude force. Subjecting the despotism of warriors, of monarchs and emperors to a sacred and inviolable authority is a singular contribution of the intellectual age. In the final days of warrior eras, the once benevolent warriors had turned into ruthless rulers, preying, in tune with passing fancy, upon their hapless denizens. Only the intellectuals could tame their caprice and despotism. In order to consolidate their hold on government, the scholars had to invent theories that paved the way for their indirect rule; in so doing they contributed unwittingly to the birth of the rule of law and constitutional forms of government. The political apparatus was, therefore, not as totalitarian as before; it was characterized by some degree of decentralization.

Of course, the martial kings resented their loss of real power; they did not give in so easily. That is why during the intellectual age, as well as during the subsequent acquisitive age when the intellectuals ran the government in the interest of the wealthy, one comes across frequent episodes pitting the king against the priest. The history of medieval Europe abounds in events of confrontation between the intellectual Pope and the warrior king, between ecclesiastical and secular authorities. At times the kings were even successful in overthrowing the priestly yoke, in ushering counter-evolutionary events, but they were of short duration—merely last-ditch efforts of warriors to cast off the noose of the intellectuals.

While the above-mentioned legacy of the intellectuals to humanity, despite their motives, is commendable, their real and eternal contribution lies elsewhere—in what they did to spread the lofty ideals of universalism. The intellectuals have the caliber for abstract contemplation which other groups do not.

Human thirst for happiness is unquenchable. We all want more and more from life; seldom are we satisfied with what we have. The reason is that our hunger for pleasure and beatitude is boundless—is infinite. However, this unlimited thirst for enjoyment cannot be quenched by material objects, which themselves are limited. Something which is limited cannot be the source of limitless joy. Thus there is a fundamental contradiction between what we really want and what we run after. We seek infinite happiness, but are obsessed with earthly objects, which, being all finite, yield only momentary pleasure.

This fundamental anomaly can be appreciated only by a superior intellect, which the intellectuals alone are fortunate to possess. That penetrating faculty which can perceive reality behind the false veneer of limited existence belongs only to the intellectual mind. Therefore some intellectuals, through intense longing and search for truth, come to attain illumination in their hearts. To be sure, very few persons have ever attained these dizzying heights, but such sages have emerged in the past and will emerge in the future. Indeed, without them the cosmic ideas of universalism and brotherly love would never have been born.

The most important bequest of intellectual eras to humanity then lies in spreading the cosmopolitan ideas of these sages who proclaimed spiritual ideals without compromising with narrowness and bigotry. However, some of their followers subsequently contrived useless rituals merely to perpetuate their own dominion over society. The sages had donated invaluable pearls, the charlatans reduced these pearls to fanatic religion; the sages had preached the sermon of God's love and mercy, the impostors proceeded to spread it by unleashing carnage on the unfaithful. And this happened not just at one place, not just in one country, but in all civilizations.

The history of warriors was written by the pen of blood. There were chivalry and valor in it, but no wisdom and sagacity. The intellectual age, on the other hand, was marked by appalling perfidy as well as gruesome warfare which—unlike the martial period where wars gave vent to personal ambition—was rooted mainly in rabid religious fanaticism. Sarkar describes all this with a vivacity so characteristic of his work:

> Going through the pages of history we find that all the crusades or jehads of the Medieval Age were engineered by these intellectual Satans. Entrapped in these intrigues, the laborers took the beatings as helpless victims and the warriors fought as crusading heroes. [1, p. 42]

The reign of intellectuals emitted nothing but rank hypocrisy. Knowing that logical reasoning was no gateway to luxury, they concocted rigid social rules which nobody could escape. Of course, all this was done in the name of some enlightened sage who, even after corporeal death, commanded esteem and reverence from the common man. On paper, and in congregations, they proclaimed lofty ideals, but in reality their lives smacked of debauchery and corruption.

Acknowledging the priest as a messenger of some sage, the common people held him in high regard. They readily handed over their labor, daughters, and wealth to religious quacks who were always the "reluctant" beneficiaries. And in case any greedy heretic had the temerity to withhold his donations or question their conduct, the priests were ever ready to put a curse on the gullible man. In order to mask their intentions, they even declared their views to be infallible. The irony of it all is that the masses trusted them, and in places continue to trust them today.

The early warrior period, as noted before, was marked by Matriarchy, a social order in which Group Mothers had dominated; this was followed by Patriarchy in which the male head of the tribe became supreme; and finally came the absolute monarchs and emperors. Due to the warriors' innate magnanimity, women continued to enjoy a respectable social status. Throughout the rudimentary warrior era she was regarded as man's co-helper, commanding sufficient, if not equal, social prestige.

In the intellectual era, however, women came to be regarded as inherently inferior to man. In the warrior era, at least in its first half, the warrior's manliness enabled him to treat women, despite physical weakness, on a more or less equal footing with men. An intellectual, however, lacks the warrior courage, and consequently is always wary of insubordination by other groups. He has to be, lest the muscular warriors and laborers see through the ruse of his shaky dogmas and cast him aside. Thus an intellectual, in order to rule, will always endeavor to subjugate other groups, much less allow them equal rights. It is therefore ironic, and pitiable, that, with his probing intellect, an intellectual can either soar to dizzying heights of enlightenment, or stoop low enough to keep his fellow-beings choked in the noose of superstition and servility.

After besting the warriors in the theological arena, the intellectual men proceeded to bind women as well in the web of theories; and in this case, the web was even tighter than that binding non-intellectual males. Women were denied access to scriptures as well as education in many countries. At some places their subservience to men came close to slavery, whereas at others they were diminished to the status of housewives: the husband was, and in places is, God Almighty to his wife. Today, we find it hard to believe that even in the West, which had supposedly shaken off religious irrationalism after the Middle Ages, women were deprived of suffrage as late as the twentieth century.

True, women have now come a long way in their emancipation from servility to men, but the idea of women as inherently inferior, as property, as playthings of men persists in many parts of the world. Women's humiliation, however, began only with the intellectual era, and if it has endured so long the blame rests squarely with agents of religion. In line with the general doubletalk of intellectuals, in theory the woman was accorded a status equal to the man. She was called "better half" or "fair sex," but in practice the essence of such labels was ruthlessly flouted.

Prostitution as a profession came into being in the intellectual era for the first time. In the laborer as well as warrior times, especially towards the end of the warrior age when men had many wives, some amount of lechery did exist in society. Warriors even went to war over women, but prostitution as an institution had not yet been born. The credit for its genesis goes solely to intellectual men, to the priests who made women totally dependent on men. Without a husband, woman economically became a cripple; prostitution presumably began when widows or some other women could not find husbands, and there was no other recourse.

More important, however, were the priestly coaxing and pressures on virgins to dedicate themselves in the service of temple-gods. This is how the so-called temple-prostitution developed in the ancient communities of Egypt, Greece, and India among others. In Lacroix's vivid words:

As soon as religions had been born, from the fear inspired in the heart of man by sight of the great commotions of nature, as soon as the volcano, the tempest, the thunderbolt, the earthquake and the angry sea had led him to invent gods, prostitution offered herself to those same terrible and implacable deities, and the priest took for himself an offering from which the gods represented would have been unable to profit. . . . Prostitution became, from then on, the essence of certain cults of gods and goddesses who ordained, tolerated or encouraged it. Hence sprang the mysteries of Lampsacus, of Babylon, of Paphos and of Memphis; hence the infamous traffic which was carried on at the gates of temples; hence those monstrous idols with which the virgins of India prostituted themselves; hence the obscene dictatorship which the priests arrogated to themselves under the auspices of their impure divinities. [2, pp. 6–7]

THE ACQUISITIVE ERA

Nothing irrational or illogical can endure forever. The strait jacket in which the intellectuals had cramped the rest of society began to loosen as other sections slowly saw through the facade of their theories. Quite fittingly, and perhaps ironically, some elements within the intellectual class itself began to question the priest's intentions. Not only the elaborate rituals but also the luxury and life-style of the priestly class came under fire. Among scholars themselves there had occurred a good deal of argumentation and doctrinal battles, and those who were thus defeated started accumulating wealth to compensate for their intellectual debility. Similarly, some warriors also followed that route. In this way, another mentality evolved in human beings; another intellect, one obsessed with money—the acquisitive mind.

In the meanwhile, all forms of authoritarianism— monarchic as well as ecclesiastic—had been challenged by certain intellectual reformers. New philosophies of individualism, as opposed to state collectivism, were gradually sinking into public consciousness. Philosophical pillars of the doctrine of divine right of kings as well as of churchmen had been fatally undermined. As a result of all these developments, the power base slowly drifted towards the opulent class—the acquisitors: thus began the acquisitive age.

In all civilizations, the acquisitive class during this period consisted of rich magnates constituting, at different points in time, such diverse groups as landlords, capitalists, and merchants. No longer was it enough to have a keen intellect to attain comforts and political power. Instead, social hegemony passed into the hands of the affluent.

An acquisitor differs from an intellectual mainly in the way he uses his intellect. The intellectual mind, while interested in comfortable living and some material acquisition, is inclined to scholarly pursuits for their own sake; it likes theorizing about any phenomenon. However, the acquisitive mind would have none of this; its intellect is obsessed with amassing, not just enjoying, wealth. It is this mentality that reigns during the acquisitive age. Yet the intellectuality of advisers does not go wasted. They now help the acquisitors stay in power by doing what they do best—devising theories that, in return for some compensation, prop the acquisitive rule. This they accomplish, as always, in a way that lures the gullible—by cloaking their support for acquisitive primacy in the unimpeachable garb of individual rights, liberty, and justice. In reality, however, such lofty principles are flagrantly violated: they are usually observed when it serves the wealthy interests.

Once intellectuals are sold out, warriors and laborers also perform services for the rich. Thus at the birth of the acquisitive age, all nonacquisitive sections willingly submit to the acquisitors who then control the means of production, be they land, factories, or financial capital. Feudalism and capitalism, for instance, are two pointed examples of the acquisitive eras of Western civilization.

Of all forms of government, the one loved by acquisitors is that where the central authority is the weakest. In the warrior era this is impossible. In the intellectual era the central imperium is not so strong, but the rigid social codes that the intellectuals contrive to perpetuate their dominion keep a tight rein on acquisitive minds. That is why one finds that the acquisitive era in every civilization was accompanied by a high degree of decentralized political authority. A centralized system can, if it suits its purpose, force the rich to share their wealth with the poor, and no other class is more aware of this hazard than the acquisitors. Therefore, whenever the affluent hold the reins, the system of government as well as the administrative apparatus are decentralized in the extreme.[2]

One distressing feature of the acquisitive epoch is that the virus of acquisitive mentality eventually infects all sections of society. Attitudes of the ruling class do not spread so much, do not become so pervasive in other eras; but in the age dominated by the affluent, the distinct marks of nonacquisitive groups ultimately succumb to the glitter of pelf. Everything is commercialized as a result—music, art, literature.

Crime also increases drastically. We will find later that a general disregard for the rule of law developed in acquisitive periods: under the coercion of ultra-selfish acquisitive mentality, all sorts of crimes—murders, thefts, muggings, rape—came into vogue in every civilization. Family ties too become loose. At some places, this was reflected in repugnant harems of the noblemen, at others in increased frequency and social tolerance of divorce.

The warrior and intellectual warfare was rooted in ambition or religion. In the acquisitive era, however, warfare stems from the acquisitor's lust for opulence, for land, or for commercial markets. Here economic rivalries, more than anything else, are to blame for sanguinary wars. The struggle to acquire commercial markets for domestic industries, to control raw materials in several underdeveloped countries during colonial times, and similar events all point to the malady of the acquisitive mind, namely the craze to accumulate wealth at all costs—at the cost of compatriots, at the cost of other countries, at the cost of every virtue in life.

The acquisitor's exploitation of society is the most difficult to see through, for in their avaricious designs they are actively assisted by the intellectuals, who continue to excel in government and administration. Some intellectuals, of course, see through the shaky dogmas justifying the acquisitor's control over the means of production; but their feeble protests are drowned in noble maxims offered by the bulk of intellectuals. In early stages of the acquisitive epoch, the rich have some humanity left in them, and the common mass inhales a fresh breath as the rigid hold of the intellectuals becomes loose. But at later stages, the semblance of benevolence evaporates like misty vapor.

Prostitution, which was born in the intellectual era, undergoes a remarkable growth in the acquisitive age. Those who have money to burn are able to corrupt many poverty-stricken women. And once the ruling class casts off its moral scruples, other sections are quick to follow suit. As a consequence, moral degeneration comes to pervade the entire society. This results not only from the lewdness of the rich, but also from the looseness of family ties, excessive stress on individualism, and a general lack of social discipline that springs inevitably from a decentralized political structure.

I have already noted that the acquisitor's mentality eventually comes to infect their subjects. The first to catch this infection are the intellectuals, who learn the art of acquisition quickly from their mentors. Such people may be called intellectual acquisitors. Specifically, such persons are intellectuals whose acquisitive intellect has been aroused through long contact with "genuine" acquisitors—those born with great wealth and excessive acquisitive instinct. Thus an intellectual acquisitor is one who, though born poor, becomes wealthy through the use of high intellect in the acquisition of wealth, whereas a genuine acquisitor is one inheriting huge wealth as well as acquisitive intellect from his parents.

Both types of acquisitors earn large incomes from their control over the means of production, but intellectual acquisitors also make money from their occupations, relying on superior intellect. For instance, during the days of European feudalism, the secular landlords were genuine acquisitors and the religious landlords were intellectual acquisitors. Similarly, today capitalists are genuine acquisitors, whereas those whose affluence derives from their brains as well as the accumulation of wealth are intellectual acquisitors.

This distinction, though minor, is quite significant for determining whether the acquisitive era is in its rising or declining phase. For towards its end, the political apparatus, and hence the entire society, come under the sway of intellectual acquisitors. And it is then that the engine of acquisitive exploitation runs at full speed. Intellectual acquisitors blend the intellectual's penchant for hypocrisy with the excessive greed of the acquisitive mind. It is under their dominion and deception that the acquisitive era gradually drifts towards the scourge of the laborer age. Eventually, as described in the previous chapter, things become so wretched that some disaffected warriors and intellectuals rise in rebellion and help bring an end to the acquisitive, or more properly the acquisitive-cum-laborer, age. Soon afterwards, the rebellious warriors take over and civilization moves afresh on the track of social cycle.

In every era, shadows are commonly cast for the advent of subsequent eras. Many prophets, for instance, were born during warrior periods, but their sublime message later fell into the hands of charlatans, whose new interpretations gave birth to the intellectual eras. Similarly, during the acquisitive epoch a warrior class begins to ascend before the actual eclipse of this age, but the acquisitors unmistakably remain entrenched at the top of the social hierarchy. In addition, and especially towards the end of this era, women begin to reassert themselves, something that foreshadows the improved feminine status in the forthcoming warrior age.

THE TESTING PROCEDURE

Before concluding this chapter, let me say a few words concerning the way I intend to test the theory of social cycle. To illustrate his hypothesis Sarkar sifts a number of pointed events from the immense landscape of the human past, but does not provide a continuum of history in terms of his four eras. Some may object to this method and suggest that it merely clothes the well-known episodes of world history with the garb of new concepts, terminology, and labels.

Perhaps the proper procedure is to explore annals of various societies and see if they can be explained by the four eras in exactly the succession that the law of social cycle determines. Of course, this methodology requires a wealth of information that may not be readily available. For detecting the mentality of the ruling class at various moments of history requires not only data about political events but also about society, the economy, literature, and so on.

Nevertheless, this is a procedure that few can question, and, wherever possible, this is how the hypothesis of social cycle will be subsequently tested in terms of three old or modern civilizations. In the next chapter, I begin with Western society, which sets a rhythmic pattern for the other three.

NOTES

1. Those warriors who had been defeated by other warriors in the struggle for supremacy sought ways to compensate for their inadequate strength and valor. Under the mental anguish and churning they set their brains to work, and there developed in them the intellectual mentality which some of them transmitted to their progeny. This is how the warrior mind evolved to become a more intelligent intellectual mind.

2. In terms of political structure, the acquisitive state may resemble the rudimentary warrior age where small groups of laborers are organized under the command of individual warriors but where no central government exists. Therefore, relative to the rudimentary warrior era, the acquisitor's polity may appear to be centralized. But this is not the proper comparison. In Sarkar's theory, each era is to be compared with the era immediately preceding it. For further details on this point, see Chapter 5 on Hindu civilization.

REFERENCES

[1] Burns, E. M., and P. L. Ralph, *World Civilizations* (New York: W. W. Norton, 1974).
[2] Lacroix, Paul, *History of Prostitution* (New York: Covici, Friede Publishers, 1931).
[3] Sarkar, P. R., *Human Society, Part II* (Denver: Ananda Marga Press, 1967).

4

Western Civilization

Of all living societies, Western civilization is the most pervasive in the world today and has been so for the last two centuries. It used to be said that the sun would never set in the West. Today the sun of the Western empire, which was once so vast and impregnable, shines no more, yet the cultural, linguistic, and institutional legacy of the West to its former colonies is alive and vibrant.

Many scholars begin their study of the West from the Graeco-Roman era, although some go back to the Minoan period and then to the Neolithic age in Europe and the island of Crete. Not all historians agree on this matter, and without judging how far back the Occidental roots can be traced, I take the first century A.D. as a convenient starting point. Western society could have sprouted from the Cretan soil, but this is a controversy I intend to skirt.

THE ROMAN EMPIRE AND THE WARRIOR ERA

By Western civilization I mean that social order which has inherited its laws, culture, and traditions partly from Roman society, a lot from Judaeo-Christian ethics and religion, a good deal from the body of socio-political philosophy first developed in Western Europe and later transplanted to the New World of the North American continent, and more recently from the ideology of capitalism. It excludes Russia, though the latter has long been a European power; it also excludes other continents save Australia, though in these places too the Western influence may have been dominant for several hundred years.

Let us then commence with the Roman Empire, which is distinct from the earlier Roman period called the Republic. At the dawn of the first century A.D., Western society was organized in the Roman state with Augustus, as the *Imperator* (or Emperor), firmly in command of its military machine and of vast European provinces. His word in Europe then swayed the modern nations of Spain, France, Italy and Greece; Britain was not yet within the orbit of the Roman Empire, but before long the Roman military might forced it to join this impressive assembly of nations. Only Germany and some parts of northeastern Europe somehow escaped the Roman colossus, which at one time towered not only over Western Europe but also over many parts of West Asia and North Africa. Later, invading hordes from unoccupied European areas pounced like sharks on the decadent Roman state, and eventually brought it down.

At the turn of the first century, a warrior era can be easily seen to be prevailing in Western civilization. This is the age of absolutism, of despotism masquerading in constitutional attire; the tradition of conquests, long established in Rome, continues unabated. The bulk of the territory constituting the Empire had been conquered by Augustus' predecessors, who lived at a time that historians have designated as the Roman Republic. The celebrated Julius Caesar belongs to those early days.

But conquest is one thing, governing is another. The republican government of the Roman city-state had been a failure; it had precipitated disorder, civil war, economic ruin and moral degradation among the people—conditions quite reminiscent of a laborer revolution following an acquisitive era. It is in this background that the seizure of power by Augustus in 31 B.C. ought to be viewed. The Roman citizens, as well as noncitizens, sick of years of anarchy, then accepted him as a savior of the ship of state, especially when his authority was bolstered by a triumphant army.

On his part, Augustus managed to avert needless affront to their republican consciousness, of which the memory was still fresh and alive. He did not dismantle old institutions and laws, and assumed only the military title of *Imperator* and the innocuous civil title of *Princeps* or first citizen. It is after this title that his rule, along with that of his immediate successors, is often called the Principate; it is a subsection of the Empire.

Even though the old Republican Senate still convened and passed some laws, Augustus was without doubt the unchallenged ruler. As commander of the army and navy, he exercised absolute control in all affairs, be they social, political, or financial. As a result of a long list of powers, which the Senate covertly or overtly delegated to him, the sovereign authority was completely centralized in his person. Here was absolutism masked under the thin veil of the constitutional structure inherited from republican times.

Augustus was an intelligent and benevolent ruler. His reign furnishes another example of how a society in the early warrior era, under the stewardship of a benign martial ruler, forges ahead with fresh vigor and reaches to heights unscaled before. One of Augustus' principal bequests to Western society, and indeed to humanity, is Roman law, of which many tributaries have survived to this day. Roman law affirmed, among other things, that all humans are by nature equal; that they are entitled to certain fundamental rights which no government has the authority to violate; that the accused is innocent until proven guilty.

Augustus' reign was not, of course, the sole contributor to this legal conception, which had actually been evolving for more than four hundred years. But it was during the Principate that ideas of humanism and abstract justice enshrined in Roman law acquired wider acceptance than ever before. Priority was given to the law of nature; it was proclaimed as something transcending the ruler, transcending the state itself. True, not every jurist of the time subscribed to this concept of natural law, yet it came to be regarded as an ideal from which the state decrees ought not deviate too far.

Augustus died in A.D. 14, and few successors could match his acumen and his regard for republican institutions. But they continued to be the absolute rulers; their regimes were marked by tyranny and sanguinary violence. As early as the second half of the first century, the army had gained considerable power in determining succession, and many rulers were military dictators. Despite this, however, unprecedented peace and prosperity prevailed in the Roman state for more than two hundred years. Never in the history of Europe, and perhaps in that of all other nations, have the people enjoyed so long a reign of absolute tranquillity, which could not but yield dividends.

More than ever before, the provinces and the state of which they were parts prospered in terms of culture, architecture, and living comforts. With respect to such achievements, the first two centuries of the Principate are more radiant than any other period of the Roman chronicle. An amazing tribute to the Roman ingenuity of the day has been paid by Rostovtzeff in these words:

> One can say without exaggeration that never in the history of mankind (except during the nineteenth and twentieth centuries in Europe and America) has a large number of people enjoyed so much comfort; and that never, not even in the nineteenth century, did men live in such a surrounding of beautiful buildings and monuments as in the *first two centuries of the Roman Empire.* [13, p. 291]

Elsewhere, writing in 1926 about Roman cities, Rostovtzeff continued in the same vein.

> We may say that as regards comfort, beauty, and hygiene, the cities of the Roman Empire, worthy successors of their Hellenistic parents, were not inferior to many a modern European and American town. [14, p. 135]

These are two incredible statements, but they have flowed from the pen of an eminent authority on socioeconomic conditions in the history of Rome. They simply confirm the view that usually during the early phase of the warrior era the achievements of a civilization surpass much that has been accomplished by it before. And the innate benevolence of the early martial ruler (or rulers) must be at least partly credited for such excellence.

This is not to say that Roman society during the Principate was without its faults. To labor the obvious, no society has reached perfection—yet. Perhaps the most stinging accusation against the

Principate society is its penchant for brutality. Judged by any standard, the then Roman people stand convicted of Philistinic sadism. They patronized bloody games and gladiatorial shows in which armed pugilists, mostly slaves but occasionally free citizens, engaged in life-and-death duels to cheers of a vituperative crowd. Such spectacles were commonplace and were watched by all people, including the Princeps.

Gladiatorial exhibitions had actually been the Roman's heritage from the Republican past, but now their savagery exceeded all bounds. The reason was that the warrior era now prevailed: the innate aggressiveness or the adventurous spirit of a warrior had to seek expression in volatile activities. Since the war activity had considerably declined in the first two centuries, the aggressive spirit had to find an outlet in other ways. And the gladiatorial shows, to which those ruling warriors were heir, offered a convenient diversion and pastime.

What was the status of women in the Principate society? This question is of more than passing interest, because according to Sarkar, women's position in the warrior-dominated society, especially in its early phase, is superior to their position in the preceding as well as the succeeding era. If this view is correct, then women must have enjoyed a better status in the days of the Empire than in those of the Republic. Furthermore, as we proceed along the track of Western civilization, their standing, according to Sarkar's theory, must decline. I will subsequently argue that this is exactly what happened, when Christianity rose to primacy in Western society.

It should be pointed out at the outset that any information pertaining to feminism in the Roman state is fragmentary and should be treated with care. This is especially true of Republican times, for which the evidence, there is reason to believe, has been tinged with the bias and prejudices of Roman scholars. More is known about womanhood in the days of the Empire simply because its records are more recent and plentiful. After issuing such caution, most students of womanhood in the Roman society argue that during the pre-Empire times women as a class were subservient to men. Their life was so miserable that at times they even poisoned their husbands to death; and that, partly because of such retribution, Roman men came to appreciate women's plight, so that gradually, over a few hundred years, most, if not all, restrictions on feminine rights and liberties were lifted. This view, for instance, is embodied in Donaldson's words:

> At the time when Christianity dawned on the world women had attained . . . great freedom, power, and influence in the Roman Empire. Tradition was in favor of restriction, but by a concurrence of circumstances *women had been liberated from the enslaving fetters of the old legal forms,* and they enjoyed freedom of intercourse in society; they walked and drove in the public thoroughfares with veils that did not conceal their faces, they dined in the company of men, they studied literature and philosophy, they took part in political movements, they were allowed to defend their own law cases if they liked, and they helped their husbands in the government of provinces and the writing of books. [5, p. 153 (italics mine)]

These words speak for themselves. It seems that women in the warrior Roman Empire matched, if not exceeded in some respects, the status of modern women in America and Europe. This is a far cry from the Republican days when a Roman man, traditionally given unquestioned authority over his progeny, treated a woman like a child, who would owe obedience first to her father and, after marriage, to her husband. In short, the woman of the Roman Empire was a "liberated" woman, at least relative to what she had been before. To reinforce this view, let me cite Emily Putnam, whose work in annals of womanhood has become a classic. Speaking of the lady as "the female of the favored social class," she describes Roman attitudes towards women in glowing terms.

> At Rome she becomes thoroughly intelligible to us. The society in which she lived there is very similar in essentials to that of our own day. We see the Roman lady helping to evolve a manner of life so familiar now that it is difficult to think it began so relatively late in the history of Europe and is not the way people have always lived. [12, p. viii]

Of course, there are some who dispute such a glowing account of feminism in the Principate society, and Bullough [3, Chapter 4] is one of them. However, what matters here is that women of the Roman Empire had won many legal and social liberties, of which they had been deprived before (and of which, as we shall see, they were to be deprived later). This point, at least, seems to have been established beyond question.

It has already been noted that following the death of Augustus in A.D. 14, the Republican form of government underwent a gradual but steady decline. Augustus had at least permitted some participation of the Senate in administrative affairs; his successors disallowed even that. However, the Senate was not completely ignored until A.D. 284 when Diocletian ascended the throne. Prior to this, the ruler, at least in theory though not in fact, was an emissary of the people who supposedly were born with some rights, but now even that semblance of "responsible" government disappeared. No longer was the Senate consulted in any matter of administration; though not abolished, it was treated as a municipal council or a social club. No longer was the ruler subordinate to natural law; he was the Law; he was the State. No longer were there any Roman citizens; only subjects servile to the divine authority of Diocletian.

Diocletian's accession thus marks a watershed in annals of the Empire, a milestone almost as monumental as the transition from the Republic to the Principate. The main reason for this change lies in the long economic decline that had its beginning in the third century: the people, having lost confidence in themselves, were ready to forfeit for the elusive hope of peace and security all their rights and freedoms. For convenience, the period of the rule by Diocletian and his successors is called the late Empire.

Actually as early as the end of the second century, the Roman polity had begun its march towards dissolution. But it was not before the third century that the symptoms of decay first came to light. Between 235 and 284, the army had wrought havoc in society. The monstrosity of gladiatorial shows had now turned backwards and fallen with uncontrolled fury on heads of Emperors themselves. Men from subjected classes, once victims of ghastly spectacles in the Colosseum, had now joined the army and lent a hand in steering the destiny of the state—if there remained any destiny. The army looted cities; it plundered provinces; it blazed a trail of terror in the heart of society. In short, the rule of brute force bedeviled the then Roman world.

Such was the tumult when Diocletian came to power, and it is hardly surprising that the Romans were ready to forfeit all cherished liberties for some order in life. The despotism, however, could only temporarily arrest the fall of the Roman Empire, whose economic and social threads had already been weakened by the decline in agriculture, population, commerce, and cities.

The first step that Diocletian took in restoring the health of the state was to usurp all power in his own person; his second step was to introduce centralization in the administrative machinery and bring it under his own direct hand. In order to make this system work in so vast an empire, he handed the governance of the western half of the state to a trusted general named Maximian. This division, effected for casual administrative reasons, was to have far-reaching effects on evolution of the Empire. It ratified the gulf that for some time had been separating the thinking of the Latin West and the Greek East. Maximian shared with Diocletian the title of Emperor, and thus was planted a germ that subsequently caused many wars of succession.

Diocletian had ushered in despotism, and his successors continued to reign in the same style. The best known among the latter was Constantine the Great, who is remembered in pages of history for shifting his capital to the eastern site of Byzantium (later known as Constantinople), as well as for his policy of rapprochement with Christianity, of which I will speak in detail in the next section.

The system of government that Diocletian had established continued with slight changes until the fall of the western side of the Empire. In the year 476, Romulus Augustulus, the last Emperor of the West, was overthrown by a barbarian chief who took over the reins of government. It is this event that is commonly supposed to have ended the dominion of Rome; but it was merely the final tip in the long Roman decline. The barbarians had assaulted and plundered Rome before. As early as 378, a Visigoth army had vanquished the once mighty Romans, thereby demolishing the myth of Roman invincibility once and for all.

Few fateful events have invited more obituaries than the fall of Rome; the literature in this respect has been varied as well as voluminous. If there is one culprit to be singled out for the demise of the Roman Empire, then it is militarism. Virtually all its problems sprang from over-aggressive warrior tendencies. The military had come to dominate society as early as A.D. 68, and after the second century all it had accomplished was disorder. The same militarism was responsible for generating such a vast empire, which in the end became so unwieldy and hard to administer.

Whatever the cause, the Roman hegemony over the West came to a definite end in 476, although the eastern half of the Roman empire lingered on well into the Middle Ages. However, as far as Western civilization is concerned the eastern empire, sometimes called the Byzantine Empire, is not of so much significance. Of greater relevance, and immediate concern, is how individual provinces in the western half evolved in the aftermath of the general Roman decline, which to all intents and purposes had begun by the beginning of the third century.

My story now takes a dramatic turn. Instead of harping on the Roman passion for cruelty and aggressive militarism, we must now speak in terms of their opposites; in terms of brotherly love and selfless sacrifice—two weapons that Christianity used in winning over hearts of pagan Romans. It is an amazing story of persecution followed by success, of perseverance rewarded by victory, of glory sinking eventually into degeneration. It is a story of initial martyrdom but ultimate debasement. It is on this that I focus in the next section.

THE CHRISTIAN CHURCH AND THE INTELLECTUAL ERA

The long period of a thousand years that bridges the gulf between the fall of Rome in the fifth century and the modern era of scientific discoveries beginning with the fifteenth, is commonly, but scornfully, called the Medieval Era or the Middle Ages. The term medieval itself has come to signify a dark age, an age of superstitions and intellectual blindness, an age where human beings endured squalor, misery, and a constant fear of perdition after death.

Many historians today regard such a wholesale condemnation of the entire period as erroneous and unfair. Yet there is a grain of truth in the saying that much of the medieval period, especially its first half, was chaotic and backward at least in comparison to its preceding as well as the succeeding age.

Throughout the Middle Ages the influence of religion was predominant; the Christian Church was the one sacred link that provided a common bond for disparate strands of European nations. Living as we do in the present, with our thinking shaped by the modern environment, it is hard for us to envisage the role that the church played in day-to-day affairs, whether religious, political, social, or economic. In Thompson's words:

> The medieval church differed enormously from modern churches, whether catholic or protestant. It exercised everywhere not only spiritual dominion, but great political, administrative, economic and social sway. Its jurisdiction extended over every kingdom in Christendom; it was not only a state within every state, but a super-state as well. [15, p. 647]

How did it all come about? Why was the Church influence during the Middle Ages so pervasive, so potent? To answer these questions, we have to go back in time and examine religious developments during the Roman Empire.

Roman society is not particularly known for its contribution to religion. It had its pagan gods, inherited from epics of Homer and Virgil; it had its temples which were places of homage to Jupiter, Juno, and Minerva; and it had its Emperor who was also its object of worship. But nothing deep did it have; nothing that would quench the thirst of the heart; nothing that would attempt to answer enigmas of the afterlife, enigmas that became all the more captivating during chaotic times of the third century. Having faced disaster and constant insecurity in the present life, men and women became more interested in knowing if there was any life after death, in questions of hell and heaven.

It is to such fertile soil that many new religions—Christianity and other oriental faiths—got transplanted from the East. The new cults had one thing in common: they all addressed themselves to issues that for a while had been besetting the Roman mind; they all offered absolution from sin, immortality for the soul, and something to look forward to in the afterlife.

But Christianity differed from the new pagan religions in many respects. The first and the foremost difference was that while other cults revolved around imaginary figures and legends, Christianity derived inspiration from a spiritual giant, Jesus of Nazareth, who had practiced what he preached, who had gloried in life as well as death, who had preferred crucifixion to compromise with principles. Secondly, it preached monotheism as opposed to the polytheism of other cults. Finally, during the early Empire Christianity had few rituals to speak of, whereas its rivals harbored a multitude of rites, sacraments, and ceremonies.

To harried denizens of Rome elaborate rituals of the new paganism were more appealing than the austere religion of Christ. For this reason as well as the fact that Christianity ran into an early collision with the Roman state, the oriental pagan cults were readily accepted by the Romans. Almost from its birth, Christianity was persecuted by the government, which was alarmed at the former's seditious teachings, barring worship of the Emperor. By A.D. 111 the new religion and its church had become strong enough to arouse the Emperor's ire; and that is when it was banned. No longer was it a legal religion, and its adherents risked severe penalties—death. Enforcement of the ban was left to provincial governors whose attitude alternated between tolerance and hostility.

This policy continued for the next hundred and fifty years during which the march of Christianity was slowed but not blocked; it was hindered but not effaced. Its progress was especially aided by a general decline in the social fiber towards the end of the second century. Its challenge to the state, with the emergence of churches and Christian communities in which it had been organized almost from birth, had grown to menacing levels by the year 250 when Emperor Decius made the first serious attempt to stamp it out of his domain. Many Christians then renounced their faith, while others continued it secretly, and some accepted martyrdom. But persecution cannot destroy anything born out of selfless sacrifice; in the end, the former merely reinforces the latter's resolve and facilitates its spread.

Among the last of the emperors attempting to crush the faith of Christians was Diocletian, but, as with his predecessors, his efforts proved abortive. It was not until Constantine the Great came to power, however, that the official repression gave way to reconciliation and even cooperation. But contrary to popular belief, he did not recognize Christianity as the state religion. This distinctive task fell to the lot of Theodosius I. The triumph of Christianity was then complete. Towards the end of the fourth century, Christians were still in a minority, but their religion had ascended the pedestal of imperial power.

Such is the fascinating history of the rise of Christianity. In Sarkar's nomenclature, its relative movement was created, and given powerful inspiration, by Christ's sublime life; it got an infusion of fresh vigor from the Crucifixion. Having been launched from so sturdy a footing, the lofty teachings of Christ could not but spread far and wide. For several years Christianity went nowhere but up; slowly but surely, it expanded until in the year 111, as noted above, it was banned by the government of Rome.

Thus the relative movement of Christianity was born when Christ began delivering his sermons; that is when it entered into a systolic phase which, with certain vicissitudes, lasted until it was banned by the Roman Emperor; then began its persecution and hence its diastolic phase which, again with ups and downs, continued for more than two hundred years. Any other movement would have been smothered by the systematic official repression; any lesser cult would have crumbled under the weight of the Roman juggernaut. But not Christianity, whose flame continued to flicker amidst rough storms.

In Sarkar's view, if a relative movement refuses to die during its diastolic phase, if its pulse continues to function, then that very movement comes back, and sometimes with vastly greater momentum; it may then climb to peaks never attained before. This is exactly what happened with Christianity, which survived over two centuries of state repression. And when it came back, it did with gusto, rising eventually to no less a status than the official religion of the Roman Empire.

The primacy of a religion, however, does not necessarily signify that its intellectual members have begun to rule; it merely suggests that in the sphere of religious policy, a particular faith has come to dominate other faiths. By no means does it imply the beginning of an intellectual era where intellectuals, by dint of their superior intellect, have the warrior rulers under their control, while, at the same time, the political and administrative system of the apparent ruler becomes relatively decentralized.

When Christianity was recognized by Theodosius as the religion of the state, its triumph over its own heretics, who had been vocal for some time, as well as over other religions, was complete; but it was far from controlling the Emperor. Time, however, was on the side of the intellectuals, for the warrior era, established in the Roman state, had been declining for a long time. Only a few years before the coronation of Christianity, Gothic barbarians had humbled the Roman army and created in the empire an unprecedented situation. Such humiliations were to become commonplace in the fifth century.

The area of modern Germany, it may be recalled, was never annexed to the empire; the northern frontier had always remained a menace to Roman security, a menace that, until the fourth century, had been kept under reasonable control. Because of the general decay, however, this task was becoming increasingly difficult, and in A.D. 376 the German tide could not be stemmed any more. In wave after wave, barbarians from the north crossed the river Danube, settling into the periphery of the Empire; and in the year 378 they trounced the Roman army. To make matters worse, at about the same time, a series of revolts against the Romans erupted in the provinces. All this could not but further weaken the social structure and morale of the Roman society.

The fifth century of Western civilization then opened with a chapter that was soon to be written in blood. The Roman retreat in the West had already started, but the rout had not yet begun. The Romans were still fighting, but it was a rear guard action, designed to delay the catastrophe. The fifth century opens with the western half of the Empire more or less intact, but ends with its disappearance; its place has been taken by a constellation of barbarian kingdoms—Italy under the Ostrogoths, North Africa under the Vandals, Britain under the Anglo-Saxons, Spain under the Visigoths, France under the Burgundians and the Franks.

The interlude, however, saw great upheavals. The fifth century is a century of barbarity at its zenith, of duplicity and treason at best, of plunder, pillage, and famine. However, the Christian Church came out of the ruins with enhanced influence and glory. It is during these turbulent times that the Christian religion gained a firmer foothold in Europe. The Church succeeded, because it provided guidance and shelter to the harried denizens at a time when the Roman Empire was crumbling under the weight of imperialism and of invading marauders who preyed on it from all directions.

In accordance with the law of social cycle, the Church in any case would have inherited power from the decadent Empire, but such succession was hastened by the onslaught of Toynbee's *Völkerwanderung*. Had it not been for the Christian Church, Western society would have found its grave at that time; under the spate of invading hordes, the relative movement which is called Western civilization would have perished, were it not for the tiny breath of life vibrating the budding Church. This is how in the West the intellectual era was born.

Perhaps the driving-force behind the survival and eventual triumph of Christianity was its efficient, compact organization which at first was refreshingly simple. There were churches in various communities, each with a number of elders and bishops whose main function was to preside at congregations and services. However, as Christianity came in touch with oriental paganism, which in the early Empire had fascinated the Roman mind, it felt the need to devise rituals of its own. In time its rituals grew to an extent that full-time priests became all but indispensable to the faithful. This is how rudiments of ecclesiastical organization, subsequently nurtured by intermittent official persecution, came into being. By the end of the third century, Christian communities, each with a bishop as its head, had been organized in almost every city of the Empire.

Still among bishops themselves there was little gradation. It is mainly after Christianity was elevated to the official religion of Rome that the ecclesiastical hierarchy came into existence. Bishops residing in large cities came to outrank those of smaller communities; those with strongholds in the capitals emerged with the highest prestige and esteem.

All these developments culminated in the primacy of the bishop of Rome who, in the fullness of time, was exclusively given the title of Pope (Latin *papa,* or father), although originally this title was given to all bishops. The Roman Catholic Church came to be regarded as the "Mother Church," because the Christians venerated the city of Rome as a place hallowed by visits from Apostles Peter and Paul. The Roman bishop also came to be looked upon as an heir to the imperial authority of Augustus who, it may be recalled, was the founder of the Roman Empire. Peter, regarded as the first bishop of Rome, was believed to be Christ's close disciple, and therefore his successors were held in great reverence.

In the eastern Empire, the bishop of Constantinople, the imperial capital, had triumphed over his rivals, but there the Church remained under the Emperor's control. In the West, on the contrary, successive invasions by barbarians had gradually emaciated the imperial power, to which the Roman Church emerged as a natural heir. Many times in the fifth century, the Emperor went into hiding in the city of Ravenna, leaving Rome at the mercy of ruthless invaders. The Roman bishops, with great equanimity and fortitude, would then take the lead, conduct negotiations with the barbarians, and quite often use their influence to save the city from destruction. The same process was repeated verbatim in other provinces as well. The end result was that bishops in many areas, under the authority of the Pope, assumed vast duties and powers, powers that at one time had belonged to the Emperor and his administration.

Thus it is clear that an intellectual era in the West was born in the middle of the fifth century. During those turbulent times, not only did Christianity remain the official religion, its leadership also came to acquire immense political power and administrative control; nor was this control to prove a fleeting affair, for, within a few years, the barbarians themselves were converted to Christianity. (Actually the conversion of the Visigoths had been begun by Bishop Ulfilas as early as the year 341.)

Furthermore, the barbarian kings proved completely inept in the art of governance, in maintaining peace, in restoring law and order. The complex administrative machine and the tax system that the Roman emperors had taken pains to establish were simply allowed to break down; in their place emerged bishops, dukes and counts with varying degrees of administrative and judicial responsibility, as well as privileges. Old regal cities were allowed to languish in poverty and squalor; in their place emerged small villages and semi-feudal estates.

It has already been mentioned that at the end of the fifth century the western Empire had split into a number of kingdoms, each ruled by a barbarian stock migrating from the northwestern frontier. Of these only two—the Franks and the Anglo-Saxons—were to survive and augment their conquests. Others were absorbed by the superior culture of the conquered people. But although the political and racial identity of the Germanic peoples was thus lost, they affixed their stamp on the linguistic, cultural, economic, and legal developments that were to take place during the medieval period. Hence medieval society was shaped by a fusion between diverse cultures, between the roughness of the victors and the civility of the vanquished, while the Catholic Church applied the healing balm.

During the course of three centuries following the fall of the western Empire, the barbarian kingdoms, through force of arms, were unified by a line of Frankish kings, while much of Spain was absorbed by the Muslim Empire. The first to make a move for this unification was Clovis, who fought many battles to expand his small kingdom, thereby establishing a strong base for the Merovingian dynasty that he founded in 481.

The next century was a witness to brutal civil war and anarchy, out of which emerged three separate kingdoms of Austrasia, Neustria, and Burgundy. These kingdoms were united under the reigns, lasting from 613 to 639, of Choltar II and Dagobert. After them followed a century of weaklings who delegated all authority to their chief ministers, called mayors of the palace; and the king played in the latter's hands like a puppet.

In 751, however, the illusory Merovingian rule ceased altogether, because a mayor named Pepin, with blessings from the Pope, installed himself as the king, thereby founding the Carolingian dynasty. In return for his benediction, the Pope received the territory of central Italy, stretching from Rome to Ravenna. This is how the 'Papal States' were born, which played a great role in the affairs of western Europe in general and of Italy in particular.

In this brief historical sketch of western Europe over four centuries (fifth to eighth), three facts are crystal clear. First, in comparison to the Roman Empire, political authority was now decentralized. Some of the Merovingian kings were strong rulers, some were feeble; some enjoyed absolute authority, while some were figureheads. But in most cases, it is the nobility consisting of bishops, counts, and dukes that reigned in matters of day-to-day administration. During the sixth and seventh centuries, the government was in the hands of mayors who ruled in the name of the king. These are instances of decentralized authority and the *indirect rule* by the aristocracy and the Church.

Secondly, in theory the king was still the absolute ruler, with an unchallenged command over his subjects. In some respects, the theoretical power of the Merovingian king even exceeded the might of the Roman Emperor. Now the kingdom was his because of hereditary rights, not because the people had delegated sovereign authority to him, an idea conflicting with the original conception legitimizing the hold of the Roman Emperor. In other words, the form of government was now more or less the same as that of the warrior era, but the reality was something else: the absolutism of the king was good in theory but not in practice. This is exactly the hallmark of an intellectual era, where the apparent ruler is under the sway of his officials.

Finally, the intellectual's influence represented by the Church hierarchy of the Pope, bishops, and priests, had by then become a fact of life. Religion was the one common bond that linked diverse cultures of different peoples living in the vast lands of western Europe. About the influence of the Church at the time, Ferguson and Brunn have this to say:

> The church played a tremendously important part in the life of the Merovingian age, barbarous and immoral though the age was in general. The bishops, who governed the church, were among the *most important* administrative officials in the state. [6, p. 166 (italics mine)]

In addition to the extensive authority that the bishops exercised, they also received veneration and wealth from the common man. While the Frankish kings themselves were the biggest donors, donations from affluent laymen also counted. All this the Church encouraged in a typical fashion—through the shrewd use of intellect. In Thompson's explicit words:

> "Give and it shall be given unto you" was the constant word. The Frankish clergy astutely utilized the zealous veneration of the saints, a remarkable religious phenomenon of the sixth and seventh centuries, for the purpose of increasing the Church's endowments. It was the saint, often a merely locally venerated one, who became the actual proprietor. For the intensely personal and proprietary ideas of the age required that the invisible Church be given some sort of personal expression, even if the patron was an invisible personage. Invocation of the saints, saints as spiritual godfathers and godmothers, became general; for the saints interceded in heaven for their protégés. [15, p. 200]

In other words, the Church utilized its immense moral appeal to gain influence and wealth. Needless to say, this influence would not have been so pervasive if the Merovingian kings had not first been converted to Christianity. The Church could not have enjoyed such primacy in society, if the kings had not paid homage to its emissaries—the Pope and bishops. This is yet another instance of the indirect sway that the intellectuals had over society through their control over apparent rulers.

It is not that greed in the Church had arisen all at once; but it had arisen with astonishing speed and magnitude. Immediately after the reconciliation between Constantine the Great and Christianity, the Church had begun to grow into a complex organization, which soon became an embodiment of degeneration as well as leadership, of sloth and simony as well as guidance and fortitude. One side of the story, the side of leadership and courage, has already been told: recall how, in the wake of barbarian attacks on the Roman Empire, the Pope and bishops would negotiate with the invaders and quite often save the cities from annihilation. The other side of the story, though not so refreshing, is no less important.

In the first three centuries, teachings of Christ were genuinely embodied in Christianity, which continued to inspire early saints and the Church. With the passage of time, however, especially after Christianity was recognized as the imperial religion, the Church succumbed to luxury and comfort. No longer was it a refuge of the poor and the middle class, of slaves and laborers. In order to acquire wealth and social acceptance, it lowered its standards, and subordinated principles to politics and secular affairs. Its bishops and saints were now concerned more with their privileges than with sublime ideals. Instead of society depending on the Church for moral guidance, the Church became a parasite on society.

Thus the moral corruption of the Church and its taste for luxury were already in evidence at the dawn of the Merovingian age. The spiritual-minded Christians had already recognized and deplored these tumors developing in the ecclesiastical body, but to little avail. And the tumors became cancerous when the Frankish kings were baptized, when Germanic peoples got converted to Christianity, when the Merovingian kings were emaciated by lust and lechery, when the mayors took over the palace. It is at these times that intellectuals, in the guise of the Pope and bishops, governed society, directly in religious and social affairs, indirectly in political matters, although in administration they had to share the spoils with the mayors.

Did the Pope and bishops govern owing to their physical prowess? Did they control the social order by dint of their manliness, valor, or adventurous spirit? No! They governed because of their intellectual superiority over the warrior king, so adept in the profession of war; because they could read and write, explain scriptures, while others could not. They governed by ministering to fears and prejudices of the illiterate masses; by elevating themselves in the common mind to the pedestal of sainthood. In short, their dominion rested on their intellectual acumen rather than on high-spiritedness and muscular strength.

The best proof of the view that the hegemony of the Church derived from intellect is furnished by the practical monopoly that it then had over education. In the Roman Empire, schools were the responsibility of the state. As the empire fell, this system gradually broke down and the Church moved in to fill the vacuum. The centers of learning in the early Middle Ages were monasteries whose gates, as far as education was concerned, were closed to the masses. Most members of the non-intellectual groups were thus illiterate. And even within the monasteries, courses of study tended to belittle science, history and, above all, a probing attitude. The emphasis was on theology; logic too was taught, but theology deemed it irrelevant. No technical skills worth the name were imparted. No wonder the early Middle Ages suffered from intellectual bankruptcy and economic decline.

With little competition from other institutions of learning, with the curriculum carefully, and purposely, designed by the Church to discourage independent thinking and scientific reasoning, intellectual achievements on the whole could not but have been mediocre. No wonder the early Middle Ages were dark.

The later Middle Ages, when this educational monopoly finally ruptured, reveal that apprehensions of the Church were well-founded. As other centers of learning emerged, many schisms, as will be seen in the subsequent section, developed in the body of Christianity—schisms that served to weaken the hold of the papacy, though not of religion, over society.

The three centuries following the fall of the Roman Empire then clearly belong to the intellectual era, to the Catholic Church. There is some amount of political decentralization; the form, if not the substance, of the absolute government of Roman times continues, but this absolutism is indirectly exercised by others—the Pope, the bishops, the mayors.

Let us now see how women fared in the new alignment of

power. In Sarkar's view, women's status in the intellectual era is inferior to that in the preceding warrior age. Let us then examine what the rise of the Church had in store for womanhood. Recall that women, by the Principate period, had already shaken off the legal, social, and political shackles which had oppressed them over the past few centuries. By the time of Augustus, women had become more outgoing, more extroverted than ever before; no longer were they chained to mere family life; no longer were they, in the modern term, mere housewives.

The early Christian views about women and their status in the subsequent intellectual era must then be examined against this background. The Roman environment at the dawn of Christianity permitted of real respect for women and their legal rights, their participation in civil affairs, and their say in family life.

So close is this Roman view of womanhood to the modern Western view that all this seems to have come down to us in an unbroken stream. But nothing could be farther from the truth. Standing between the West of the present and of the Roman Empire are more than fourteen centuries during which a woman was at times treated no better than a slave. Not only was she then considered inferior and servile to man in all respects, but even the existence of her soul, in a world where every man was privileged to have one, was at times open to question. On the one hand, she was denied the right to participate in religious affairs, on the other she was called upon to submit to her husband as she would to God, give the best care to an army of children, and perform all other household chores without a murmur.

Is it a coincidence that such subjection of women occurred during an age of which the first half belonged to the intellectual era and the latter half, as subsequently argued, to the acquisitive era? The bulk of the Middle Ages is said to have been dark; but much of this period was not as dark for men as it was for women. Is it a mere coincidence that the intellectual era, and the acquisitive era, were the darkest as far as feminism in the West is concerned? Not in Sarkar's mind! Not in terms of the theory of social cycle!

Right after the birth of Christianity, its saints reserved a role for women that was, to say the least, unbecoming and less active than her Roman counterpart. This was certainly not Christ's attitude, for, where there are purity and sublimity transcending the mental plane, there is no room for chauvinistic ideas of any sort. Christ is believed to have uplifted both men and women without discrimination. He did not get married, but this does not mean that he looked down upon women, or that he exalted celibacy over marriage as a social institution. He had many female followers and is also believed to have taken part in matrimonial ceremonies. Actually his compassion for women flouted the mores and customs of the community in which he lived.

But as soon as we come to St Paul and the later Church Fathers, there is an abrupt turn in the Christian attitude towards women. In the first blush of the Christian movement, women did much towards its spread. Their contributions did not go unnoticed, and we find St Paul appreciating them with great warmth. Apparently he lauded many outstanding women, imbued with love for Christ, as coworkers. But when it comes to relations between man and woman, between husband and wife, his tone takes a stern turn. He exhorts women to obey their husbands as their Lord, observe silence in churches, and refrain from wearing jewelry or expensive clothing. His words have been quoted time and again in justification of woman's inferiority in society. How is one to reconcile the two apparently contradicting positions that St Paul has taken in his view of womankind? Georgia Harkness has come up with an explanation:

> Of individual women, Paul could speak highly and gratefully and feel with them a fine fellowship in Christ. But of the man-woman relation, he spoke his inherited rather than his Christian conviction when he said that as the head of man is Christ, so the head of woman is her husband, and that man is the image and glory of God while woman is the glory of man. [8, p. 71]

Indeed, to this day Paul's contribution to woman's status in Christianity continues to be debated, with some accusing him of as much as misogyny and some absolving him of any such malevolence. Regardless of Paul's views, what is beyond dispute is that his sermons have been used time and again by churchmen to denounce women. He has been frequently cited to show that the Bible condones, nay, demands the exclusion of women from religious affairs. In the early Christian organization, there were three tasks, too menial to be performed by men themselves, that were reserved for women. In the New Testament and in subsequent ecclesiastic writings, brief mentions are made of deaconesses, widows, and virgins who were assigned duties that were usually paltry relative to those assigned to men. Later, however, the Church leaders, ignoring Paul's warmth for feminine coworkers, denied women even this bit of respect and responsibility.

The saints who steered Christianity through storms of the first four centuries are called Fathers of the Church. Most renowned among them are Clement, Tertullian, Jerome, and Augustine. Without slighting what they did for Christianity, I must say that the Church Fathers hummed one and the same tune in their tirade against women. To be sure, the pagan converts, who respected feminine rights, did not take kindly to the exclusion of Christian women from all religious functions. But their murmurs were submerged by the rhetoric and eloquence of the Fathers.

Why? What was the reason? Why did otherwise compassionate, scholarly, and unpretentious saints take positions so abhorrent to women and to the rational mind? The reason lies in asceticism, which has been woman's scourge in most, if not all, religions. In every religion which extols communion with God to beatify the soul, there have been some people who renounced everything to taste that rare beatitude, of which every prophet speaks in glowing terms. Asceticism is the name given to such renunciation and self-denial.

The ascetic usually feels that to achieve oneness with God, natural instincts and senses have to be brought under control; and of all the instincts, the biological urge of sex is perhaps the most difficult to conquer. Thus when the ascetic fails in this herculean task, which he usually does, he blames it on temptations hurled at him by woman. Quite sweepingly, he holds the charm of Eve responsible for Adam's fall; he detests woman's propensity for makeup as well as rich clothing. Little does he know that self-adornment is an integral part of human nature, inherent in both women and unascetic men; little does he realize that, because of his very effort to suppress the sex instinct, woman appears more seductive to him than to ordinary men; that if there is any moral pollution, it is in his own mind and not in any extraneous object.

As soon as Christianity came in contact with oriental cults, it was also infected by the latter's ascetic bent. The result was all those anti-feministic sermons by Tertullian, Jerome, Augustine, among others. In Donaldson's words:

> Now what the early Christians did was to strike the male out of the definition of man, and human being out of the definition of woman. Man was a human being made for the highest and noblest purposes; woman was a female to serve only one. She was on the earth to inflate the heart of man with every evil passion. [5, p. 182]

As long as Christians themselves were objects of official repression, as long as they were in the minority, as long as their leaders were out of the saddle of power, the new chauvinistic ideas afflicted only Christian women. But when the Church, its Pope and bishops, gained the upper hand in Western society at the beginning of the Middle Ages, portents for feminism could not have been more ominous. The customary Roman respect for woman's rights and liberties had then as much chance of survival as the gladiators of older days. Steadily and surely, the attitude of the Church Fathers made its way into the common law and custom, as well as the family and private life of Western society. So complete was the subjection of woman during the Middle Ages that relics of these customs and mores have survived to this day. In some ways, they still shape social attitudes towards woman in Western countries.

The first idea to gain currency in society was that celibacy is superior to matrimony. Priests were barred from marriage, something that vented the ascetic impulse of the Church Fathers. But more than that, it created a distinction between the clergy and the common, married people. Automatically it conferred a diploma of sainthood on the celibate priest, a diploma that was the time-honored gateway to creature comforts.

The ideas that the sexual urge is intrinsically evil and that woman is purely a temptress could not but color the public view of family life and of adultery, for which woman was held solely at fault. A lewd man, because of his immunity to pregnancy, could deceive the public, could, if exposed, even win forgiveness for his excesses, but not a lewd woman, not a prostitute, who would inevitably end up a social pariah. For a long while, this double standard underlay many of the laws concerning rape as well as prostitution, and only now is the West lukewarmly trying to free itself from this mockery of justice.

Curiously, as the sex instinct got slighted, the size of the family increased manifold with inevitable consequences for women's health and household chores. The Church Fathers permitted sexuality within marriage solely for procreation. The weakling layman, the laborer, the warrior, or the acquisitor, who looked up to the Church for guidance in every affair, had to justify in his mind his every carnal act. This he did by begetting as many children as possible; hence the emergence of large families and an aversion to birth control. However, although a layman could thus expiate his sensual sins, woman had to bear the brunt of man's taboos which the Church had foisted on him, and which were not at all of woman's own making. Thus, woman in the intellectual era was not only condemned as a temptress, not only condemned as inherently immoral, she was also, as it were, called upon to help man atone for his indulgence that biologically was unavoidable. Such then was the status of women in the early Middle Ages that belong to the intellectual era.

Does the Church have anything salutary to add to the cause of womanhood in Western society? I believe it does; and I say this because of the positive role that the Church in some respects has played. I have already referred to the absolute authority that the Roman father used to have over his offspring; even the decision whether his children, especially those with handicaps, should be allowed to live or perish was his and his alone. Infanticide was, therefore, quite common, and although, by the time of the Principate, this heinous practice had somewhat abated, its vestiges took many centuries to die. Till the very end of paganism, this prerogative of the Roman father was accepted by the pagans. However, its brunt fell on infant girls, who were considered a liability in those days.

The Church Fathers did not take kindly to this practice, and denounced it as plain murder. Therefore when the Church came to prevail over the West, this practice was slowly eliminated; the chief beneficiaries, of course, were women, whose population must have thus risen. In this way the Church ironically promoted increased numbers of seductive creatures whom the Fathers had dreaded for fear of falling from their elevated pedestal of sanctity.

On the political scene, the history of the West has already been traced through the eighth century. We have traveled in time up to a point where Pepin, with the approval of the Pope, had deposed the king in 751, and taken direct control over the reins of government. With Pepin's rise, there was a further increase in collaboration between the state and the papacy. But the Carolingian king was made of a stuff sterner than the Merovingian weakling he had replaced. On Pepin's insistence, many reforms were instituted to eradicate clerical corruption; but unwittingly he helped the papacy by strengthening its hold over the clergy.

For our purposes, Pepin's rule is significant in yet another way. Through his strong and benevolent government, he prepared the ground for his more famous son and successor, Charlemagne, who quickly assembled a vast empire, and in the process took command of the Church as well. Thus the supremacy of the Pope and bishops remained more or less unchallenged until the accession of Charlemagne, who reigned from 768 to 814. The new king, never the one to let anyone else rule in his name, was a man of superlative martial qualities. He was tall, healthy and stout; had a superabundance of energy and vigor. With his excellent health and stamina he was able to mount innumerable campaigns of conquest, which resulted in a vast empire, covering all central and western Europe save England. At the same time, he assumed control of the Church. He was an absolute ruler who supervised administrative and church activities through an institution called *missi dominici* (emissaries of the king).

Actually the star of the Pope, Leo III, had been going down-hill for some time. Leo had been accused of profligacy and tyranny, and in 799 was chased out of the city of Rome. However, Charlemagne promptly came to Leo's aid, and reinstated him as Pope. In return, on Christmas day of the year 800, the beholden Leo took Charlemagne by surprise and, in a melodramatic cere-mony, crowned him Roman Emperor. The king was thus elevated to the majesty of Augustus.

Despite this, Charlemagne never acknowledged the papal primacy over himself, although Leo, of course, regarded it as a precedent whereby the king's *imperium* derived directly from God, of whom the Pope was on earth the only representative. True, Charlemagne was now an emperor, but it was the papal action that had sanctified his position; and the Pope could recant what he had bestowed. At the turn of the ninth century, such assertions were empty, for the fact of Charlemagne's primacy over government and the Church had already been established; was not the Pope obliged for his own survival to the Emperor? But during the next four centuries, this precedent was to become the source of eternal conflict between secular and ecclesiastical authorities.

The shift of power from the Pope to the warrior king, this shift from indirect rule and decentralization to direct rule by a centralized authority, is a striking example of what Sarkar calls counter-evolution, because this entire episode signifies a backward movement of the social cycle from the intellectual to the warrior age. However, the fact that this change to autocracy and the corre-sponding diminution of the papacy were not to endure long sug-gests that counter-evolutionary events are usually short-lived.

In the long procession of history, one discovers that counter-evolution usually occurs when a particular era of the social cycle is about to run its course. This is not an inexorable law, but it gener-ally holds good with annals of most societies. Charlemagne's domi-nance over the Church was, therefore, a premonition of things to come. For the ninth century opens with a government as central-ized as it can be, but terminates with such dilution of political power as was not seen in the West before: it begins with autocracy, but ends with unprecedented decentralization. It is towards this new situation that I now turn.

FEUDALISM AND THE ACQUISITIVE ERA

Charlemagne's death in 814 was followed by a century of turbulence, chaos, and disorder. None of his successors was to inherit his forceful personality, with the result that within a few decades after his demise the Carolingian empire just disappeared. The central government was so badly weakened that more than ever before the counts, bishops, and big landowners usurped rights and duties of the state—if there remained any state. It is here that we detect the elements of extreme decentralization, culminating in feudalism that for the next few centuries prevailed all over Europe. The Church also then underwent a vast change in composition and character. It regained a measure of its sway that had been the rule before Charlemagne, but only in a limited area of Europe.

In most European nations in which Charlemagne's empire was divided, political and economic dominion was exercised by feudal kings and feudal lords or nobles who exhibited an acquisitive mentality. They ruled because of their control over the means of production—land or fiefs. They were always on the prowl to increase their wealth through matrimony and petty feuds in which usually their vassals had the honor of participation. And it was during the ninth century that ground was prepared for the impending acquisitive age.

As defined in the first two chapters, an acquisitor is someone whose intellect for the most part runs after wealth, and when the rich gain social primacy by purchasing services of the other three classes, the acquisitive era begins. The intellectuals then zealously serve the wealthy, and devise theories justifying the acquisitor's dominance as part of some natural order. Many scholars themselves now behave like the acquisitors, because the acquisitive virus, once dominant in society, quickly infects the intellectuals: for the privileged classes, mammon becomes the sole objective. This is what transpired in Feudal Europe around the end of the ninth century and the beginning of the tenth.

Charlemagne was succeeded by his son, Louis the Pious (814–40), whose chief claim to fame in history is his mediocrity; he could have been as strong a ruler as his illustrious father, had he not been overawed by the Church as well as an indomitable wife. Hardly had Charlemagne been laid to rest than conspiracies and conflicts broke out among his grandsons, who were eventually subdued with some difficulty—a poor augury for coming generations. In 841, immediately after Louis' death, simmering embers of internal strife erupted into an open war among the three claimants of the throne. The sequel was the Treaty of Verdun in 843 and the empire was divided into three parts—France, Germany, and a "middle kingdom." All this simply prepared the soil for emaciated central authority that was to be the hallmark of Europe in the near future.

Just as assaults of Germanic barbarians had helped intellectual priests into power on the debris of Roman empire, so did invading marauders called Northmen help acquisitive landlords at the end of the ninth century. From their original base, situated in the three Scandinavian countries of Norway, Sweden, and Denmark, the Northmen, also called Vikings, moved out in droves, and demolished much of civilized life that was in their way. Having been cut off by the Baltic Sea from the rest of Europe, they had not yet been injected with the serum of Roman and Christian influence. Their incursions into Christian Europe had begun as early as 787 when they first preyed on the British Isles; thereafter their raids continued in a crescendo of destruction, until, towards the end of the ninth century, they were repulsed by nobles who by then had erected impregnable castles. It is then that Vikings began to settle down in England as well as in the outskirts of the erstwhile Carolingian empire.

The Vikings were as much a barbarian element as had been their Germanic predecessors, and their advent proved calamitous to parts of Europe they visited. They destroyed many monasteries, and hence the centers of learning, over which the Church had exercised a monopoly. But in the end they were absorbed by the culture of their more civilized victims. Their adventures, of course, helped determine the evolution of Western society for the next five centuries. By their daring assaults, the central authority of the Carolingian kings was emasculated beyond repair.

Everywhere power passed into the hands of the nobles—dukes, counts, bishops, big landlords. And the Carolingian empire split further into many kingdoms: one in Italy, two in Burgundy, one in Germany and one in France, while Spain was still under the Muslim yoke and England divided into two royal domains. In short, the Europe of the later Middle Ages, commonly called Feudal Europe, followed a course determined partly by the enterprise of the Northmen.

The hallmark of the new kingdoms was their essentially feudal character. The medieval European society from the tenth century onwards was a feudal society that differed radically from its predecessor. The scholars of European feudalism define it as a social order where the political and economic power is exercised by big landlords, and where the rest of society serves them in terms of well-defined contractual obligations. The entire fabric of feudal society is woven together by myriad contracts whereby every person—the serf, the noble, the clergy—is called upon to submit to his immediate superior. Everyone is a vassal to someone else, including the overlord who is a vassal to his king. In the words of Burns and Ralph:

> Feudalism may be defined as a structure of society in which the powers of government are exercised by private barons over *persons economically dependent on them.* It is a system of overlordship and vassalage in which the right to govern is a contractual relationship involving reciprocal obligations. [4, p. 390 (italics mine)]

In other words, the aristocracy under feudalism enjoys duties and privileges of government simply because its subjects are "economically dependent" on it. This is precisely what distinguishes an acquisitive age: the acquisitors rule not because of superior intellect or muscle power, but because of their command over productive resources, which in the tenth-century Europe consisted primarily of land. Thus Western society of the later Middle Ages, or of the period lasting from the tenth century to the fourteenth, belongs to the acquisitive era.

Not that feudalism was the same everywhere in the then Europe, for what prevailed at one place might not prevail at another, or what was true of one time might not be true of any other. At one place feudal barons might be kept in check by a centralized authority, while at the same time extreme decentralization ruled the roost in other parts of Europe. At one time a warrior king might be the ruler, in theory as well as in fact, of as much as a quarter of European lands, while at others acquisitive overlords reigned everywhere in the name of a feeble king. At times even the Pope might be at the helm of temporal affairs, and at some places, as in big cities, wealthy merchants might wield the scepter.

Thus no picture of the later Middle Ages displays a harmony applying to the whole of Europe all through this period. But differences, for our purposes, are mostly in terms of nuances or shades of colors. This much can be said with little doubt that, looking at Europe or Western society as a whole, disregarding some of its parts that may at times strike an aberrant note, the four to five hundred years of the late Middle Ages were dominated by the acquisitive aristocracy which ruled, usually in the name of the king, solely because of its wealth.

Not only that, its rise to power in the first place occurred because of its wealth; because of its vast estates or, as in cities, because of its control over commercial capital. And when the king, for some short intervals, became powerful, he could never lose sight of disgruntled barons ready to strike back at the first opportunity. Whenever the kings ruled, they did so usually by appeasing the aristocracy or by taking momentary advantage of the factional strife among the barons themselves.

How did medieval feudalism come into being? In most respects, it was an embodiment of that fusion among the barbarian, Roman, and Christian elements of which I have spoken in the preceding section. Roughly speaking, the germ of feudalism was planted in the eighth and ninth centuries; it attained adolescence during the twelfth and thirteenth, withered into senility during the fourteenth, and gave way grudgingly to a system of centralized monarchies, reminiscent of a warrior epoch, beginning with the fifteenth. In England it met an early death, but in many parts of Europe its vestiges lingered on well into the nineteenth century.

To find the roots of feudalism, we must retreat in the dimension of time to as far back as the late Roman Empire. There, to thwart the decline in agricultural population and production, imperial decrees had bound many laborers and tenants to the soil as serfs during the third and fourth centuries. In time these serfs became completely dependent on big landlords. Eventually, as the central government weakened, the landowners usurped all powers of governing their estates and their serfs.

Then there were the Merovingian and Carolingian kings who contributed much to feudalism by rewarding the loyalty of their warriors and governors with vast tracts of land. Later, these nobles grew very powerful and arrogated to themselves the sovereign authority of the king himself. However, without the unexpected assistance from the Vikings, feudalism perhaps would never have developed into the kind of pervasive system that emerged at the turn of the tenth century.

The Frankish central government, which seldom rose to the efficiency and authority of the Roman Emperors, simply collapsed under the steady onslaught of invaders from the North. Emasculated by years of internal strife and civil wars, Charlemagne's successors were simply unable to defend their citizens from the northern *Völkerwanderung*. The people, in desperation, then turned to the nobles for protection behind their fortified castles. Once the nobles assumed responsibility for the main function of the state, namely the provision of defense, other rights and privileges of government naturally passed into their hands.

In those days of skimpy communications, the emaciation of monarchy automatically meant a rise in the powers of local magnates who were more accessible to the people than the remote king. The vacuum of power could then be filled only by the Carolingian counts, dukes, and other nobles, who also managed to make their offices hereditary. Still they paid homage to their king, but it was merely ceremonial, designed to perpetuate the *status quo* and avoid unnecessary affront to an institution that in the popular mind had been hallowed by centuries of presence.

What was the theory of government under feudalism? This issue is of much relevance here, at least for purposes of comparison, because it may be recalled that all through the first eight centuries, the king was entitled to an absolute authority over his subjects. Regardless of whether this absolutism was directly exercised by the ruler, as in the Roman Empire, or indirectly by the Church and the mayors, as during the Frankish reign, the king's absolute sovereignty was in theory never questioned. However, during the later Middle Ages, this view underwent drastic surgery at the hands of the intellectuals, who by now had become hirelings of the rich. In so doing, they were simply singing tunes of the times, capturing in their writings new realities, the new spectrum of power which, to their chagrin, had slipped out of their hold.

Many medieval theologians and philosophers seriously examined complex questions regarding the origin of state and of political power. And in these matters, if in nothing else, they generally agreed with each other. Though deriving from different reasoning, their thought converged on one essential point: man should not yield to the tyranny of any sovereign—an idea sharply conflicting with that of the Church Fathers, who had preached that the state was created by God to help man atone for his sin, so that the ruler, however ruthless, had to be obeyed.

No longer was the state regarded as inherently evil in feudal times; rather, it could be an engine of unqualified goodness, provided the sovereign governed with fairness and justice. No longer did political philosophy recognize the absolute authority of the ruler; rather, the ruler's main function was to administer the law, not to make it or shape it of his volition.

This legal conception is somewhat reminiscent of the concept of natural law that was meant to underlie the civil law in the early Roman Empire (where ideally the state was not above the law), except that under feudalism there could exist no law as an expression of the sovereign's will; for there seldom was a sovereign strong enough to enforce his decrees. Instead, customs and tradition ruled the roost. The medieval social fiber rested on a system of reciprocal services and obligations intricately woven through a hierarchy. The overlord provided protection in ex-

change for certain services that his vassals were supposed to perform. It is as simple as that. The feudal system was then guided by
the force behind customs, and the concept of law, natural or civil,
had no place in it. The medieval philosophy of government thus
championed the cause of extreme decentralization, of what was
actually a clearly accomplished fact.

Among the political ideas of medieval thinkers, there was at
least one bone of contention. Who should be the supreme overlord
was a question that created a gulf in the thinking of two schools.
One, headed by Dante, believed in the ultimate supremacy of the
Emperor, and the other, headed by St Thomas Aquinas, argued,
not unexpectedly, for the supremacy of the Pope over everyone
else, including the king. In fact this conflict is the ideological
counterpart of the actual conflict that poisoned relations between
the Pope and the Holy Roman Emperors during the eleventh,
twelfth, and thirteenth centuries. Of this I will shortly speak at
length.

What was the role played by the Church during the feudal
regime? Note that the main difference between intellectual and
acquisitive eras is that although in both cases the intellect, not
physical prowess, governs society, in the acquisitive era the ruling
class rules because of its wealth, whereas in the intellectual era it
rules because of its high acumen. The power of intellectuals in the
acquisitive era diminishes somewhat, as they now become agents
of the rich, but the intellectuals still exert influence in society. In
fact, their influence is second only to that of the acquisitive class.
Even in their activities and thinking, the intellectuals get infected
by the acquisitive mentality, and the two groups at times become
indistinguishable.

During feudal Europe the Church, like every other institution, could not remain immune to the acquisitive contagion. Gone
were its other-worldly concerns fostered, at least in theory, during early years of Christianity and during the Merovingian age
with which the intellectual era, as argued in the preceding section, had coincided. Religion underwent so much dissection, that
Christianity emerged with almost a new face. The essential elements of monotheism and other cardinal principles were, of

course, not discarded, but then the Church seldom took these fundamentals very seriously. If it had, it would not have accumulated so much wealth and land as it did as early as the fifth century. Its proclivities had always been for new dogmas, new doctrines interfering as much as possible with individual, family, state, and religious affairs. And it is in the doctrinal arena that Christianity was now markedly altered.

Up to the early medieval period, the Church regarded the present life as essentially miserable; the picture of this world appearing on its optical screen was one of fatalism, gloom, and doom. For this reason, man, whose nature was inherently wicked, had to disregard the sensual world and focus on the world beyond. However, as the acquisitive era emerged by the tenth century, even the Church doctrine succumbed to mundane melodies of the times. The forces of wealth were now dominant, and Christian theology could not but take them into account.

The transformation of Christianity, set in motion around 1050, was mainly effected by the triumvirate of St Thomas Aquinas, St Francis, and Pope Innocent III. These theologians cast aside garments of pessimism they had inherited from the Church Fathers, and painted a rosier picture of the present world, wherein life, for its own sake, was of supreme importance. No longer was a compromise with this world regarded as demeaning or devilish.

However, it would be too much to expect the Churchmen to be guided by lofty, unselfish sentiments in the new sermons. During the early Middle Ages, the state was still theoretically centralized in the person of Merovingian kings, and by controlling them the Church had been able to extend its umbrella over the entire society. But ever since the advent of Charlemagne and subsequently of the Northmen, its status had been declining. And when feudalism arose on the ruins of the Carolingian empire, the Church still could not regain its old power; for it could influence one feudal lord, or ten of them, but not all those hundreds of local magnates who were quite often inaccessible owing to poor communications.

This is not to say that religion was less pervasive in Western society than before, but simply that the ecclesiastic sway in political affairs had steadily gone downhill. It would be wrong to think that the Church watched these developments with complacency. What it had lost in terms of political sway, it tried to make up by tightening its noose around individual and family matters; and in this endeavor it came out with flying colors.

We are already acquainted with how the views of Thomas Aquinas, who exalted the Pope as the supreme overlord, towering even over the kings and the Emperor, had been disputed by the notable philosopher Dante among many others. However, some other rulings of Aquinas, especially those dealing with theology and individual life, went unchallenged. While he elevated the present world, he also entitled the priest to greater interference in family affairs. The latter now came to inherit, albeit indirectly, some of the authority and magnificence of Christ. By virtue of this power the priest became the medium through whom God could perform certain miracles, heal the sick and grant absolution to the sinner.

The moral strength and character of the priest were of no relevance in this regard. How could they be, it was theorized, when he had been ordained, through the instrument of the Pope, by Christ himself? No matter how unworthy the priest, no matter how tainted his mind, the rituals and sacraments that he administered were to be regarded as pure and sacrosanct. Something similar to this effect had first occurred in Egypt some thirty-five hundred years ago: the Egyptian priest thus seems to have been resurrected as the Christian cleric.

Whatever its other ramifications, the new theology succeeded in strengthening the hold of religion on society. It is not clear, however, that the Church grew more powerful than before in matters of religion, for there were other cross-currents at work and they tended to offset its influence. What is undisputable is that it became ever more worldly, conceited, and mechanical.

Perhaps the most potent of these cross-currents was the breakdown of the former Church monopoly over education, a breakdown that was effected first by Charlemagne who had invited many new scholars to his court, and then by the Northmen who had demolished many monasteries, which were the only

centers of early medieval learning. In the eleventh century, education began to move from the remaining monasteries to cathedral
schools which are somewhat reminiscent of modern colleges.
Later, these schools were overshadowed by the rise of medieval
universities, founded initially to produce and train teachers. But,
other educational programs, notably liberal arts, were gradually
added. Between the tenth century and the twelfth, impressive
centers of learning emerged at Salerno, Paris, Oxford, Cambridge, and Naples.

The rise of new schools and universities did not augur well
for the Church. Their contribution to the surge of new ideas ever
since the tenth century shows precisely why the Church so zealously guarded its monopoly over education in the early medieval
period. The priest's forte is his intellectual superiority, and the
Church sought to maintain this superiority, and hence its power-
base, by first rendering education inaccessible to other classes and
then regulating the curriculum in its own schools. The erosion of
the Church monopoly over education was then a symptom as well
as a cause of its decline in the acquisitive age.

In the medieval universities, the emphasis generally was
more on secular learning, especially law and medicine, than on
theology; particular attention was given to the study of rhetoric
and logic. The sequel in the twelfth and thirteenth centuries was
an intellectual revival that later flowered into the Renaissance as
well as the Reformation.

Scholasticism is the name given by historians to literary
achievements of the late Middle Ages, a name which does them
ill-justice. For the term Scholasticism signifies an effort to ratio-
nalize theology in terms of dialectics and philosophy, whereas late
medieval thought was by no means limited to questions of religion.
If anything, some of the then philosophers were interested in
examining only secular issues, ranging from social and philo-
sophic to economic and political. In their methods of research,
logic or rationalism took precedence over empiricism or personal
experience.

We have already seen what the new theory of priesthood

meant for the power of the clergy over lay people. However, side by side emerged the medieval humanizing attitude, of which the Church was not particularly enamored. It manifested itself in the cult of the Virgin Mary whose prominence tended to exalt the status of woman, of whom the Church Fathers had spoken with contempt. It is not surprising to find that the rise of the Virgin sprang mainly from popular sentiment foreign to the Roman Church. The words of Mary Beard are highly convincing in this regard:

> Thus the Virgin signified to the people moral, human, or humane power as against the stern mandates of God's law taught and enforced by the Church. As such, her position made trouble for the Church; but the Papacy, if it had been so minded, could scarcely have suppressed the urge of the people to Virgin worship, however successful it was in excluding women from the priesthood and the musical services of its choir. [2, p. 206]

The upshot of this whole discussion concerning the Church is that, although religion in the late Middle Ages was as pervasive as in the early part, new attitudes, new symbols, new centers of learning were emerging during the tenth and eleventh centuries, and they all served to undermine the formerly undisputed hold of the Church over the public mind. Why? Because this was the acquisitive age, where the real say in social, political, and economic matters belonged to the acquisitive overlords. Actually the Church itself was feudalized; it was by far the largest owner of land, with its territories administered by ecclesiastical overlords who behaved like secular overlords.

Thus the former intellectuals also now displayed the acquisitive characteristics: they had become intellectual acquisitors. In fact, some of the Church power then derived from its vast holdings of land. Hunt and Sherman, commenting upon the feudal noose around the serfs who labored on the manors or fiefs that the lords owned, confirm Sarkar's claim that in the acquisitive age, acquisitors and intellectuals behave alike and work in unison to perpetuate their hold on other sections.

Thus the manor might be secular or religious (many times secular lords had religious overlords and vice versa), but the essential relationships between lords and serfs were not significantly affected by this distinction. There is little evidence that serfs were treated any less harshly by religious lords than by secular ones. The religious lords and the secular nobility were the joint ruling classes; *they controlled the land and the power that went with it.* [9, p. 7 (italics mine)]

Let me now turn to the life-style of the lords themselves. Did they possess the acquisitive mind which runs after wealth? Did they control the warriors who would do their fighting, as well as the intellectuals who would devise theories to justify their dominion in society? Answers to these questions reinforce my argument that the period of European feudalism belongs to the acquisitive era of Western civilization.

We have already seen how the churchmen and philosophers alike had advanced the political theory of a decentralized state. This theory, itself a drastic revision of the former belief in absolute government, plainly justified the primacy of important nobles who purchased the loyalty of their vassals by granting them land. Each noble held his estate as a hereditary fief from the king, divided it into pieces of varying size, and then parceled them out to vassals of lower rank, and so on. This practice is called sub-infeudation. Whoever thus held the hereditary fief was called a lord. Those on top of the feudal hierarchy of lords, vassals-in-chief, were then the acquisitors, who in different places were called dukes, counts, earls, or margraves. Barons, who ranked next to the vassal-in-chief, may also be included in the acquisitive class.

Actually, some barons were bigger proprietors than the dukes, as were some dukes than their kings. In comparison to the total population, even to the population of lords, the chief vassals were few in number. Below the overlords were other nobles of various ranks, depending upon the size of their fiefs. Lowermost in rank among the nobles were the knights, whose life-style brings to mind the interests, ideals, and activities of the warriors. As a matter of fact, the vassal's chief duty to his overlord was the provision of military service, but the brunt of this duty fell on robust shoulders of the knights who have become legendary in medieval folklore and poetry.

To the term knight, two meanings were attached during the feudal period. The medieval theory entrusted the defense of the other two classes, the clergy and the peasants, to the nobles. All nobles, therefore, were knights in the sense of warriors; they were all, in terms of social prestige, a cut above the non-warring class of peasants and other physical laborers. At the same time, the term knight was reserved for the lord holding the smallest fief. Thus in the sense of military obligations to other classes, all nobles up to the dukes and counts were knights, whereas in terms of manorial size, the knight was one with the miniature fief. (It is in the latter sense that the term knighthood has been commonly used by historians, and unless otherwise specified I follow the same practice.)

Regardless of the medieval usage of this term, all nobles were expected to lead a bustling life of adventure and warfare. Medieval literature exalts the chivalry and heroism of knights in battlefields and war. Especially during the tenth and eleventh centuries, knighthood was a title that measured the noble's ability and stamina to fight for the honor of his lord. However, to earn this title was no easy matter. Being born of a noble family was only its first prerequisite. A noble could be awarded knighthood only after a prolonged period of training in the use of variegated weaponry and in the military arts.

From this account it appears that all nobles were born warriors; that they all loved to wage warring campaigns and thus keep themselves busy in an adventurous life. Nothing, however, could be farther from the truth. What is true is that the knights holding small fiefs loved to go to war for its own sake, especially when fighting, not nearly as hazardous as in modern times, was at times a profitable business. Fighting behind the shield of his heavy armor, the knight was usually not killed in the battle, and if victorious he could obtain a large booty, or a sumptuous reward from his overlord. But the great overlords, the dukes, counts, and barons, did not directly participate in battles unless they had to fight for their king or for their lives.

Not that they were pacifists, desirous of leading a tranquil life. On the contrary, feudal warfare was common; sometimes too common. But usually the knights did the fighting at the command of their overlord. And whenever the great duke fought by the side of his knights and foot-soldiers, it was usually not for the sake of adventure but for the sake of riches and land. For on the size of his fief rested his social prestige, political power, as well as income and other prerogatives. Therefore, as far as the barons are concerned, the term adventure is a misnomer for their warring campaigns. It was concocted by the intellectuals (philosophers and poets) simply to mask their patron's greed for land.

The fief-size could be increased in two ways—through marriage or war; and the rapacious overlord employed them both. Thus in feudal society, the chief overlords were the acquisitors, the clergy and philosophers the intellectuals, knights the warriors, and peasants and serfs the laborers. At some places, as in Germany, lines of demarcation among social classes were not as clear, but these are roughly the groups into which feudal society was organized.

Reasons for much of the private warfare were petty and local in character. Quite often feudal obligations were ignored, the oath of loyalty breached, and the bond of trust destroyed by both the vassal and the lord. And in redressing their grievances, real or imaginary, the nobles would assault their foes first and ask questions later. No section of society, the Church, peasantry and nobility alike, felt safe from this useless strife which was started on the flimsiest excuse. Monasteries were quite often its victims, so that many bishops, abbots, and other clergy were forced to seek shelter with the barons, who, of course, were only too glad to oblige them for money.

Sometime the extent of the private warfare has been exaggerated by historians, because much of it could have been brigandage, and hence pure crime, usually involving the mugging of merchants and other travelers.

What was the lot of women in the acquisitive age? In the first three centuries of the feudal period, tenth, eleventh, and twelfth, social attitudes towards women were still fashioned by teachings of the Church Fathers, and therefore feminine status could not have improved from its low point in the intellectual era or the early Middle Ages. If anything, it was perhaps lower than before, because now a large class of serfs had come into existence and the serf-women were, of course, abused by their lords. Prior to feudalism, serfdom had existed but not as a preponderant feature of society. The female serfs, of course, shared in the oppressive physical labor that the male serfs had to perform on the manors, but, in addition, they were also called upon to satisfy the lust of their lordly masters.

In some places, the lord reserved the right to sleep with his serf's bride on the first night of the honeymoon; while in others, the husband had to bribe his way out of the Church injunction exhorting chastity on the first wedding night, or even the first three nights. This inevitably worked to the benefit of the priest, who would let the poor groom off the hook in return for a paltry fine of, so to speak, expiation. I draw upon Thompson to reinforce my argument that women in the early acquisitive age fared worse then they did in the intellectual period.

> Medieval marital relations, far from being the sentimental attachments which romance depicts, were very often marriages of convenience and were brutally enforced. Young and tender girls were compelled to marry rough, and often lecherous, husbands. . . . Marriage was often a contract entered into to make an advantageous alliance, to escape escheat of a fief, to keep a particular piece of land in the family, to acquire new lands. [15, p. 711]

Thus the acquisitive mentality found free expression in matrimonial contracts which were administered by the lord with an eye on personal wealth. And in such marriages, designed either to increase the size of the fief or to strengthen the familial status and power, women were treated like chattels. Upon the death of a vassal, his property as well as his widow reverted to the jurisdiction of the lord, who usually made money from the tragedy. The lord's chief interest was in the services, military and otherwise, of a masculine vassal, and for this reason he usually forced the widow to remarry, as it were, a healthy "bull" of his choosing. Her own preferences mattered little in this regard.

Of course, the heiress could buy her way out of the predicament by paying the lord a goodly sum of money. The threat of forced marriage to the widow was thus blackmail which she could escape only by paying a large ransom.

All in all, the lord's contempt for women's rights was not just limited to female serfs, who, of course, bore the brunt of it, but it also extended to women of his own class. The ugly double standard which the Church Fathers had fostered in public attitudes towards adultery now struck at womankind with full fury. We have already observed how the serf-women were not safe from their lords, but in this respect the noblewomen fared only slightly better. Within his own fief a noble could not dishonor any woman, including, in theory, the peasant girls, but outside its bound, his conduct was under few reins. Speaking of a knight in this regard, Sidney Painter makes this observation:

> Thus it was a serious offense for him to rape the daughter of his lord or one of his own vassals, but he could rape anyone else's daughter with impunity if we was powerful enough to ignore the ire of her relatives. [10, p. 7]

In other words, rape in feudal custom was not a criminal offense if a knight committed it under propitious circumstances. This is the kind of esteem in which women were generally held in early feudal society. Thus up to about the twelfth century, woman's status was no better, if not worse, than that of the intellectual era. Vern Bullough's words vividly capture the picture of the times:

> The feudal male was chiefly absorbed in war and the chase. His wife bore him sons, his mistresses satisfied his momentary lusts, but beyond this women had no particular place in life, and he was not particularly interested in them as individuals. When they appeared in the feudal literature, at least in the literature prior to the twelfth century, they were pictured either as sex objects or as noble and virtuous wives and mothers, nursing their children, mourning their slain husbands,

and exhorting their sons to brave and often cruel deeds. If they dared to confront a male in any other role they were resented and vilified. [3, p. 165]

However, during the twelfth century there emerged two new currents that tended to soften the social attitude towards women, especially towards those belonging to the nobility. One was the concept of chivalry with its emphasis on platonic love, and the other, perhaps an offshoot of the first, was the cult of the Virgin Mary.

The concept of chivalry, or courtly love, owes its origin to French lyrics and romantic literature embodying the love-songs that troubadours would sing in feudal courts. The essence of these effusive lyrics was romance and selfless love. Woman, that seductive tormentor of the Church Fathers, was now idealized as a being whose love is to be sought and won through one's heroism and gentle manners. Whatever else it achieved in society, the concept of chivalry gradually moved out of French poetry and replaced, during the thirteenth and fourteenth centuries, the former feudal ideal of excellence on the battlefield.

The other powerful current shaping the aristocratic attitude towards noblewomen, the cult of the Virgin, was the ethereal counterpart of the mundane idealization of courtly love. The Fathers of the Church were not the ones to glorify Mary as the mother of God, and it was not before the twelfth century that Mary-worship struck roots in society. But once started, it spread with astonishing speed. Mary was raised to the pedestal of a goddess, something reminiscent of the pagan times. Men and women of all sections came to her fold and offered her their veneration; several imposing cathedrals were erected in her honor.

Whether all this idealization of woman—as an embodiment of tender love and as the Mother goddess—really bettered ordinary woman's treatment in society is open to serious question. Georgia Harkness raises this issue by asking, "but did this lift the position of the ordinary earth-bound woman?", and then answers it by affirming: "There is no evidence that it did" [8, p. 80]. In the same vein, Eileen Power suggests: "It is probable that the idea of

Chivalry has had more influence upon later ages than it had upon contemporaries" [11, p. 407].

Such a theoretical elevation of femininity must have had some impact in the heyday of the feudal order, but whether it was strong enough to ease woman's plight at the time is not altogether clear. What is indisputable, however, is that it marked a beginning of the end of the scorn that womanhood, ever since the intellectual era, had encountered in Western literature. It also anticipates much of the improved status that women were to enjoy in the new warrior era which, as subsequently argued, emerged in the West during the fifteenth century.

In terms of economic conditions, the acquisitive epoch is usually superior to the intellectual age, and a glance at the early and later Middle Ages quickly confirms this view.[1] As a result of so many circumstances, some fortuitous, some emanating from general pessimism of the Church Fathers, the intellectual era had suffered a considerable economic decline. Both Italy and France of the times paint a dismal picture of economic ruin and disaster; elsewhere in Europe conditions were little better. And the decline was reflected in all economic units—industry, commerce, agriculture, population, cities. At the dawn of the acquisitive era around the end of the ninth century, such, then was its heritage—pestilence, famine, stagnation.

By the early part of the tenth century, the landlord had become *de facto* master of his serfs, who lived in poverty and misery as their toil mainly benefited the landowner: consequently, labor-productivity and economic efficiency continued to suffer. But during the eleventh century, the diffusion of new technology replacing the old two-field method of crop rotation by a three-field system resulted in an agricultural spurt that was unprecedented at the time. In the words of Hunt and Sherman:

> A dramatic increase in agricultural output resulted from this seemingly simple change in agricultural technology. With the same amount of arable land, the three-field system could increase the amount under cultivation at any particular time by as much as 50 per cent. [9, p. 16]

Other changes, quite significant by standards of the day, took place in modes of transportation. Horses superseded oxen in plowing, and this turned out to be a labor-saving innovation; in the thirteenth century, the four-wheeled wagon took the place of the two-wheeled cart, thereby substantially reducing the costs of traveling. Such technical improvements by modern standards are slight, but during the feudal period they culminated in great economic strides. The marked increase in agricultural output and surplus laid the foundation of industry, and urban and commercial centers. It also paved the way for a rapid increase in population that almost doubled in the three hundred years between 1000 and 1300.

With a bulging population, the growth of cities could not stay far behind, and this in turn fostered industry and international commerce. All these developments tended to interact on each other, and thus provide further economic stimulus. The growth in agriculture nourished the growth in population, urbanization and small-scale industry, and all this nourished the demand for agricultural goods and hence further agrarian improvements; the lords and a prosperous peasantry in turn nourished the demand for industrial products. Thus the acquisitive era opened with a murky economic horizon, with the desolation of deserted towns and widespread hunger, but within a few generations it witnessed an economic revival.

What did this revival have in store for serfdom? All these strides could not but loosen the straitjacket of servility in which the bulk of the peasantry was caught by the tenth century. Right from its inception, feudalism was oppressive of free peasants and serfs, who were not slaves in the strict sense of the term, but their lot was no better. In theory both the serf and the lord were bound by reciprocal obligations, but in practice the lord's obligations were minimal in comparison with the array of services that the serf had to perform. For his hereditary right to plow the land, the serf owed various fees to his lord who collected them to the last penny, with no shade of mercy. The lord levied these fees arbitrarily, varied them according to his own needs and, with little coin money around, obtained them in kind. In Tuma's words:

. . . the serf had to pay a fee, the *merchet,* upon marriage of his daughter; he paid another, the *chevage,* for any absence from the manor; upon a serf's death, the lord was entitled to take his horse and war equipment, *heriot* and *relief.* [16, p. 53]

In addition to all these dues, the serf also had to provide the lord with free farm labor for part of the week. However, as the agrarian economy expanded, some innocent changes occurred in the composition, though not in the essential character, of manorial labor relations, changes that were to alter the course of the feudal polity. With the growth in agriculture had come the growth in heavily populated and industrialized towns, which, for food and raw materials, depended on the rural sector. The result was a two-way flow of goods between manors and the cities, which opened up new opportunities for the manorial peasant who could thus sell his surplus grain for money. He found it increasingly convenient, as well as profitable, to offer the lord a fixed sum of money as rent in lieu of physical labor.

This practice, known as commutation, did much to alleviate the plight of the serf, who now began to enjoy the fruit of his work rather than see much of it expropriated by the lord. While labor dues were replaced by pecuniary rentals, other arbitrary dues also, much to the relief of the serfs, gave way to fixed monetary payments. Thus the acquisitive era began with the serfs trampled under the wheels of grinding repression, but by the thirteenth century many of them had attained economic freedom. Even the lords themselves, ever in need of cash to taste luxuries of industrial goods, came to prefer money to physical labor. As a result, by the fourteenth century money rents in many European areas surpassed the monetary value of labor services. Thus all sections of society eventually benefited from the general affluence that the acquisitive age had brought about.

This is not to say that feudalism was on the decline or that the stature of the nobility had diminished—not yet. If anything, the new-found prosperity, by eliminating the thorn that for a while had poisoned the lord-serf relations, furnished a sounder agrarian base upon which the rest of the feudal edifice could stand firmly. But later on these very developments helped bury feudalism in the grave.

What were the economic, social, and political conditions in medieval cities which practically existed outside the sphere of the feudal order? There things look different, but in reality are much the same. There one discerns the same political decentralization with acquisitors, this time in the guise of wealthy merchants, firmly in control. Most of the city governments then were generally under the sway of an oligarchy of merchants, also known as burghers, although some places were fairly democratic, with power nominally exercised by the electorate.

In the intellectual era, it may be recalled, cities and commercial towns had succumbed to the general state of economic decline. But during the tenth century an agrarian base was created for the resurgence of cities, at times around the old, diminished centers, at others around new centers in which the burghers had come to live and pursue their commercial activities. A good section of European population began to reside in cities and towns, and from the eleventh century onwards the urban centers had as large a role to play in Western evolution as the feudal institutions. In fact, much of the intellectual advance of the acquisitive age occurred in the lap of the cities—Venice, Florence, Paris, Milan.

At first, most cities were dominated by the feudal nobility, but in time they sought, and obtained, freedom from such control. The typical medieval city was governed by a council and some executive officers who were mostly elected from ranks of the burghers. The feudal lord, depending on the extent of his dominion over the city, sometimes intervened in this election, but more often than not paid lip service to the city administration.

The urban economic ideology was, not surprisingly, constrained by the web of Christian doctrines and ethics, which generally condemned the greedy attitude towards profit as well as the practice of charging interest for any kind of loan. Needless to say, such prohibitions were flagrantly, though covertly, violated. The distinct features of city economies were the merchant and craft guilds, of which all burghers operating in the city were supposed to be members. A guild's principal interest was to ensure monopolistic conditions for the goods bought and sold by its members, and for this purpose its membership was usually denied to foreign merchants. Also, for the same purpose, the guild took it upon itself to regulate market prices and wage rates as well as the quality of goods produced within its jurisdiction.

For women the cities generally offered a freer and more bustling life, even though there too male attitudes as well as the literature displayed the misogyny of feudal society. Many women, single as well as married, engaged in an assortment of trades, with dominance in some industries. However, economic discrimination, designed to shield male vocations from female competition, was commonplace, and, of course, for the same work, then, as now, women were underpaid relative to men. Of such women in the cities, Bullough has this to say:

> Throughout Europe they dominated the manufacture of beer and much of the processes of textile manufacture. In fact, the very word "spinster" would indicate that spinning was not only the regular occupation of all women but also the habitual means of support for many of the unmarried. Still many craft regulations excluded females, and when they did work they often did so at wages lower than that of the man. [3, p. 179]

By now I have touched on the main aspects of the feudal society and established that its characteristics fit well into Sarkar's description of the acquisitive age. This, when added to conclusions already reached, implies that the evolution of Western society up till now has followed the tracks of Sarkar's theory of social cycle. A rotation of the cycle will be complete if the closing stages of the feudal period are marked by uprisings of the oppressed laborers—the peasants, the serfs—and then followed by the age of absolutism so that the warrior era begins anew. The fourteenth and fifteenth centuries turn out to be the centuries of such transition, of the kind of anarchy that bedevils the terminal phase of the acquisitive age.

Seeds of strong monarchies that were to emerge in Spain, France, and England during the fifteenth century had actually been planted earlier in the feudal age. We have already heard of various feudal kingdoms, of which all, at one time or another, had succumbed to the power of the nobles. The map of tenth-century Europe displays a number of royal domains in England, France, and in the Holy Roman Empire comprising Germany and Italy, with the real rulers, of course, being the host of dukes, counts, and barons.

In France, the Carolingian dynasty ruled until 987 when it was replaced by the Count of Paris, Hugh Capet, whose descendants then became the French kings for the next three hundred years. During these centuries, the fulcrum of power shifted between the Capetian kings and their nobles, but, by a series of maneuvers lasting over several generations, the kings were eventually able to lay the foundations of a national monarchy. Through one excuse or another they expropriated the fiefs of their vassals, with the result that by the end of the thirteenth century the king had become the most powerful of all the rulers in France. There still were some independent fiefs, but they now paid more than ceremonial homage to the king, who had begun to reassert the royal right to levy taxes. In the main, the royalty succeeded because it broadened its support by seeking help from the cities.

In England, the basis of national monarchy was laid by William the Conqueror, whose conquest of the British Isles in 1066 spelt disaster for the native Anglo-Saxon rulers. Although William transmitted some features of feudalism from France into the British feudal structure, the monarchy he founded was stronger than the one he displaced. By assuming the right to coin money and by prohibiting petty feuds among his vassals, he kept the nobles under some degree of control. After William's demise, power alternated between the kings and nobles, a process quite reminiscent of neighborly French developments during the same period. William's forceful personality had somewhat diminished the baronial sway, but the subsequent rulers were not always so successful.

In 1135, the country was ravaged by an internecine civil war between two pretenders to the throne, and the nobles swiftly moved in to take advantage of the weakened monarchy. This is the way the pendulum of power switched to and fro between the royalty and the barony up to about the middle of the thirteenth century, when there occurred yet another civil war in which the king was defeated and captured. I have singled this event out, because it paved the way for the British parliament which was later to play a monumental role in the nation's affairs—when Britain did eventually emerge as a nation.

Under the stewardship of Simon de Montfort, the leader of the rebellious barons, an assembly was convoked to discuss constraints on the king's authority. The assembly was attended not just by the great nobles and ecclesiastical authorities, but also by representatives of knights and city-dwellers. Thus a precedent was established for assembling a group of men, representing the three classes—of acquisitors, intellectuals, and warriors—who could thus discuss political and economic affairs in unison.

However, credit for fathering parliament is usually given to King Edward I, who, in 1295, summoned the so-called Model Parliament—not, of course, for considering limits over the Crown, but for obtaining a broad-based support from the populace; this is how he sought to lessen his dependence on the nobles. Such then was the political map in England at the end of the thirteenth century.

Let us now move to Germany and Italy, and examine their political developments following the breakdown of the Carolingian empire. In 911 the last of the Carolingian kings died, and the German dukes, with no one powerful enough to unify them into one entity, reverted to the expedient of choosing a king who was meant to be no more than a titular overlord. In 936 Otto the Great was elected, but right from the beginning of his rule, he had grandiose designs of glorious conquests. Not content to remain a mere German king, he soon got involved with Italy and eventually with the papacy. As with Charlemagne, Otto too came to the assistance of the Pope, this time John XII, against papal adversaries, and was in return recompensed with the crown of the Roman Emperor.

This is how the Holy Roman Empire came into being. For its philosophical base, it rested on the contemporary theory of government whereby the Emperor was recognized as the supreme secular overlord, superior even to kings, with a mandate coming directly from God.

Whether Otto's coronation did anything to enhance his territory or power is questionable, but it did deflect his attention from his home base, Germany. Subsequently it brought his successors into open conflict with the papacy. In essence, all kingdoms of those days were feudal, resting on slippery shoulders of the nobles who, in accordance with the swing of the pendulum of power, switched their allegiance from one overlord to another. Thus to hold on to both Germany and Italy in feudal times was no easy affair. Yet there was prestige, though of an empty shell, involved with the imperial title, and this allure ultimately proved to be the scourge of Otto's successors. They neglected Germany, poked their noses into Italy, and consequences were just as predictable: while the German nobility often dictated political affairs, Italians rose in sporadic revolts.

Another inevitable consequence was the collision between the papacy and the Emperor. Ever since the onset of the acquisitive era, the weakling popes had been under the sway of the nobles of Rome. The reason was that the papacy had lost face with the public because of its own rapacity and degeneration. After Otto came to the Pope's help, the latter had to contend with even more powerful rulers; consequently, for a while the Church was completely embroiled with feudal institutions. However, the Emperors did something which ultimately proved to be their nemesis: they set out to reform, in good conscience, the papacy and purge it of its corruption. The culmination was a gradual revival of the Church which soon endeavored to free itself from secular fetters. Its conflicts with almost all governments, and especially with the Holy Roman Emperor, were then unavoidable.

For more than two hundred years, there occurred a struggle for supremacy between the papacy and the Emperor, a struggle in which the latter was eventually trounced, so much so that even in Germany the real governing power reverted to the myriad duchies. Unlike the kings in England and France, the Emperors failed to seek support from growing cities and thus spread their roots deep into the heart of the general population. After 1273, when Rudolf of Hapsburg was elected to the ceremonial crown, the Holy Roman Empire could never rise above the shadows of its checkered past. But for the Hapsburg Dynasty, this event marks the beginning of prominence, which was to set its imprint on future generations—a story that, for its present irrelevance, must be postponed until a suitable occasion.

There remains the question of Spain, which had been conquered by the Muslims during the early part of the eighth century, thereby evolving along a track differing from that of other European countries. But during the late Middle Ages, most Spanish domains had become independent to rejoin the ranks of western Europe and to share, as it were, in its essentially feudal character. The Spanish struggle for liberation had lasted well over two centuries during which both the Christian and the Muslim sides had seen violent ups and downs. By 1248, however, only the small kingdom of Granada remained under the foreign yoke, with the rest of Spain split into four Christian domains of Castile, Aragon, Navarre, and Portugal.

The end of foreign rule did not, of course, mean the end of warfare. It now occurred among the Christian kingdoms, which fought each other from habit. All this weakened the central governments to such an extent that the feudal nobles became predominant in much of Spain, especially in Castile, which was its largest kingdom, comprising more than sixty percent of its area.

Such was the political map of Europe at the end of the thirteenth century and the beginning of the fourteenth. The characteristic flower of feudalism was then in full bloom: petty private warfare had somewhat subsided, and economic expansion and the resulting commutation had defused possibly the most explosive source of social and political instability—serfdom. Thus at the onset of the fourteenth century, the prospects for feudalism could not have been brighter. Historians or social philosophers of the time cannot therefore be faulted for believing in the perpetuity of contemporary life. How myopic were they though? Because, within a few years after feudalism had reached its peak, there began its slide, a period of war, desolation, anarchy, and laborer revolutions in which, sadly, every acquisitive era is destined to end.

The fourteenth century was then a witness to major up-heavals. It was a century that saw the inauguration between England and France of a war that lingered on for more than one hundred years. This conflict was so destructive that the private warfare of the entire feudal period pales before the ravages of this so-called Hundred Years War. It was a century in which the bubonic plague of 1348 did to feudalism what the past three centuries of agricultural and industrial expansion could not: there was a tremendous shortage of manorial labor, because over a third of the population succumbed to the so-called Black Death—the most horrifying epidemic in European history. This fortuitous development could not but sever arteries of the feudal structure, which had rested all along on pillars of excess labor supply.

PEASANT REVOLTS AND THE ACQUISITIVE-CUM-LABORER ERA

The closing phase of the fourteenth century is a period of sheer anarchy, of the chaos of ever more savage war in which thousands of nobles were killed, of unprecedented bitterness between the former serfs and the lords suffering from the paucity of labor, of the inevitable peasant revolts.

Right from inception, feudalism had been oppressive of the peasants and the serfs who were squeezed to the last penny by the nobles. To be sure, there were some just lords who felt responsible for the security of their laborers, but even the best of them insisted on timely payment of severe manorial dues. In general, the life of physical workers was incredibly wretched, at least until commutation, by the thirteenth century, had enabled many serfs to free themselves from contractual obligations. But then came the fourteenth century during which wars and pestilence had wrought havoc with the population; wages had risen high, but rents of relatively plentiful land had drastically declined.

The natural response of the nobility was to revoke the freedoms they had granted to serfs under commutation, and to reinstate their labor service obligations. But in this, the lords met with stiff resistance from the peasants, who knew from experience what serfdom had meant for their lives. From the vantage point of today's observer, nothing in that acquisitive age was more natural than the head-on collision between the peasantry and the nobles. Feudalism had begun with the lords on top and the workers toiling for their masters. What is astonishing is that the system endured so long—for more than four centuries. But no era meets the grave before attaining its peak, which feudalism had scaled during the thirteenth century.

Thus when, beginning with the fourteenth century, anarchy in the guise of peasant revolts broke out all over Europe, the acquisitive era was simply following the tracks set forth by the law of social cycle. Such revolts were marked by crescendos of brutality and widespread destruction. And in this ferocity, both the peasantry and the nobility strove to excel each other.

When the peasants first erupted into violence to protest against economic oppression is not clear. One outburst, rooted in social and economic grievances, occurred in West Flanders as early as 1323, and set an example for the neighboring regions of England and France. But it was not until 1358 that the peasantry in northern France took up the cudgels, and rebelled in the wake of rapacity and brigandage of the French nobles and knights. For a while, nothing had been safe from these marauding lords who plundered villages at will, dishonored women with impunity, and destroyed anything that came their way either for the booty or for the sport.

Therefore, when the peasants hit back in exhaustion, they had but little choice. Known by the name of the Jacquerie, this rebellion was led by two men of completely diverse origins and disposition: Guillaume Cale, a peasant by birth, was a warrior by disposition, whereas Etienne Marcel belonged to the merchant class, which sympathized with the peasants' animosity towards the feudal lords. However, despite this alliance, the peasants were eventually put down. About the fundamental cause of this rebellion, Norman Gras has this to say:

> The Jacquerie seems to have been the peasants' sudden reaction to the loss of security and happiness and of the slowly developing

emancipation from servile status and tenure. The peasants had been bettering their lot. Suddenly the tide turned against them. The despised countrymen having tasted of better things, refused to accept worse. [7, p. 109]

Similar causes were at work in the peasant uprising of 1381 that briefly shook the roots of England. The revolt has been given various appellations—Wat Tyler's Rebellion, the Peasant Revolt, the Great Revolt, the Social Revolt. As in France, the outbreak in England was also more than a peasant revolt, because it was not just confined to the peasantry; it was social, with causes ranging from economic and political to religious and legal. In its immediate objectives, which called for economic reforms and for complete emancipation from serfdom, the revolt was a failure. But taking a long-run viewpoint, it had some measure of success in that the alienation and plight of the peasantry gained nationwide attention. Sixty to seventy years later, nearly all peasants had achieved freedom from manorial labor and serfdom.

Other parts of Europe too—especially Germany and Austria —felt the tremors from the peasant rebellions at the advent of the sixteenth century. Everywhere they were abortive, but they succeeded in pinpointing the festering social wounds which demanded nursing and careful treatment. Although feudalism was not laid to rest in their aftermath, its anachronism had been proved beyond any shade of doubt. By the fifteenth century, it had been exposed and weakened beyond repair.

SOCIAL REVOLUTIONS

Much of the fourteenth and fifteenth centuries of the West belongs to the acquisitive-cum-laborer age, because virtually every corner of western Europe—England, France, Germany, Spain— was then plagued by anarchy, of which the peasant revolts and the resulting horror were not the only symptoms. While England and France were locked in bitter conflict for more than a century, the kingdoms of Spain were not sitting idle either. The Christian kingdoms fought and fought, not just with the Moors but also amongst themselves. To this the Spanish nobles made their own contribution by generating, as Ferguson and Brunn put it, "a frightful amount of lawlessness and disorder." [6, p. 385]. And in this respect, what held true for Spain held true for the rest of western Europe as well.

It is in such tumult that new leaders emerged to put an end to the anarchy in France, Spain, and England. The credit for the laborer revolution (or revolutions), therefore, goes to Louis XI in France, Isabella and Ferdinand in Spain, and Henry VII in England, as they all eclipsed anarchical forces of the feudal nobility during the latter half of the fifteenth century. What is interesting is that such momentous events occurred within a short span of a quarter-century beginning with the 1460s. Is it a coincidence that such revolutions occurred so close to each other? Not according to Sarkar's hypothesis!

So far then, Western civilization has evolved along the track of social cycle. Now, if Sarkar is right, comes the turn of those with physical prowess and high-spiritedness to rule again. The new age must again reflect the spirit of adventure as well as subordination of the other three sections to warriors.

NATIONAL MONARCHIES AND THE NEW WARRIOR ERA

I have already traced the history of the West up to the fourteenth century. We have seen that by then national monarchies had risen in England and France, while Spain was dominated by the kingdom of Castile. These early developments towards centralization turned out to be portents of absolutism, which emerged in France, Spain, and England between 1460 and 1485. Thus, a new warrior era appeared in the West during the fifteenth century, and then spread over much of Europe in the course of the sixteenth and the seventeenth.

The French monarchy emerged from the debris of the Hundred Years War (1337–1453) with unquestioned authority. Credit for effecting this centralization goes to Louis XI, who ascended the throne in 1461. Shortly after his accession, he had to face a revolt by the nobility, whose influence he finally effaced by military action as well as by bribing some of the nobles. Slowly but surely, in place of the feudal control over the army of knights, over taxation and over the administration of justice, arose the monarchical system of national taxation, a national structure of royal courts, a huge standing army of mercenary soldiers recruited from the ranks of the peasantry and the nobility. Most of the acquisitive lords were steadily diminished to the status of courtiers, with their titles and prerogatives deriving principally from the monarch's whims, of which he had an abundance. Thus in the 1460s direct, centralized rule by one king took the place of the earlier indirect, decentralized rule of the French nobles.

At just about the same time (in the 1470s), centralization also emerged in Spain after Princess Isabella of Castile and Prince Ferdinand of Aragon were bound in matrimony, which thus laid a sturdy foundation for the Spanish monarchy. Together the two monarchs not only crushed the feudal nobles but also annexed Granada and Navarre to their territories. In the early part of the sixteenth century, their successor, Charles V, was elected as Holy Roman Emperor, and, as a result, the Spanish absolutism was also extended to southern Italy and much of central Europe including Austria, which was to become a respectable power during the eighteenth century.

In England, on the other hand, absolute monarchy was not established until the rise of the Tudor Dynasty, of which Henry VII was the first ruler. While the Hundred Years War had all but destroyed the French nobility, the British nobility, though considerably weakened, was still breathing and alive. It took another thirty years of internal strife, called the Wars of the Roses, before the English aristocracy was suppressed. In 1485, in the aftermath of this civil war, Henry VII emerged with an unchallenged *imperium*. In Britain, in contrast with France and Spain, absolutism was tempered, and perhaps strengthened, by the presence of a legislative assembly. The Tudor kings have appropriately been called absolute monarchs in parliament.

Italy also emerged during the fifteenth century with despotism, but of a different variety. No nation-state took shape, but a number of city governments, notably in Milan and Florence, were organized into dictatorships of which centralized authority was the chief characteristic.

Thus towards the end of the fifteenth century, despotism dotted many areas of western Europe, and even though in some parts, as in Germany, decentralization in the guise of rule by many princes still prevailed, there is little doubt that thereafter it is the centralized nation-state which shaped Western destiny. With the advent of this centralization arose other features which usually highlight a warrior age, features that in some respects reflect its superiority over the preceding wealth-dominated order. The new warrior era, as subsequently argued, lasted till the end of the seventeenth century, when it too gave way to another intellectual age.

The fabric of feudal society has been frequently compared by historians with organized anarchy, which it certainly was. The very fact that absolutism was accepted by the populace in many nations is a telling commentary on the kind of disorder that had prevailed in the feudal age, especially at its terminal point. In the new warrior epoch, the monarchs restored law and order by controlling the rapacity, brigandage and private warfare of the barons with an iron hand. In this respect alone, the early phase of the new warrior era is superior to the preceding acquisitive age. But this alone is not the former's claim to preeminence.

More than anything else, the new warrior era is an embodiment of the spirit of adventure—adventure for its own sake and not just for booty or plunder that was the hallmark of the acquisitive age. Many activities of the time remind one of the direct struggle through which a warrior battles with hostile forces of nature, and strives for prestige and a sense of fulfillment. Quite a few daring spirits of this age immediately come to mind: Christopher Columbus, Vasco da Gama, Ferdinand Magellan are luminaries among numerous explorers who dedicated their lives to the discovery of new lands, of frontiers unknown at the time to Europe and indeed to much of the world.

In all these campaigns launched over tempestuous seas, over endless oceanic waters, amidst uncharted currents and winds, state help was indispensable. And the state, of course, rose to the occasion, matching the ardor of certain individuals with generous funds and other assistance. Why? Because the West was then in the early phase of the new warrior era, and the sense of adventure and vivacity permeated most European nations—Spain, Portugal, England, France. America was then discovered; so were new oceanic routes to India, to the South American continent and to numerous obscure islands.

In terms of intellectual and artistic attainments also, the new era surpassed the preceding age. In terms of the theory of social cycle, it is not a coincidence that the full bloom of what is sometimes called the civilization of the Renaissance overlapped with the early phase of the new warrior age. Renaissance means intellectual revival, especially that in the secular arena. True, the interest in secular learning had surged with the rise of universities in the acquisitive period, yet the intellectual revival did not reach its zenith in Italy until the fifteenth century, and elsewhere in Europe until the sixteenth. The artistic genius of Leonardo da Vinci (who painted the Mona Lisa), Giotto, and Botticelli belong to the Italy of this age; so do the literary works of Machiavelli, as well as the scientific discoveries of Galileo. Regarding other intellectual centers of Europe, such celebrities as Shakespeare, Bacon, Newton, and Spenser of England, Rabelais and Montaigne of France, El Greco and Cervantes of Spain are lasting bequests of the new warrior age to the world.

Women too could not do poorly in the new epoch, for this was the warrior age. The spirit of Humanism inspired by the cult of chivalry and of the Virgin, had already arisen in the later parts of the acquisitive age, but it could seep into the fabric of society only gradually, not before the Renaissance had spread its fragrance first in Italy and later in the rest of western Europe. To be sure, the social view of woman did not improve radically in the new warrior era, but it improved enough to be noticeable. The attitudes of subordination of woman to man, of wife to husband, were still prevalent, and indeed have been prevalent till this day, but the general public was now exposed to such blasphemies as women's right to education, even to priesthood. Remember that such views in preceding eras would have earned their author nothing but social ridicule—ostracism.

To humanists, education was essential to all human beings, to men as well as women, because it helped everyone to become civilized, gentle, and virtuous. After the first treatise emphasizing women's education was written by Leonardo Bruni in 1405, this idea steadily filtered into the mainstream of Italian life, and a number of princes employed learned scholars to tutor their daughters. In other parts of Europe too the humanist scholars expressed the same concern for women's education when the Renaissance spread beyond the Italian borders in the fifteenth and sixteenth centuries. There might be constraints on what women could read, but they were not to be denied the essentials of learning.

Another sign of woman's improved stature in the early phase of the new warrior period is the rise, during the fifteenth and sixteenth centuries, of ingenious and powerful women all over Europe. Italy of the time was witness to outstanding achievements of two sisters, Beatrice and Isabella; a part of credit for the discovery of America in 1492, regarded by many as an epochal event, must go to the Spanish Queen Isabella. It is she who, in the face of her courtiers' opposition and skepticism, gave Columbus all possible help in his herculean task that promised nothing but enormous risks and, at best, uncertain dividends.

Then there are the French regents, Anne de Beaujeu and Queen Anne of Brittany, who, for many decades in the fifteenth and sixteenth centuries, overshadowed men in political and cultural spheres. To top them all, there is Queen Elizabeth I (1533–1603) who gave England its Golden Age. Although the general subservience of women was accepted by the new warrior society, even by female rulers, yet the rise of so many extraordinary women all over Europe could not but lend a feminine touch to the social view of womanhood. Bullough makes interesting observations in this context:

> Probably even more important than the humanist emphasis on learning in encouraging education for women was the fact that women played an important role on the political scene in the sixteenth century

in their own right. That they were able to do so is indicative of some change in societal attitudes. Earlier women like the Empress Matilda, mother of Henry II of England, and Eleanor of Aquitaine, his wife, had tried to rule independently of their husbands, but they had been severely handicapped and in the long run unsuccessful. At the end of the fifteenth and beginning of the sixteenth centuries, however, there were a number of women who were important as rulers in their own right or as regents. Isabella of Castile was a queen of Spain, while in England Mary and Elizabeth were reigning monarchs. In France Catherine de Medici fought like a tiger to see to it that her minor sons succeeded to their inheritance. The influence of these women rulers is evident from the fact that they were instrumental in forcing a reassessment of education of women. [3, p. 211]

The influence of the papacy and the Church, of course, drastically declined. The words of Ferguson and Brunn make this clear:

> In a great many ways the fourteenth and fifteenth centuries were disastrous ones for the Catholic Church. The papacy, with its wide claims to supremacy over all Catholic Christians, had come into violent conflict with the growing power of the centralized territorial states and had been defeated. National interests had combined with moral disapproval to break the vast authority that the church had wielded during the High Middle Ages. [6, p. 375]

Thus by the fifteenth century, the rising power of the national monarchs had humbled the Popes, who in matters of religion were the supreme overlords as late as the fifteenth century. However, the knockout punch to the papacy had yet to be delivered. It was left to storms of the sixteenth-century Reformation which originated in Germany under the guidance of Martin Luther, and eventually overwhelmed the Catholic Church in many nations. But in the process Europe was drenched with blood. So pervasive had been the influence of the papacy for the past thousand years, that it took more than a century of sanguinary Wars of Religion among European despots before anyone could realize the futility of it all, the futility of imposing the word of God by gunpowder. Whatever else might be the achievement of the Protestant Revolution that Luther had inspired, the back of the Catholic Church was broken beyond repair. Never again was it to play as wide a role in common life as it did during the thousand years of the Middle Ages.

Economically too the new era surpasses the previous one. In Tuma's words:

> The period extending roughly between A.D. 1500 and 1700 has been recognized as a critical one in the economic history of the western world. Some observers in fact suggest that the foundations of the economic upsurge of Europe and the West which occurred in the next two centuries were laid during this period. [16, p. 131]

Actually many economic changes occurring in this period derive from the industrial development of Europe starting as early as 1300, but it was not before the discovery of America towards the end of the fifteenth century that European economies really forged ahead, evolving eventually into the modern system of commercial banking and capitalism. All this suggests that, in many important respects, the new warrior period excels the preceding acquisitive age.

So far we have looked at the luminous side of the new age of centralization; let us now examine its seamy side, by which unfortunately every age is possessed. I have already alluded to the Reformation, and the Wars of Religion it inspired. Almost the entire period of the new warrior era is scourged by these conflicts. Petty private feuds of the feudal age now gave way to wars of the despots, but the warfare was petty no more; it was carried on by huge armies of professional soldiers, with weapons far deadlier than ever before, with stakes involving usually religion but occasionally dynastic succession in many nations. In fact, years of peace in the new warrior era fall far short of the years of turmoil. It is indeed a miracle that despite this, European economies achieved impressive advances.

PRIME MINISTERS AND THE NEW INTELLECTUAL ERA

My prognosis now reverts to England, which has been the cradle of many an institution distinguishing modern Western society. I have already spoken of Henry VII, who had founded the Tudor

Dynasty in 1485 and inaugurated in England a new age of central-ization. The last of the Tudor monarchs was Elizabeth I who died in 1603, and then her cousin, James VI of Scotland, was invited by the British Parliament to wear the crown.

The arrival of James, the founder of the Stuart Dynasty, was a poor augury for futurity, for the new king had none of the practicality of the Tudors who had maneuvered the Parliament to their own advantage. He was exceptionally gifted with medi-ocrity, but it is his loquacity that really got him into trouble. He was not content with the reality of autocratic power, he had to brag about it as well. As a result, he quickly managed to anger the Parliament. It is James who proclaimed the doctrine of the divine right of kings in England—something he borrowed from the neighboring French autocracy.

Thus when James died in 1625 and was succeeded by his son Charles I, the English people were looking forward to better days. However, the proverbial truth, "like father like son," was never more appropriate. Charles continued the high-handed policies of his father, and eventually England plunged into a virulent civil war in which the king was defeated and then, in 1649, beheaded. The forces of Parliament had won a decisive victory, but constitu-tional monarchy was still a breath away. England escaped the fry-ing pan of absolute monarchy, only to be hurled into the fire of dictatorship of the Protectorate, of which Oliver Cromwell was the first sovereign. However, in that charged atmosphere, the new autocracy disappeared within a year of Cromwell's death, and a Stuart prince, Charles II, was invited by a newly-elected Parlia-ment to wear the crown.

Charles II did not want to repeat his father's follies, but secretly he sought to restore the health and former power of the monarchy. He, and subsequently his successor, James II, had high hopes of reviving the autocratic rule. However, the warrior era in England had been going downhill right from the accession of the Stuart Dynasty, and it was only a matter of time before an intellec-tual era was to appear. The final blow was delivered by a bloodless coup in 1688—by the so-called Glorious Revolution that climaxed first into James' abdication and then into diminished powers of the new king, William of Orange. The king was not then shorn of all authority, but soon after 1700 he had to play second fiddle to the Prime Minister, who came to head the Parliament.

In the aftermath of the Glorious Revolution, the Parliament had emerged supreme, but it was a heterogeneous entity with little prior experience or precedent of an authoritative body. Anyone who could then manipulate it with oratorical skills, intrigues, high-minded platitudes and, above all, with the lure of sinecure offices thus became the supreme ruler of British society. Such skills are possessed only by an intellectual. Therefore after 1700, through a confluence of peculiar circumstances such as a later king's inability to understand English among others, real power converged to the head of the Parliament—the intellectual Prime Minister. Thus began a new intellectual age in Europe, and, of course, the Prime Minister, as in every intellectual era, could rule only indirectly, in the name of the King who was still esteemed by his subjects.

The British Parliamentary system at 1688, even up to 1867, was much different from the institution one finds today. It was anything but democratic, for democracy signifies the rule by a majority of people, and at the beginning of the seventeenth century, an oligarchy of landed interests, headed by the Prime Minister, controlled the English Parliament. Almost from its inception, the legislative assembly had been organized into two distinctive chambers—the House of Commons and the House of Lords. The House of Lords, also called the upper house, was totally undemocratic, for it was composed of two highly privileged groups— hereditary peers and bishops of the Anglican Church. Elections were open to the House of Commons or the lower house, but to all intents and purposes were controlled by a group of big landowners who were members of the upper house. This suggests that acquisitors, not intellectuals, governed the British society after the revolution of 1688. But a deeper investigation reveals something else.

It is true that social supremacy in eighteenth-century England rested with the peers and the landed gentry, while the political power converged to the Prime Minister. It is also true that the upper house was dominated by a few big landlords who shamelessly controlled elections to the lower house by means of bribery, nepotism and intrigues. But this nobility, consisting of peers and the gentry, was far from the richest class. That distinction belonged to the rising class of wealthy merchants and capitalists, who then possessed all the money but only a bit of social stature and prestige.

The prestige by tradition derived from land. Some of the biggest landlords were men of humble means, but their sway in the House of Lords as well as the lower house would certainly belie this impression. Furthermore, land was no longer the principal engine of production; it was capital, financial as well as industrial, and that, of course, was owned by the select group of capitalists, bankers and merchants. In other words, it is not the land-owner but the capital-owner who now belonged to the acquisitive class.

How did the landed aristocracy wield so much influence? The answer lies in the force of traditions and ideas. The aristocracy governed by means of time-honored ideas that exalted the dignity of owning land above everything else; by means of the injunctions of the Christian paternalistic ethic—preached earlier by the feudal barons and bishops to justify their exploitation of the serfs—which condemned not so much landed wealth as wealth acquired in the form of interest and profit, the twins that made the capitalist so rich; by means of intellectual trickery which enabled the hereditary peers as well as the Prime Minister to keep the lower house under their thumb.

Ever since the Middle Ages, the Church (whether Catholic or Protestant) had set its vast moral authority against usury, profits and in general the acquisitive mentality, although its injunctions were carefully disregarded by some of its own members, not to speak of others. Still, this ethic served to slight the acquisitors who made money from business and lending. And who controlled the Anglican Church during the eighteenth century England! The aristocracy, of course! "Its influence over the Church of England," asserts Daniel Baugh, "was practically absolute." [1, p. 3]

The landed aristocracy was dominant, because it took an active role in politics of the time, while the bourgeoisie were busy making money. The rule of the game then, as now, was to secure a majority for one's party, Whig or Tory, in the House of Commons whose members were generally elected, or recruited, from the ranks of the landed gentry dominating the countryside. "Management" is the word that has been commonly used by historians to describe the way the aristocracy, under the guidance of the Prime Minister, kept the lower house in line. The first British Prime Minister was Robert Walpole, who came to power in 1721 on the shoulders of the Whig party. I cite Baugh again to describe the intellectual trickery in which the Prime Minister had to be adept in those days:

> Management constricted the political influence of the independent country members [of the lower house]. Sir Robert Walpole, the greatest of eighteenth-century managers, elaborated the system. By melding the patronage of the court, the interests of the great financial institutions, and the influence of the aristocracy, he secured a corps of loyal M.P.s. [1, p. 19]

Actually there is yet another angle through which the mentality, in Sarkar's sense, of the upper-house peers ought to be viewed. Some peers were indeed men of affluence, but they evinced little interest in the accumulation of wealth—one infallible trait that distinguishes the acquisitive mind. In the feudal age, the big landlords were frequently on the warpath so as to accumulate wealth by increasing the size of their fiefs, which at the dawn of feudalism were the only instruments of production and power. In the eighteenth century, and a few centuries before, capital was fast emerging as the chief source of production, income and wealth, and it is a person's interest in the accumulation of capital that now mainly determined whether or not he possessed the acquisitive mind.

But the interest of the aristocracy in this capital accumulation, in frugality that ultimately leads to it, was, if not negative, negligible. Some of the biggest landowners were in debt; traditions of the time demanded that all peers live a life of pomp and ostentation, which rendered capital accumulation, despite fabulous incomes, well-nigh impossible. In short, primacy of the landed interests stemmed not from their economic power but from the force of tradition, contemporary ideology, and the guile in which the Prime Minister had to be a virtuoso; if he was not, his job did not last long.

Actually the fact that eighteenth-century England was ruled by the Prime Minister, who did not possess absolute power but rather depended on a small oligarchy consisting of seventy-odd peers, accords well with the intellectual character of the new age. All it displays is the relative decentralization of political power which the aristocracy exercised, as in every intellectual epoch, in the name of the apparent ruler, the English King. Later on, as we shall see in the ensuing section, governmental authority became dispersed among the bourgeoisie, and the power-base became extremely decentralized, thus paving the way for a new acquisitive age.

Once England moved into the new intellectual era, other important nations of Europe did not, or could not, stay far behind. Not that, at the onset of the eighteenth century, parliamentary forms of government also developed elsewhere, only that in the European countries molding Western society at the time real power passed into the hands of indirect rulers—the Prime Minister, the Chancellor, or diplomats, who all reigned in the name of their king. Fittingly, it is the almost perpetual state of war that the warrior despots had waged against each other for more than a century—the wars of religion, the wars of succession, and the like—that increased their dependence on their ministers. Quite often had the monarchs found that they would win battles at the front but almost lose the war at the bargaining table, or that the treaties of peace did not measure up to their expectations, to their investment of time, national energy, and lost manpower, to the degree to which the foe had been trounced. For these reasons, there arose the need for diplomats, for men of intellect shrewd enough to preserve what the army had accomplished at the battlefield.

This was one of the main reasons for the rising star of the intellectuals. Another was that after 1700, many monarchs were simply too feeble to govern their nations amidst crescendos of international conflicts. And when the apparent ruler is feeble, the vacuum of authority has to be filled by the indirect ruler.

Let us examine the developments in France and see how the intellectual period reappeared there at just about the same time as in England. It has already been noted that a centralized French state had emerged in the 1460s on the debris of the Hundred Years War. Flames of the Reformation also eventually engulfed France during the sixteenth century; at the same time it had to fight a long war with Spain over Italy. The result was a weakening of the monarchy along with a resurgence of the old feudal forces.

The absolute French monarch thus embroiled with Spain was Henry II who died in 1559, whereupon two factions of nobles —one Catholic and the other Protestant—came to dominate the political scene. For the next thirty years, their rivalry plunged France into civil wars of religion, until Henry of Navarre, the founder of the Bourbon Dynasty, brought order to the scourged land in 1593. Not only did Henry restore peace, he also revived the absolutist tradition to which the rest of Europe, as well as France, had already been accustomed. In his goal of national recovery, he was ably assisted by his Chief Minister, the Duke of Sully, who could not have lived in France at a more opportune time. Both Henry and Sully were energetic warriors and exceptional leaders, but Sully was a better administrator.

Henry's promising rule was, however, cut short in 1610 by an assassin's dagger, and after a disturbing interlude of fourteen years, the new king, Louis XIII, practically handed the reins to his Chief Minister, Cardinal Richelieu. For the next eighteen years, France lived and prospered under the shadow of this capable, energetic, intellectual minister who set out to efface all internal opposition to the monarchy. Both the king and his minister died about the same time, and while the new king, Louis XIV, was a lad of four, the new Chief Minister was Cardinal Mazarin, whom Richelieu had carefully groomed for this appointment. Until his death in 1661, Mazarin was the real power in France.

It then appears that the intellectual era of rule by Chief Ministers had begun in France at the beginning of the seventeenth century, a full century ahead of its arrival in England. Even if Sully's rule is disregarded in this context, for his own king, Henry of Navarre, was the real ruler, Richelieu and Mazarin between them provide four decades of intellectual reign during which the kings, owing to infancy of age or of intellect, had to take a back seat. However, by Mazarin's demise in 1661, the king Louis XIV had come of age, and then began a long, direct, iron rule, lasting for over fifty years, during which the ministers and other administrators played only a phantom role.

In the person of Louis XIV, absolutism reached its apotheosis; he was the Law; he was the State; he was the sun around whom his subjects, like planets, revolved. However, after his death in 1715, most of the kings were weaklings and their absolutism was in reality exercised by others—their mistresses, the ministers, the bureaucrats—and it is then that the intellectual era really began. The reign of Richelieu and Mazarin thus turned out to be a harbinger of the new intellectual epoch, not its beginning. Every era casts its shadows in the preceding age, and Richelieu and Mazarin were in this sense the shadows of their counterparts who reigned for much of the eighteenth and parts of the nineteenth centuries.

From 1715 until 1789, the memorable year of the French Revolution, France was in reality governed by ministers of the royal council, of which Cardinal Fleury, the *premier ministre* from 1726 to 1743, was the one and only effective administrator. In the aftermath of the Revolution, the renowned Napoleon Bonaparte was catapulted into power, and the direct warrior rule reappeared. But this proved to be a counter-revolutionary event (in Sarkar's sense)—for Napoleon's star collapsed as fast as it had risen—and after twenty years of his rule, the intellectual era returned, only to be tested soon by the forces of direct, monarchical rule. This story, however, must be reserved for a later occasion.

At the beginning of the new warrior era, Spain, France, and England were, in that order, the three dominating powers of Europe. Spain particularly was among the leaders in oceanic exploration, and this activity, as noted before, played a monumental role in determining the future of Western society. But by the beginning of the eighteenth century, the Spanish orbit of influence had shrunk and two new powers had emerged in its place— the Austrian House of Hapsburg and Prussia. Both had been more or less centralized during much of the seventeenth century, Austria under the scepter of Leopold I and Prussia under that of Frederick William I.

During the eighteenth century, while Prussia continued to be under the direct rule of its king, the Hapsburg ruler came increasingly under the sway of his advisers, of whom some became the state Chancellors. Leopold himself had been ably served by his foreign ambassadors, who, in those days of poor communications, held wide powers in international affairs. This was the age of diplomacy and the European balance of power was on the mind of each and every diplomat. Political fortunes were made or marred in this arena, and it is to the shrewdness of the Hapsburg ambassadors that credit must go for enhancing their king or queen in European affairs.

The House of Hapsburg during the first half of the eighteenth century was represented by a weak ruler, Charles VI, who reigned from 1711 to 1740. But he received sound advice first from Count Wenzel Writislaw, who helped maintain an intricate alliance with England, and then from Count Karl Friedrich Schönborn who went on to become the state Chancellor. Thus in the case of the Hapsburg Dynasty, with its vast domains in Europe, the germ of the intellectual era had been planted in the second half of the seventeenth century, in the reign of Leopold. But the intellectual influence came to light only during the eighteenth century, especially in the second half, even though the then Austrian rulers themselves—of whom Queen Maria Theresa is the most renowned—were persons of sound intellect and judgment. This is because their Chancellor, Prince Wengel Anton Kaunitz (1753–92), was intellectually more than their match. Later in the nineteenth century, the intellectual dominance displayed itself in the person of Prince Clemens Lothar Metternich, who was undisputed master of Austrian affairs from 1809 to 1848.

Thus we see that in three of the four most important centers of western Europe during the eighteenth century, in England, France, and Austria, it was not the King (or the Queen) who actually ruled, but the intellectual minister or the Chancellor.

The intellectuals were then the real arbiters of Western destiny, not the apparent rulers.

Womanhood had made great strides during the new warrior age, and without much difficulty, because during the preceding acquisitive age the social respect for women had reached a point so low that it could not sink any further. We have already seen how, around the sixteenth century, education was no longer regarded in Europe as just the prerogative of men. Furthermore, so many outstanding women had surfaced on the European political scene that the social attitude towards them had to become more cordial than before. Louis XIV himself had furthered the cause of feminism by inviting some noblewomen to the royal court and by granting them positions of honor. However, as the warrior era drew to a close and the new intellectual age got under way, the progressive forces working for feminine rights received a serious setback. This became evident in France after the death of Louis XIV, when the reaction of the privileged male nobility set in.

The discussion of social attitudes towards women in eighteenth-century France, and elsewhere in Europe, is tied with an institution called the salon. The salon had been transplanted from Italy into France as early as the sixteenth century when royal women provided it patronage; gradually it filtered into the lower stratum of society, and by the eighteenth century permeated the intellectual fabric in major cities. Basically, a salon was a place of congregation for many kinds of social functions—balls, dancing, gambling, gossiping. Gradually it became an outlet for new ideas, philosophies, the latest literature, religion, and any other subject that could be the focal point of intelligent conversation. It is through this conduit that the fervor of revolution eventually spread all over France.

Women had a particularly important role to play in this haven of the intelligentsia; they were particularly adept in the functions of a hostess who would start the ball rolling by introducing new guests, by initiating conversation, and, at times, by entertaining guests with witty comments. In the working of the salon, therefore, women enjoyed a good deal of say and responsibility. Some women themselves were creative, intelligent, and influential, although intellectual discourse was not something society expected of the hostess; nay, it discouraged it. From France, the salon was exported to many other European nations. In fact, with women of an intellectual bent, it became more popular in England than anywhere else.

It thus appears that women in eighteenth-century Europe were breaking new ground, opening up new careers, and even assuming equality in some intellectual circles. But unfortunately, time was not on their side; Europe had passed into the new intellectual era, and seeds of women's liberation from age-old clutches of servility were to fall on barren and hostile soil. For one thing, in the then European society there were to emerge few outstanding women who could have inspired feminism at a time when many of the *philosophes,* the philosophers of France, were beginning to see through the real cause of women's subordination in society: they were beginning to realize that men, not God, were to blame for women's so-called inherent inferiority. However, such ideas, for some reason, made little headway.

The age of Louis XV was an age of debauchery in which the king himself was the ringleader. He had quite a few mistresses, and numerous other men quickly stepped in his shoes, eventually arousing the ire of many citizens. However, the blame, as usual, was to fall on women, for men, who actually dictated society, could not by time-honored tradition be faulted in this regard. This was then one force retarding the feminine cause. Another such force appeared in the writings of some *philosophes* themselves, who, ignoring their king's lechery, emphasized women's penchant for sexual pleasure. Thus, through their erotic works, they were spewing the same venom which for different reasons the Church Fathers had once taken pains to spread. As a result, the general attitude towards women reached a new low in literature and society, which, because of its medieval training, was quick to accept the amatory thought demeaning womanhood. And in this respect, what was true of France was also true of the rest of Europe.

Even some of those who championed human liberty from the tentacles of absolutism, whether of the king or of his ministers, limited their progressivism to the male population. Jean-Jacques

Rousseau, that progenitor of the concept of democracy, himself argued for the subservience of women. To him woman had been created on earth for only one purpose: to please man by her presence, and entertain him by her grace and skills. In short, while the ideas of individualism, of freedom from everything superstitious and totalitarian had been gaining ground in many parts of Europe, especially in England and France during the seventeenth and eighteenth centuries, woman was not meant to be their beneficiary. Man was supposed to have monopoly over liberty, woman over servility. The reason: while the warrior era was on the decline, the intellectual age was on the rise.

CAPITALISM AND THE NEW ACQUISITIVE ERA

The new intellectual era in the West lasted till the middle of the nineteenth century, when it too gave way to a new acquisitive epoch in which capitalists, embodying the new forces of wealth and the means of production, came to dominate society. We are already familiar with how undemocratic the British parliamentary system was at the outset of the eighteenth century; how the landed aristocracy and gentry controlled the House of Commons by manipulating elections. And in any case, less than four percent of the population exercised the right to vote. In this setup, not only the poor masses, but also the emerging middle and upper classes (in terms of income) were clearly at a disadvantage. Not only did this system poorly reflect the glaring shifts that had occurred in the composition of population following the rise of industrial cities and centers, it also tended to pass laws that favored the landed interests and hindered economic development, capitalism as well as industrialization.

This anomaly, of course, did not go without protest. But the aristocracy was so deeply entrenched in the seat of power that little corrective action was undertaken until 1832, when the famous Reform Bill somehow sailed through narrow crevices of the House of Lords. The upper house had all along stood in the way of all progressive legislation that originated in the lower-house, and it was only when the King threatened to create new peers that the Reform Bill was enacted. However, it was merely a palliative, raising the number of voters to no more than five percent. Thus political power remained with the Prime Minister, who had enough intellectual trickery to control the lower house and have his way in most affairs.

It was not before the Reform Bill of 1867, when almost a million names were added to the list of voters, that the powerbase was sufficiently decentralized to herald the beginning of a new acquisitive era wherein elections to Parliament were controlled by none but the rising class of capitalists. Control over the House of Commons also then slipped out of the Prime Minister's hands as elections could no longer be as easily managed as before. Prior to 1867, there were several Prime Ministers, such as Robert Walpole, who got themselves elected for three or four consecutive terms, lasting altogether for as many as twenty years; but after 1867, there is not one who reigned for more than eight continuous years. Of course, there were some who intermittently came to office many times—Disraeli and Gladstone are conspicuous examples—but in the two-party system prevailing in England, this is not surprising.

Thus after the passage of the second Reform Bill, political power got much more decentralized as it passed into the hands of affluent capitalists who displayed all the features of the acquisitive mind. They represented the forces of wealth, believed in its accumulation, and controlled factories and banks—the new engines of production.

In France too, a new acquisitive era emerged around the 1870s. We have already noted that a council of ministers ruled France after the Sun King, Louis XIV, died in 1715. This indirect rule, however, was cut short in 1789 when the famous French Revolution cast off the *ancien régime* like old garments. In the ensuing turmoil, Napoleon Bonaparte came to power in 1795, and with him the direct warrior rule as well as absolutism made a resounding comeback. This, however, as stated before, turned out to be an episode of counter-revolution, for in 1815 Napoleon met his Waterloo, which sealed his fate once and for all.

France then reverted to constitutional monarchy, in which Louis XVIII, a descendant of the deposed Bourbon Dynasty, was the first ruler. This is how the French Republican tradition was born; extensive executive powers were then given to the king who was to govern with the help of a Chief Minister and a two-chamber parliament patterned after the British model. However, stiff property qualifications were introduced for voting rights, with the result that less than one percent of adult males enjoyed the privilege of suffrage. The Republic had been born amidst defeat and pandemonium, and its essentially unstable character soon came to the surface. In the next fifteen years, ministries frequently changed hands, until another revolution took place in 1830, and the last of the Bourbon kings was deposed. The next king was Louis Philippe, who promised to be a titular ruler and to govern in the interest of the bourgeois and the working class.

In his promise, the new king was faithful to the letter; he tried his best to be as nominal a ruler as possible, and when one's objectives are lowly, success is inevitable. The policy of prosperity and peace at home and abroad is what the new king pursued in cooperation with his more influential ministers, of whom the name of Guizot immediately comes to mind. The government did little to change the constitution and make it more democratic so as to secure in parliament a better representation of the bourgeois class. But ultimately it is the excessive caution of the Guizot ministry in providing everything but leadership in foreign affairs that proved to be its undoing. In 1848, France was on the brink of another crisis, with the majority of the people demanding a more open government and democracy.

However, another counter-evolutionary event was to take place, before the forces of decentralized democracy were to prevail over those of the relatively centralized intellectual rule. In yet another revolution of 1848, Louis Napoleon Bonaparte (or Napoleon III), a nephew of the celebrated Napoleon, was elected President with a resounding margin. Monarchy was thus abolished, but the new Napoleon gave free reins to the old Napoleonic penchant for self-aggrandizement and power. In three years, he proclaimed himself as the dictator and later as the Emperor of France. This way despotism and the warrior rule staged an unexpected return, but they could go no further than 1870, when a Paris uprising overthrew Napoleon and with him the final vestiges of autocracy.

In 1875, a new constitution was introduced, and this time the French Republic really became democratic, with universal manhood suffrage, a cabinet system borrowed from Britain, and a titular President elected by the Parliament. The influence over elections, of course, passed into the hands of the affluent capitalists within the bourgeois class. Thus it is only after the 1870 crisis, three years later than the British Reform Bill, that a decentralized government and a new acquisitive era were born in France.

By the end of the nineteenth century, democracy, and hence the new acquisitive era, had also been established in many other countries of western and central Europe—Italy, Switzerland, Belgium, Norway, Denmark. In fact, in some of the smaller nations, democracy was more advanced than in their bigger English and French neighbors. Similarly, in the United States of America, whose story as an offshoot of the West must become a part of my story (to be told in Chapter 8), the democratic tradition had struck firm roots by this time. There were, however, some notable exceptions in Austria and Prussia, which by then had evolved into a unified German state.

In Austria the real power during the eighteenth century had been by and large exercised by its state Chancellor, and even though, in the second half of the nineteenth century, a constitutional monarchy had emerged, democracy was still far away. The Austrian House of Hapsburg and its empire actually lingered on until the end of the First World War in 1918, when the undemocratic monarchy was abolished and a republic took its place. However the forces of democracy were soon trampled by those of fascism, and it took another world war before the republican governments could emerge again.

In Prussia and Germany, a somewhat different evolution took place. We have already noted that while most other important European centers were in the intellectual era, Prussia still chafed under absolutism. However, other German states were only partially centralized under the rule of many princes who were so jealous of their independence that a German nation remained undeveloped as late as the middle of the nineteenth century. Stirrings of democracy had, of course, occurred in both Austria and Prussia ever since the 1789 French Revolution, but the Prussian monarchs and the Austrian Chancellors had managed to keep them under control. In 1849, following the revolution of 1848 in neighboring France, the Prussian king granted his subjects a token constitution embodying a bicameral parliamentary system. Even though royal absolutism did not then abate in Prussia, the new development did foreshadow the advent of its intellectual age, which soon found a powerful spokesman in the famous statesman Otto von Bismarck.

Raised in a conservative tradition, Bismarck entertained grandiose visions of a vast Prussian empire, with all German states unified under its command in one nation. He got his opportunity in 1862 when King William I appointed him as Chief Minister. Bismarck wasted little time in restoring the military strength of the diminutive state, and soon his foresight yielded dividends. Within a short span of the next eight years, Prussia was embroiled in three wars, and in each it emerged triumphant. This is how a German nation, and its empire, were born in 1871; and the credit for all this must go to Bismarck's ingenuity, statesmanship and machinations. Thus, Prussia, which had long played a pivotal role in the destiny of Europe, moved into the intellectual era when Bismarck came into prominence. Up to 1890, when he was finally removed rather brusquely, Bismarck was the unchallenged master of the German Confederation.

At the end of the nineteenth century then, while most of the prominent centers of the West, England, France, and the United States, were in the acquisitive era, two other regions—Germany, and vast European domains controlled by the Austrian House of Hapsburg—had lagged behind in terms of Sarkar's evolutionary cycle as they were still languishing in the intellectual age. A tussle for supremacy between these divergent forces was then inevitable, a tussle that in 1914 erupted in a world-wide conflagration of unprecedented horror. When the First World War was over in 1918, the acquisitive forces, after paying a frightful price, had won, and Austria and Germany were forced to accept democratic regimes.

However, the energies of absolutism, whether of warrior or of intellectual variety, were not yet spent. Soon Austria, Germany, and even Italy were caught in the straight-jacket of dictatorships. The international atmosphere became so combustible that even a little spark could then ignite it into an infernal fire. The climax was the Second World War (1939–45), even more tragic, more formidable, more cataclysmic than the first. However, time was still on the side of acquisitive forces, and before them the agents of absolutism eventually had to kneel. Ever since, at most places which once nurtured Western civilization, the acquisitive era has prevailed.

In most democratic countries today, parliamentary representation can be bought with money. The capitalistic wealth rules the roost; the political structure is extremely decentralized, and there is scarcely any respect for authority, for law and order. Most laws, civil or criminal, are designed to further the interests of the rich: they can escape taxes through legal loopholes, while the poor and the middle class pay disproportionately high amounts; can usually avoid prison sentences for committing the so-called white-collar crimes. Social and political hegemony thus now ostensibly belongs to the acquisitive class

SUMMARY

This has been a long narrative and a compendium is in order, if only to keep a clear track of the pattern to which I have reduced the vast narrative of Western society. I have argued in the foregoing pages that annals of the West provide an exquisite fit for Sarkar's law of social cycle. As we have seen, the period of the Roman Empire conforms with the warrior era, of the early Middle Ages with the intellectual era, of the later Middle Ages or Feudalism with the acquisitive era, of the peasant rebellions with the laborer era, culminating in the laborer revolution that was brought about by Louis XI in France, by Isabella and Ferdinand in Spain, and by Henry VII in England. The evolution of this entire period of about fourteen hundred years following the birth of Christ completed one rotation of the social cycle. Another cycle commenced with the new warrior period of centralized national monarchies, followed first by the intellectual age portraying the influence of the Prime Ministers and then by the acquisitive era dominated by affluent capitalists. That is where the West now stands.

NOTES

1. Some comparisons between one era and the other become invalid if the new era is imposed on society by a foreign power. This, for instance, happened when the British imposed an acquisitive era on India and unleashed the engines of exploitation. This is one case where the acquisitive age was economically worse off than the preceding intellectual age. For details, see Chapter 6.

REFERENCES

[1] Baugh, D. A. (ed.), *Aristocratic Government and Society in Eighteenth Century England* (New York: Franklin Watts, 1975), Ch. 1.

[2] Beard, M. R., *Woman as Force in History* (New York: Macmillan, 1946).

[3] Bullough, V. L., *The Subordinate Sex* (Urbana: University of Illinois Press, 1973).

[4] Burns, E. M., and P. L. Ralph, *World Civilisations* (New York: W. W. Norton, fifth edition, 1974).

[5] Donaldson, J., *Woman; Her Position and Influence in Ancient Greece and Rome, and Among the Early Christians* (New York: Gordon Press, 1973).

[6] Ferguson, W. K., and G. Brunn, *A Survey of European Civilisation* (Boston: Houghton Mifflin, second edition, 1947).

[7] Gras, N. S. B., *A History of Agriculture in Europe and America* (New York: F. S. Crofts, 1940).

[8] Harkness, G., *Women in Church and Society* (Nashville: Abingdon Press, 1972).

[9] Hunt, E. K., and H. J. Sherman, *Economics: An Introduction to Traditional and Radical Views* (New York: Harper & Row, 1975).

[10] Painter, S., *Feudalism and Liberty*, ed. F. A. Cazel, Jr. (Baltimore: Johns Hopkins Press, 1961).

[11] Power, E., 'The Position of Women,' in *The Legacy of the Middle Ages*, eds. C. G. Crump, and E. F. Jacob (New York: Oxford University Press, 1926). Reprinted in *Women from the Greeks to the French Revolution*, ed. S. G. Bell (Belmont: Wadsworth Publishing Company, 1973).

[12] Putnam, E. J., *The Lady* (New York: G. P. Putnam's Sons, 1910).

[13] Rostovtzeff, M., *A History of the Ancient World, Vol. I* (London: Oxford University Press, 1928).

[14] Rostovtzeff, M., *The Social and Economic History of the Roman Empire* (London: Oxford University Press, 1926).

[15] Thompson, J. W., *Economic and Social History of the Middle Ages* (New York: The Century Co., 1928).

[16] Tuma, E. H., *European Economic History* (New York: Harper & Row, 1971).

5

The History of Russia

The early history of Russia, to borrow a phrase from Florinsky, is shrouded in an "opaque veil of oblivion." As a matter of fact, it may not be an exaggeration to say that more is known about ancient Egypt, which basked in splendor long before the birth of Christ, than about Russia of even as late as the seventh century A.D. It is only the eventful episodes of the eighth and ninth centuries that first bring Russia into the limelight of history. The main sources of information in this regard are the Russian *Chronicle*—regarded by some as unreliable—and foreign historical records and writings, especially those furnished by Byzantine and Arabic scholars.

As elsewhere, but more so in Russia, geography has played a paramount role in shaping social evolution of the Russians, who are basically of Slavic ancestry. Russia today is the biggest nation with an area sprawling over two continents—Europe and Asia. In its early history, however, only the geography of its European wing mattered, because until the sixteenth century no Russian set his footsteps in Siberia, which constitutes its Asian arm.

At this point one wonders why Russian history is not studied as an integral part of Western civilization. The reason lies in the vast social, economic, political, cultural, and even religious gulf that right from its inception has separated the Russian state from the rest of Europe, a gulf explained chiefly by radical geographical differences between them. According to Toynbee, for instance, Russian narrative is a tributary of the Orthodox Christian society and not of the West.

136

Since its early history is so murky, it is not surprising to find the origin of the Russian state riddled with controversy, which has mostly centered around the formation of what is known as Kievan Russia. It is not my intention to get embroiled with this debate, and for the purpose in hand it turns out to be refreshingly unessential. I therefore take note mainly of those Russian events and characteristics on which the historians are in substantial accord.

From the third century to the ninth, it is believed that parts of European Russia were inhabited by several Slavic tribes—the Alans, the Antes, the Goths, the Huns, the Lithuanians, the Finns, the Khazars. In the course of the ninth and tenth centuries, many of these tribes were overwhelmed by the Normans (or Vikings), and it is this event which is credited with opening a new chapter in the annals of Russia. As in the West, the Normans gradually merged with the native population.

Early Russian history is closely linked with the body of a people called Rus, who later lent their name to Russia. Now the question is: did the Rus have anything to do with the Normans and, if so, when did the former set their feet on the Russian soil? If we accept the *Chronicle's* word verbatim, then the Rus was a Scandinavian tribe, and the first ruler of the unified Russian state was Riurik, a famous warrior and pirate, who around 862 founded his regime in Novgorod and restored order in turbulent Russian affairs. He was succeeded by Oleg, who in 882 enlarged his domain by conquering Kiev, a commercial and military town situated in the Dnieper basin. This is how Kieven Russia was born. The center of activity shifted from Novgorod to Kiev because of the latter's geographical advantage as a confluence of trade routes to the Black Sea and Byzantium, and as a fortification against the constant menace of assaults from the eastern and southern nomads.

There are those, however, who question first the Scandinavian origin of the Rus and then the existence of any Riurik. They also go a bit too far by objecting to the use of the word "state" in describing Kievan affairs. A quote from Riasanovsky, who represents the majority view on Kievan historiography, may be used to settle this argument:

To sum up, the Norman theory can no longer be held in anything like its original scope. Most significantly, there is no reason to assert a fundamental Scandinavian influence on Kievan culture. But the supporters of the theory stand on much firmer ground when they rely on archaeological, philological and other evidence to substantiate the presence of the Normans in Russia in the ninth century. . . .

In any case, whether through internal evolution, outside intervention or some particular combination of the two, the Kievan *state* did arise in the Dnieper area toward the end of the ninth century. [5, p. 30 (italics mine)]

As far as Sarkar's hypothesis is concerned, it matters little if Kievan Russia was, throughout its history, organized as a centralized system or as a loose federation of city states. What matters most—for which there is little margin of doubt—is that in the period between the ninth and the eleventh century, Russia, as subsequently shown, was politically more centralized than in the immediately succeeding period. My argument is that, as far as can be judged from the information we have, at least the first half of the Kievan period belongs to the warrior age.

KIEVAN RUSSIA AND THE WARRIOR ERA

The foundation of the Kievan state (or federation) rested on military activities, on fire and the sword. The expansion of the State— first founded by the legendary Riurik and then augmented by Oleg—continued unabated, until by the year 1000 it extended from the Finnish Gulf in the north to the Caspian Sea in the south, and from the Don River in the east to the present-day Hungary in the west. Much of this territory was conquered by a prince named Sviatoslav whose reign—lasting from 964 to 972—was cut short, not unexpectedly, by war. Most of the early Kievan princes were thus endowed with martial qualities and disposition. About Sviatoslav, for instance, Vernadsky has this to say:

Sviatoslav seems to have gloried in the hard life of the military campaigner. In the words of the old chronicler, he was as brave and quick as a panther. When he attacked, he scorned stealth and sent messengers ahead announcing "I come against you." [6, p. 34]

Similar traits, perhaps to a lesser degree, also distinguished other princes, especially Sviatoslav's predecessors. Whenever, the succession to the throne was in question, it was settled by fratricidal wars. Such blood-baths occurred after Sviatoslav's death, when Vladimir won the day, and then again following Vladimir's demise, when Iaroslav was the victor. Upon Iaroslav's death in 1054, however, the tradition of bloody feuds of succession was broken, albeit temporarily, and Russia was divided into many principalities ruled by his sons. The fecundity of princes, however, culminated in a great multiplicity of these city states, and the so-called Rota system had to be devised to determine, among a multitude of relatives, seniority for purposes of succession. Thus until 1054 the Kievan state was centrally ruled by one prince, but following Iaroslav's reign the political *imperium* was divided among many princes, although one prince, depending on the prestige and commercial significance of the town under his governance, continued to be regarded as the first among equals.

In spite of the subdivision of Russia in 1054, the militaristic foundation of the Kievan state did not immediately disappear. The princes, even before Iaroslav, were not autocratic rulers and shared power with their retinue, called *druzhina,* which was a privileged group of persons known as boyars, a term whose origin still eludes us. The privileges of the boyar-aristocracy, however, arose not from material acquisitions and wealth but from naked military might. The prince and his boyars, though holding large domains, were relentlessly ready for warfare, which was quite frequent among the princes, who all coveted the prestigious principality of Kiev. Their main function was the defense and expansion of the territory under control. In short, the boyar-aristocracy then displayed the warrior mentality.

Some areas were, however, fairly democratically organized, and there—especially in Novgorod—a modicum of power was exercised by the *veche,* a city assembly composed of all the adult townsmen, who occasionally engaged in armed skirmishes to reach agreement on decisions and policies. With the passage of time, and especially during the twelfth century, the *veche* became more important in almost all cities.

From the facts presented above, it is safe to conclude that relative political centralization and hence the warrior era prevailed in Kievan Russia at least until 1054. The exact origin of this era must still evade us, because the critical information regarding the sociopolitical setup in early Russia is unavailable. The embryonic stage of the warrior period could have started with the third century, or even before, when the Russians were organized in various tribes under, possibly, the tutelage of warrior chiefs. What is unequivocal, however, is that the onslaught of the Vikings during the ninth century heralded, if not reinforced, the advent of the Russian warrior age, which, as argued above, lasted at least until Iaroslav's demise in 1054.

MONGOL DOMINATION AND THE INTELLECTUAL ERA

One of the memorable events during Vladimir's reign (978–1015)—one that played a monumental role in steering the ship of the subsequent Russian state—was the conversion of pagan Russians to Christianity. Vladimir repudiated paganism, and in 988 accepted the Christian religion—of the Greek Orthodox variety with its center at Byzantium—as the official Church of Russia. One would suppose that Russia's official baptism drew it closer to the West in thinking, attitude, and culture, but in fact the effect was just the opposite. Richard Pipes tells us why:

> The fact that Russia received its Christianity from Byzantium rather than from the West had the most profound consequences for the entire course of Russia's historic development. Next to the geographic considerations . . . it was perhaps the single most critical factor influencing that country's destiny. By accepting the eastern brand of Christianity, Russia separated itself from the mainstream of Christian civilization which, as it happened, flowed westward. . . . Thus, the acceptance of Christianity, instead of drawing it closer to the Christian community, had the effect of isolating Russia from its neighbors. [4, p. 223]

The late arrival of Christianity in Russia derives mainly from its geographical remoteness from the hub of the Roman Empire where, it may be recalled, the religion of Christ was at first rejected but later patronized by the government. In the West, Christianity had spread from the grass roots to the top, whereas in Russia it was imposed from above—as a state religion. Therefore right from its birth the Christian Church in Russia enjoyed privileges unavailable to the lower strata of society. It did not, however, overshadow the princes, at least not until 1054, and perhaps not before a foreign power—the Mongols—was firmly entrenched at the head of the Russian political structure.

Despite the unflinching official patronage that it enjoyed at its introduction, Christianity was not readily accepted by the common people. Its dogmas and rituals, especially of the Greek Orthodox variety, were too cumbersome for the illiterate masses to understand. Therefore, for a long while both Christianity and paganism endured in Russia in an unhappy but unavoidable alliance. The state, as in most other countries, did try to impose the divine love of religion by the earthly vigor of fire and sword, but the old Russian faiths just would not die.

Vladimir's successors did not share his enthusiasm towards the Church and the latter was dependent upon them to a greater degree. Following Iaroslav's death in 1054, however, when the relatively centralized rule by one prince gave way to joint rule by many princes, the Church, through its own status and through its influence on the *veche,* to which I have already alluded, assumed a more vocal role in political affairs. Fedotov, an authority on Russian religious history, corroborates this in a forceful way:

> The loose monarchy of Kiev, after reaching its climax under Vladimir, who died in 1015, and his son Iaroslav, who died in 1054, began to split into a multiplicity of local principalities. . . . Their ties were very weak, and of moral rather than legal character; the primacy of the prince of Kiev was merely honorary.
>
> In every local state the prince had to face many social forces. . . . The Church was the most powerful of these social elements and the princes could not even dream of dominating it. [2, p. 22]

One of the most celebrated episodes representing Church intervention in secular affairs is what Clarkson [1, pp. 37 and 45] calls the "democratic revolution" that rocked Kiev in 1113. There, in response to the appeals by prelates and local magnates, a junior prince, Vladimir Monomakh, condescended to the wishes of the people and accepted the throne in the full knowledge that his action directly violated the Rota system—the then law of primogeniture.

Events such as these do not prove that during the twelfth century the Church and hence the intellectual era had been firmly established, but they do signify a general decline of the warrior era, of relative centralization, and the beginning of the intellectual ascendancy which, as we shall presently see, was to receive help from a completely unexpected source—the Mongols. The latter thus played the selfsame role as Germanic barbarians who had earlier, in the fifth century, inflicted a lethal blow upon the Roman Empire, and thus enabled the Roman Church first to fill the power-vacuum and then to emerge supreme in Western society.

At the beginning of the thirteenth century when Kievan princes were preoccupied with their own petty feuds and the nation was torn with strife, in distant Mongolia occurred a momentous event that a little later virtually shook the foundations of civilization. Around 1206 fierce Mongolian nomads dwelling on the periphery of northern China were united under the chieftainship of Temuchin, later known as Chingis Khan (or Genghis Khan). After soon conquering North China and Turkestan he set his ominous footprints on Russian soil, and inflicted a crushing defeat on the half-hearted response of feuding princes now seemingly unified behind a common cause. The Mongols, however, withdrew as abruptly as they came, leaving behind an unprecedented cataclysm of devastation, slaughter, and rapine.

Unfortunately the breathing-space for the Russians was very short. The Mongols returned, but this time as overlords of the Tatars, a people who themselves had been overwhelmed by the fearsome nomads. The Mongols had now come to stay; they had brought their wives and children with them.

It is not clear what the Russians could have done to block the triumphant advance of the Mongolian colossus, but trifling squabbles among the princes did not help either. The then loose federation of the city-states would perhaps have crumbled anyway under the burden of its own disharmony, but the Mongolian *Völkerwanderung* added the finishing touch to its decline. By 1241 the entire country, except Novgorod, had fallen under the alien rule.

Among the European nations only the Russian polity had long contact with the Mongols. For more than two centuries certain parts of Russia were to pay tribute to the Asian nomads, while its western portion, including the Dnieper basin, after a century of Mongolian rule fell under the subjection of other non-Russian powers—Poland and Lithuania. It is worth noting here that the area relevant to the Russian history shrank drastically during the Mongol domination. It was confined to a region called Oka-Volka Mesopotamia that included the principality of Moscow, whose rise was to steer Russia's destiny to a somewhat familiar track of centralized government. Only this time, the centralization would be far more pervasive and imperious than that encountered by early Kievan Russia.

Russian history during the thirteenth to fifteenth centuries is referred to as the "Tatar Yoke" or the "appanage period." Catastrophic as the Mongol conquest had been, it created few immediate ripples in the internal politics of Russia. Economically, of course, the country was decimated for a very long time, but politically there were only subtle changes in native ways of governance, not drastic surgery involving amputation of political institutions.

There is perhaps one exception—the *veche*. The city assembly, which used to be the vehicle of any popular discontent, ceased to function. In China, as in Persia, the Mongols had overthrown native regimes and assumed direct control. In Russia, by contrast, they found no centralized state and the princes seemed too feeble to pose any menace, especially when most of them were eager to accept subservience and alms. Russian princes, all those successors of the mythological Riurik, were allowed to remain in power as long as they timely paid the tribute and swore fealty to the Khan of the so-called Golden Horde. In fact, no prince could gain legitimacy without first currying favor with the Khan and obtaining from him a charter of investiture, which was granted to those promising the maximum amount of tribute. To secure this sanction, the prince had to journey, through long, formidable terrain, to the city of Sarai and sometimes even as far as Karakorum. In so doing, some princes ran the risk of terrible humiliation and even of losing their lives.

While the princes were thus humbled, the Church emerged out of the holocaust considerably stronger and glorified. This is certainly remarkable, for Christianity and the Mongolian hordes had little in common. But the time was ripe for the intellectual era in Russia, and the nomads simply played their role in furthering the advance of Sarkar's law of social cycle.

At first the Church met the same fate as princes and the masses. The Mongols did not discriminate, and their axe fell with equal severity on the bishop and the commoner, on the privileged and the underprivileged. The Russian Church, however, had one thing working in its favor—the religious tolerance of the Khans. Despite the savagery with which the Mongols demolished their enemies, they were an intensely religious people, and, regardless of religious denomination, respected those engaged in the profession of preaching the love of God. Once the dust settled after the wars, the Church was granted a series of charters (*yarlyki*) which not merely confirmed but also expanded its former prerogatives. Priests, monks, and most others associated with the Church were exempted from all fiscal obligations and also from the Tatar tribute, which, it may be remembered, even the princes could not escape. From 1267 onwards, the Church was also allowed to send a bishop to the Khan's capital.

However, the grant of such charters was by no means a one-sided exchange. The Metropolitans of the Church promised to perform the exacting task of publically praying for the Khans. They also served as Mongolian agents in calming the rebellious masses who had to bear the brunt of the tribute which the princes, in order to stay in good graces of the Mongols, would collect so ruthlessly.

There is another dubious way in which the Mongol invasions and the resulting carnage proved of lasting assistance to the

Church. It may be recalled that Christianity had been imposed on the Russians by the state. It had failed to capture the illiterate masses, who despite centuries of official prodding did not care much about it. The widespread destruction caused by the Mongols, however, enabled the Church to provide some leadership; for once the Church played a useful role in Russian affairs. Priests moved from place to place, and provided much needed spiritual guidance and solace to the people dazed by misfortunes. As a result, Christianity spread very fast: for once the Church, which heretofore had been accepted out of fear, actually gained ground in people's hearts.

The latter part of the thirteenth century therefore is a witness to the Russian Church at the zenith of its glory and power. The intellectual era—whose beginning is discernible during the twelfth century—had thus been firmly established in thirteenth century Russia. At least on this issue, there is little dispute among historians. Pipes affirms this in convincing words:

> The *Golden Age* of the Orthodox Church in Russia coincided with Mongol domination. The Mongols exempted all the clergy living under their rule from the burdens which they imposed on the rest of the subjugated population. . . . The main beneficiaries of Mongol favor were the monasteries. In the fourteenth century, Russian monks undertook vigorous colonization, and before it was over built as many new abbeys as had been established since the country's conversion four hundred years earlier. [4, p. 226 (italics mine)]

Sometimes it is argued, and with good reason, that the Russian Church was never as powerful as its Roman counterpart; that the former, under the Byzantine tutelage, never made a sustained effort to proclaim its supremacy over the state. Does this in any way impair or even negate my basic conclusion that by the end of the thirteenth century, intellectuals wearing the Church garments, enjoyed the highest status and esteem among native Russian classes? The answer cannot but be no, because what matters here is not the comparison between the Russian and the Roman Church, but between the social standing of the Russian Church at two points of time in its own history.

What happened elsewhere in the annals of a different civilization makes no difference to my argument here. What is of greater interest is that though the Russian Church believed in the ultimate superiority of the state in secular matters, it did emerge to overshadow the princes during the early part of appanage Russia. This is because, under the pressure of circumstances, the princely authority had been so emasculated that the state, if there remained any, could not possibly prevail over the Church, even though the priest had been long tutored to submit to the ruler. All this accords so well with Sarkar's doctrine of social cycle, because here we have an instance where intellectual priests rose to primacy in spite of their habitual subordination to secular authorities.

The positive role of leadership played by the Church during the convulsive years of Asian conquest did not, of course, last long. It would be too much to expect continued morality from the priest who had become used to all the creature comforts which the Kievan princes had provided. Soon after the return of normality in Russia, the Church resumed its accumulation of land and wealth. Church property had grown, though at a sluggish pace, even during Kievan Russia, but now tax exemption and other privileges enabled it to acquire land at an unprecedented rate.

The clergy, always willing to perform the demanding task of praying for others, received large estates from princes and other wealthy classes in return for its services. It constantly preached that the generous bequest of wealth to the Church was the one infallible means to achieve, even though posthumously, the security of eternal peace. At the same time it made sure that religious rituals and dogmas remained too complex to be intelligible to the common people, thereby making its intermediary role in prayers all but indispensable. Thus the same drama played by the Roman Church in the European Middle Ages was replayed in appanage Russia by new characters. The plot was the same, the script was the same, only the stage was different. There were, to be sure, important changes on the Russian scene, but the methods that the Russian Church used to enrich itself had been with success tried before.

The assiduity with which the Church sought to acquire land ultimately made it the biggest landlord. A similar distinction had been achieved by the Roman Catholic Church in medieval Europe, but in Russia it came somewhat later—during the sixteenth century. Florinsky, among many others, may be cited to confirm this point:

> It is believed that in the middle of the thirteenth century the holdings of monasteries were relatively modest, but three hundred years later the Church owned about one-third of the entire area under cultivation. [3, p. 133]

The upshot of this discussion is that towards the end of the appanage period, the churchmen gradually turned into acquisitors. Bishops and other prelates came to acquire the acquisitive mentality that mocks the plight of others. Their interests became identical with those of other aristocratic groups which were single-minded in exploiting the toiling peasants and serfs. More will be said about this in the ensuing discussion.

The intellectual era in Russia lasted until the end of the fourteenth century. As may be expected, the fortunes of the Church varied in proportion to those of the Mongols. As long as the Tatarian yoke appeared robust and impenetrable, the Church enjoyed the esteem and envy of all other people—princes, boyars, merchants, peasants. About the middle of the fourteenth century, however, chinks began to appear in the Mongolian armor. The nomadic behemoth, which thus far had crushed all rebellions by the Russian masses with the help of some princes and the Church, no longer seemed invincible.

The first to take advantage of the situation were Lithuanians who, after defeating the Mongols around 1362, occupied Kiev and a large part of western Russia. Had Russian princes been unified under a single command, they could have liberated their states then and there; but they had everything but unity, and as a result the Mongolian rule of eastern Russia was to linger for another century.

This is not to say that some princes, especially the prince of Moscow, did nothing to profit from the tottering alien rule. They occasionally rebelled and even bested the Khans in some battles, but until 1480, when the Tatar yoke was formally put to an end, they had to pay tribute to one Khan or another. At times the tribute was substantial, at others inconsequential.

In short, the Mongolian noose around Russia had considerably eased at the outset of the fifteenth century, and as a result the intellectual influence could not but decline. At the same time the intellectuals themselves had been steadily evolving into landed aristocracy of the acquisitors. Riasanovsky is of the view that "the Mongol domination over the Russians lasted from 1240 to 1380 or even 1480 depending on whether we include the period of a more or less nominal Mongol rule." [5, p. 72] It is thus safe to conclude that the intellectual era, commencing around the twelfth century, came to an end with the weakening of the Mongolian yoke at the end of the fourteenth.

THE QUESTION OF FEUDALISM AND THE ACQUISITIVE ERA

Let me now digress a bit to facilitate further exposition of the Russian social evolution. There has been considerable controversy regarding the question of feudalism in appanage Russia, although this one cannot be blamed on the lack of informative and unjaundiced archives. The controversy has arisen because both the Marxian and non-Marxian historians have taken inspiration from the Western brand of feudalism which, as seen in the previous chapter, prevailed in the late medieval Europe.

To be sure, many economic, political, and social features prevailing at the conclusion of Mongolian rule in Russia are sadly reminiscent of the feudal West. The feebleness of central political authority, the debasement of the Church into citadels of land, wealth, and corruption, the existence of large private estates, the delegation by princes of fiscal and judicial powers to the ruthless landlords are all tragic reminders of conditions that almost contemporaneously bedevilled western Europe.

However, there are others who make much of the principle of sub-infeudation that characterized medieval Europe but was only partially present in Russia; of the fact that some peasants in the appanage period were free to move from one estate to the other, whereas in western Europe they had been mostly tied to particular landlords; and of the premise that the princes conferred judicial and fiscal privileges on the landlords only for a few years.

Some, especially Marxists, suggest that differences between medieval Europe and medieval Russia (as appanage Russia is sometimes called) are purely semantic, more apparent than real. For one thing the peasant mobility in Russia was more or less theoretical, and in reality the financial strength of the landlords and active collusion among them frequently curbed the peasant's movements. Similarly, the judicio-fiscal prerogatives of the governors, landholders or otherwise, were usually extended indefinitely.

However, the main point missed by many historians before is that in the latter half of both medieval Europe and appanage Russia, the acquisitive era prevailed. In both places the Church, which usually helped everyone but the needy, had amassed an incredible amount of land and wealth; in both places the landlords, secular as well as ecclesiastical, had become instruments of oppression over the common masses who were forced to pay extortion to their *de facto* masters. In short, in both places, the acquisitive mentality was predominant.

Most contemporary scholars outside the sphere of Marxian influence argue that feudalism never existed in Russia, or at the least the Russian brand was vastly different from the Western variety. In his summation of this issue, Riasanovsky strikes a deft compromise:

> In sum, it would seem that a precise definition of feudalism, with proper attention to its legal characteristics, would not be applicable to Russian society. Yet, on the other hand, many developments in Russia, whether we think of the division of power and authority in the appanage period, the economy of large landed estates, or even the later *pomestie* system of state service, bear important resemblances to the feudal West. . . . Therefore, a number of scholars speak of the social organization of medieval Russia as incipient or undeveloped feudalism. [5, p. 128]

For my purpose, it is immaterial what label is assigned to socio-economic conditions prevailing in the late appanage period. As the

intellectual influence declined with the Mongols towards the end
of the fourteenth century, social primacy passed into the hands of a
new class, a new aristocracy which rose on the strength of its
landed wealth. It is the acquisitive mind which then swayed the
Russian society, and that is just the hallmark of an acquisitive age.

How did all this come about in medieval Russia? How did
Sarkar's social cycle move from the intellectual to the acquisitive
era? It is towards these questions that I now turn.

One of the striking political developments in the appanage
period is the meteoric rise of the principality of Moscow from
a virtual nonentity until the middle of the thirteenth century to a
force that, by the end of the fifteenth century, succeeded in unifying scattered fragments of Russia under one banner. The credit
for this goes mostly to Ivan III who, as grand duke of Moscow,
reigned from 1462 to 1505. A pragmatic ruler of great foresight,
Ivan not only brought the cities of Novgorod and Tver under his
control, but, with his declaration of independence in 1480, he also
put a formal end to the Mongolian yoke.

The Tatar domination, however, did not end overnight. The
Russian road to emancipation was long, precarious, and tortuous.
It also resulted in a considerable diminution of the Church coupled with a swift ascendancy of the boyar aristocracy. The new
boyars, however, were no longer the warriors that they were during the early Kievan days; they now possessed an acquisitive mentality as well as vast estates and wealth. Years of subservience to
the alien rule had completely sapped their strength and vitality,
while the princes, who needed them badly first in inter-princely
feuds and then in the struggle against the Mongols, rewarded
them generously in terms of land.

In point of fact, as the struggle for supremacy among princes
grew bitter, the influence of the boyars increased manifold. Actually some boyars came from the princely families which had been
forced by other princes to retire from politics and administration.

During the late Kievan Russia, the princely authority had
been limited by many social elements including the boyar duma
(*druzhina*) and the *veche* (the city assembly). In the early appanage
period, the *veche* had all but disappeared and the Church had

come to dominate society. All this time the landed boyars had remained on a high point of the social pyramid, but they had not been able to get to the top. During Kievan Russia their presence had served to restrain irresponsible actions of princes, but at that time they were constantly ready for warfare and possessed martial qualities. As landed proprietors, however, they attained social dominance only during the fourteenth century when Church influence began to decline with the Mongolian power, and when princes continued to need their assistance to fight other princes.

Thus the acquisitive era, i.e., the period dominated by landlords, secular as well as ecclesiastical, was born in Russia around the end of the fourteenth century. As in the feudal West, the dominion of landowners in late appanage Russia stemmed from their ownership of vast areas of land and their resultant economic power. This is then an unmistakable sign of the acquisitive age. About some of the boyars, Pipes has this characterization:

> Rich boyars were *virtual sovereigns*. The administrators of the prince's household rarely interfered with these people [boyars], and sometimes were formally forbidden to do so by immunity charters. [4, p. 46 (italics mine)]

Princes themselves displayed an acquisitive mentality as they made frequent grants of land to those who would wage their battles and wars. About Moscow's grand princes, who were typical of other princes at the time, McKenzie Wallace has this to say:

> They were not a chivalrous race, or one with which the severe moralist can sympathize, but they were largely endowed with cunning, tact and perseverance, and were little hampered by conscientious scruples. Having early discovered that the liberal distribution of money at the Tatar court was the surest means of gaining favor, they lived parsimoniously at home and spent their savings at the Horde. [7, p. 202]

This quote from Wallace should dispel any remaining doubts about the acquisitive mentality of the princes of medieval Russia. The control over society by a handful of persons through their wealth is exactly what characterizes an acquisitive age. The princely acquisitive mentality is also emphasized by Pipes who observes that the appanage prince

> had an obsession with accumulating real estate. He bought land, traded it, married into it and seized it by force. This preoccupation had the consequence of transforming the more ambitious of the appanage princes into ordinary businessmen, strengthening in their mind the already well-developed proprietary instincts. [4, p. 54]

There were two sources of the boyar's power and supremacy in society: they were rich, at least some if not all, and by long established tradition, had been independent of their so-called masters (or employers)—the princes. This tradition, inherited from the old *druzhina*, held that boyars were not obliged to stay with their employer through thick and thin; that they were free to choose their master and desert him at any time, if necessary. At times disgruntled boyars chose to exercise their right of desertion at precisely the time when their employer needed them most—at the time of war with other principalities. In the contractual agreement between princes and boyars, therefore, the former clearly were at a disadvantage. The princes, of course, did not care for this practice, but they were too powerless to abolish it, at least until the sixteenth century.

At first, perhaps, the boyars acquired their land through direct purchase or occupation. Such estates were called *votchina*, where the owner had complete freedom of management without any obligation to the prince save the collection and payment of taxes. It is worth noting, however, that some *votchina* estates, especially those belonging to the Church but also those belonging to some boyars, were exempt from taxation. Around the middle of the fourteenth century, as cultivable land became scarce, there arose another form of landholding called *pomestie*, where the tenure was obligatory. In this case the landholder obtained his land from the prince and in turn agreed to perform some duty— usually military service. The *pomestie* form of landholding increased in importance with the passage of time, and became the general rule in the sixteenth century when some form of government service was required of all landlords.

All landholdings, *votchina* and *pomestie,* were cultivated not directly by the landowners but by peasants and slaves. As with the boyars who were free to choose their masters, the tenants in the early days were free to move from one landlord to another. The economic disadvantage of this practice was not lost on the landowner, who did his best to restrict their mobility. However, legal rights of the peasants to move freely were by tradition as unimpeachable as those of the boyars. Accordingly, the princes, especially those of Moscow, eventually made pacts with other princes, agreeing not to accept the free tenants of each other. Of greater significance in limiting peasant mobility, however, were the financial obligations of the tenants to the landowners, who exacted high interest rates for their loans. In Florinsky's words:

As early, perhaps, as the thirteenth century, the debtor-creditor relationship became an important source leading to the *de facto* enslavement of people who were *de jure* free. [3, p. 107]

Thus, as in Western Europe, it is a combination of several forces and circumstances that culminated in the Russian acquisitive age. Regardless of what label is attached to socioeconomic conditions prevailing in late medieval Russia, there is little doubt that society then was dominated by the acquisitors: wealth ruled everything and the government was highly decentralized. The state had been split into miniature, quasi-sovereign entities, and private law had emerged in place of the law of the state.

The acquisitive era in Russia lasted roughly from the end of the fourteenth century to the end of the sixteenth. By then a series of tumultuous events and revolutions had given Russia a face-lift. While the boyars and feuding princes were humbled, the governmental machinery became extremely centralized under the *imperium* of Moscow's prince, better known as the tzar.

OPRICHNINA AND THE SOCIAL REVOLUTION

As happens during every acquisitive era, medieval Russia slowly drifted towards extreme economic disparity, lawlessness, and anarchy of the acquisitive-cum-laborer age. Also, as with ancient Egypt prior to the emergence of the Middle Kingdom and as with feudal Europe, the end of the acquisitive era in Russia was preceded by a move towards political centralization and a number of social rebellions.

It may be recalled that the burden of onerous taxes and tributary payments to Mongols fell largely on frail economic shoulders of tenants, independent farmers, artisans, and other common people. While princes and landlords basked in their fortunes, the masses lived in squalor and misery. In time, especially during the fourteenth and fifteenth centuries, the financial noose of landowners around the tenants became really tight, so much so that the once free peasants were reduced to serfdom.

Meanwhile the influence of boyars increased manifold as Moscow's princes needed their support to bring other principalities and princes under subjection. This the Muscovite rulers were able to accomplish, though not without a protracted struggle, with all machinations, trickery, and wealth at their command. By the onset of the sixteenth century, all of Russia's princes had been subdued by the grand prince of Moscow, and some of them were settled away from their earlier domains; they thus joined the ranks of boyars.

The unification of Russia under one banner produced unexpected results for the landed aristocracy which had been Moscow's staunch ally through the dark days of struggle for dominion. No longer did the Muscovite princes need the boyars. Furthermore, the chief source of the boyars' hegemony, namely their threat to switch from one prince to another, vanished with the consolidation of political command under one prince. These developments portended convulsions of a kind Russia had never seen before.

The supremacy of Moscow also spelt further trouble for the peasantry's phantom freedom of mobility. For instance, in the economic interests of ecclesiastical landlords, Vasily II of Moscow decreed around 1455 that the free tenants working on certain Church estates could no longer abandon their tenancy. Developments such as these contributed further to serfdom, which to be sure was not yet fully developed: its fullblooded rise was to occur much later—during the eighteenth and nineteenth centuries. Nevertheless, in medieval Russia partial serfdom, combined with oppressive taxation, made the tenant's physical survival all but impossible.

As expected, the strife between boyars and Muscovite rulers intensified during the sixteenth century and continued with inevitable vicissitudes into the early part of the seventeenth. The rise of Moscow in the political firmament had become a fact of life by 1533 when Ivan IV succeeded his father, Vasily III, at the age of three. Ivan, better known as Ivan the Terrible, was a mercurial, some say pathological, character; he was at once capable of extreme cruelty and deep piety. Ivan was a typical warrior; he believed in family discipline with himself as the head of the family, except that his family extended to the entire state. Ivan was thus a champion of the ruler's absolutism, an idea that the Mongolian despotism, still fresh in Russian memory, had left behind. He was the first prince to assume the title of tzar, which previously had been associated with the Mongols. In fact from the long-run viewpoint, absolutism is perhaps the only Mongolian legacy to Russian society, which is scourged by it even today.

No historical narrative of Russia, even the one as brief as mine, can afford to neglect Ivan's childhood impressions of boyars' misconduct, if only because they vividly portray acute strife between the then Muscovite rulers and the entrenched landed aristocracy. Throughout his life, Ivan had to live with the childhood memory of scenes of violence in which feuding factions of boyars, jockeying for power, had freely participated; how they would tear up the robes of the Metropolitan and frequently help themselves to palace jewelry and valuables; how his own mother had to constantly fight them for her survival.

When Ivan turned sixteen in 1546 and took over the rule from boyars, he had perhaps already made up his mind to efface their influence. Towards this end he was ably assisted by a council of advisers. A series of important reforms were instituted and a new assembly called *zemsky sobor* convened in 1550 to counter the exclusive sway of boyars in governmental affairs. The judicio-fiscal powers of landlords and boyar governors were also curbed.

However, none of these reforms could erase from Ivan's mind his innate distrust of boyars; he began to suspect even his own advisers. In time, this suspicion grew so deep that he began to ignore their advice. For instance, when in 1558 he waged war against Livonia, which in turn sought protection from Lithuania, he did this despite his advisers' strenuous objections. The Livonian war produced the normal ups and downs in battles, but each defeat Ivan would ascribe to the treachery of boyar commanders, of whom several were arrested or executed. This policy merely added fuel to the fire. Ivan's own associates began to fear his whims. After losing a battle in 1564, a former adviser to Ivan, Prince Kurbsky, defected to Lithuanians for purely this reason. Shocked by what he considered treason, Ivan finally decided to take peremptory action.

Ivan had it all planned. In December 1564 he secretly left Moscow for a nearby town, and then sent a message to the people, declaring his intention to abdicate on account of the boyar's perfidy. However, upon receiving earnest requests, which he must have fully expected from the people of Moscow, he graciously agreed to return. But he insisted on the grant of absolute power to punish those who had betrayed him, to confiscate their lands, and to form a new administration unencumbered by the existing aristocracy. Around these confiscated estates evolved a new social contract, called *oprichnina*, which literally means a separate household (or a private court).

In the *oprichnina*, Ivan was the supreme master. Of all the people, he trusted the lower gentry, merchants, and commoners, and it is to such people that he parcelled out land he had seized from boyars. In return the new landowners were enjoined to provide military service as recruits of the *oprichnina* guards, who at one time numbered as many as 6,000.

At first the new political order adversely affected only the boyars, and their status and power were all but annihilated. Many had to pay the price for earlier excesses in terms of their lives. Later on, however, the *oprichnina* guards spread so much terror that they became a menace to Ivan's own government. In 1571 they were disbanded, although some were allowed to join the regular army. The boyars also then heaved a sigh of relief. They were assigned new lands in restitution for properties confiscated before. Never again were they able to rise in society.

How is one to appraise the momentous event of *oprichnina* in terms of the theory of social cycle? I am inclined to interpret this episode—and others occurring at the turn of the seventeenth century that finally broke the back of the boyars—as Sarkar's laborer revolution in which the lower strata of society, oppressed by years of boyar rapacity and strife, directly or indirectly participated.

It may be recalled that the laborer revolution, according to Sarkar, is one where the warriors or intellectuals, reduced to laborer ways of living, revolt against the entrenched acquisitors and cause an abrupt change in conventional ideas about the established sociopolitical order. There are two prerequisites: the successful revolt of non-acquisitors, and the sudden introduction of new ideas. The *oprichnina* satisfied them both. For one thing the revolt by Ivan, a warrior, against the boyars was elaborately prepared; and when he proclaimed his abdication, the boyars as well as other privileged groups were keenly aware of the strong military force —recruited from the masses—that was ready to back his ultimatum with vigorous action. Much as it despised capitulation, the aristocracy was really left with no choice.

Secondly, the *oprichnina*, more than any other action by Ivan and his predecessors, demolished the social status of boyars, the acquisitors. True, they were subsequently resettled on different, perhaps more fertile, lands, but they had been uprooted from their strongholds and then banished to new areas where traditionally they had mattered little. And it is the tradition—inherited from the old *druzhina*—that lay at the basis of their hegemony in society. Thus the fact that a boyar's rights to freedom and inheritance were no longer inviolable was a revolutionary new idea that found ready acceptance following the *oprichnina*. It is in these respects, rather than the systematic terror which Ivan perpetrated on the landed aristocracy as well as on others, that the *oprichnina* episode qualifies as the laborer revolution in Russia. Florinsky's words add further weight to this conclusion:

The two most significant consequences of *oprichnina* were the final destruction of the political influence of the old landed aristocracy and the forcible transfer of land on a huge scale. [3, p. 202]

It is worth adding here that according to some historians the real impetus for social revolt against the boyars came not from above, not from Ivan, but from below, from other nonacquisitors. Their chief spokesman was Peresvetov, who belonged to the class of lower gentry. Peresvetov frequently attacked certain aspects of the Muscovite political hierarchy of which he himself had been the victim. After Ivan's coronation, he wrote several treatises, exhorting the tzar to tame the boyars and form a strong and just government based on the Turkish system of administration, a system for which Peresvetov had nothing but admiration. In Vernadsky's succinct words:

Peresvetov may be considered a mouthpiece of the lower Russian gentry, expressing their readiness to become the mainstay of the tzar's power. [6, p. 110]

The upshot of this discussion is that *oprichnina* was instigated by the non-acquisitors against the undeserved, but extensive, privileges of the affluent aristocracy of the boyars. It was a laborer revolution that turned violent and oppressive because its leader, Ivan the Terrible, was by disposition a warrior.

Following Ivan's death political and social antagonisms came to the surface again, and Russia had to go through what is usually described as "The Time of Troubles," which is really reminiscent of a period of adjustment following a laborer revolution. It lasted only for fifteen years, from 1598 to 1613, but during that short span, the Russian economy and morale were all but exhausted. This is a period when factional strife among boyars bedevilled society again; Russia was again catapulted into revolutionary turmoil and a civil war, and although peasants and slaves in the end gained little from their revolt, remaining vestiges of the boyarpower were annihilated.

It may then be concluded that tremors of the laborer revolution shook the Russian polity not only during Ivan's reign but also during "The Time of Troubles." Russia had passed through so many upheavals that its anarchical order could not sink any further; it had to give way to some peace and relatively better times for all concerned.

TZARDOM, ABSOLUTISM, AND THE NEW WARRIOR ERA

My discussion so far has shown that the Russian historical experience accords well with Sarkar's hypothesis. We have seen that, in accordance with the law of social cycle, the Russian society evolved from the warrior to the intellectual era and then to the acquisitive era, culminating in social revolutions against the wealthy. This completes one rotation of the social cycle. Now, if Sarkar's thesis holds good, it is the turn of the warrior era, of political centralization to rise again. In the ensuing discussion I argue that it is precisely this era that has prevailed in Russia from the turn of the seventeenth century till today. Now and then the fulcrum of power has briefly swayed from absolutism to relative decentralization, but on the whole the Russian body social has been caught in the straitjacket of totalitarian regimes for the last four centuries.

"The Time of Troubles" came to an end when Michael Romanov was elected as the tzar by a *zemsky sobor* convoked in 1613. Thus was founded a dynasty that was to rule Russia for the next three hundred years, until in 1918 its last ruler, tzar Nicholas II, met a violent end at the hands of Bolshevik revolutionaries. The chief asset of the first Romanov was his mediocrity, a trait from which his supporters fully expected to profit. Actual political control during his reign and during the times of his two immediate successors was exercised by the tzar's relatives. From 1619 to 1633 tzar Michael was dominated by his father, Filaret, who, as the Patriarch, headed the Church.

In theory both Michael and Filaret were to share power in governance, but in practice Filaret was the master. Therefore, it seems that Russia, following the laborer revolution and the period of adjustment, sidestepped the warrior era and rushed into the intellectual age. In the state of utter confusion that attends a social revolution, a non-warrior group may come to dominate the polity, but it cannot stay in power for long. This is precisely what happened with Russia following the accession of the first Romanov as the tzar, as Filaret's rule lasted only fourteen years. Later, a similar attempt by Patriarch Nikon to regain power proved abortive and led to his downfall. As a result no subsequent Patriarch staked claims to primacy in secular affairs.

The first three Romanovs had one trait in common: they all seem to have specialized in ineptitude and feebleness of mind. On their supple shoulders had fallen the gigantic task of national reconstruction for which they were sadly ill-equipped. The movement towards political centralization—which was discernible during the fifteenth century and which, following the *oprichnina,* reached its heyday during the reign of Ivan the Terrible—was temporarily thwarted during the times of the first Romanov. The next two rulers were weak, but the state nevertheless moved towards totalitarianism, which was spearheaded by a new militaristic nobility. Thereafter came the short, but vigorous, reign of Sophia, followed by Peter who was anything but a figurehead of state.

During the first four decades of the Romanov regime the institution that attained some prominence was *zemsky sobor* which, it may be recalled, was the one that had elected Michael as the tzar. The *sobor* appeared to show some promise at the time, but it was a medley of heterogeneous social groups openly suspicious of each other. Thus the internal friction in *zemsky sobor* allowed it to be no more than a consultative body, even though the first three Romanovs were incapable of strong rule: they were weak, but the restraining influences on their power were even weaker. The last significant *sobor* was summoned in 1649 to create a code of laws.

Social primacy gradually passed into the hands of *pomestie* landowners called *dvoriane* who, it may be recalled, had been granted land by Ivan the Terrible in return for military service for the state. It was their military prowess or martial qualities, of which the tzar was always in great need, that enabled the *dvoriane* to become the new aristocracy. Warrior domination, and the concomitant centralization of authority initially in the hands of *dvoriane* and later in the hands of the tzars, had become the order of the day even in the final years of the first Romanov. The interregnums, during which the Patriarchate, first headed by Filaret and then by Nikon, was dominant, thus merely provided the brief novelty of intellectual supremacy in the general monotony of the new warrior age. As a matter of fact when Fedor, the third Romanov ruler, died in 1682, the Church had already become subservient to the state.

Fedor died childless, whereupon a bloody struggle ensued for succession, and, through a military coup, a tzarina named Sophia won out. Her rule, though eventful, was very brief and the same tide that had swept her on to shores of power swept her aside in 1689. Upon Sophia's forced retirement, Peter, later known as Peter the Great, ascended the throne.

In 1689 Peter was merely a youth of seventeen, but even then he possessed a physique unusually tall and developed for his age; he had a remarkable penchant for military discipline and skills. It is said that at barely the age of eleven, he formed a *poteshnye* regiment, which by 1689 had grown to a force strong enough to determine Peter's accession to the throne. In short Peter was a first-rate warrior, a trait that explains why during his reign absolutism reached a new high. He believed in glorification of the Russian state, not necessarily of the Russian people: no longer was the tzar a titular head of state.

The reign of Peter the Great opened new chapters in the annals of Russia, which perhaps for the first time heavily imported Western culture. Russia truly became a member of the European comity of nations, as many of its institutions were restructured along the Western archetype. At the same time, the Church suffered a further decline. The tzar became the head and arbiter of its destiny, its internal administration, its policies. The Patriarchate itself was abolished.

Many new reforms in trade and industry were introduced, and, as a result, economically Russia developed apace. Peter's absolutism as well as progressive reforms have moved some historians to conclude that his reign was marked by benevolent despotism. His reforms, however, were marred by some backward steps, as the *zemsky sobor*, the last remaining bastion in which the masses had a say, was dismantled in 1708. The government, as a result, completely lost contact with the people at large. Eventually it faced popular unrest, which it silenced with much brutality and harsh measures.

The army was also reorganized along Western lines. Peter created a first-class navy which won him not only laurels in battle, but also the formal titles of Father of his Country, Emperor, and "the Great."

One result of his military reforms was that privileges of the *dvoriane* increased further. Of course the new nobles detested the element of compulsion in the military or civil service that until then some of them had escaped, but the heavier burden was not without its compensation. The hold of the *dvoriane* nobility over the army and the administration augmented manifold. At the same time it retained rights to its estates which were farmed by serfs, who had every reason to resent the reforms that in effect bound them as slaves to their landlords. The army officers, especially regiments of guards, were mainly recruited from the nobility. These regiments were soon to play a decisive role in the succession to the Russian throne.

The rest of Russian history until 1917 may, for our purposes, be disposed of very quickly. The warrior era associated with direct absolutism continued with few interruptions. There were some episodes which make it appear that Russia moved into the intellectual or the acquisitive era, but they were either short-lived or their impact on society is subject to multiple interpretations.

Consider, for instance, the indirect rule by the regiments of guards following Peter's demise in 1725. The tzar had named no successor, and naturally there were many pretenders to the throne. The next thirty-seven years produced an era of intrigues and a series of coups in which the regiments took more than a helping hand. It is not clear what label should be assigned to the so-called period of palace revolutions, when power truly belonged to the *dvoriane* from which the regiments had been recruited. During Peter's regime the *dvoriane* had been forced to provide lifelong military service and fight his myriad wars. In his grandiose designs they were the reluctant partners even though their perquisites had substantially increased. After Peter's death,

however, the *dvoriane* got the best of both worlds. They continued to retain their privileges, especially their stranglehold on the
serfs, and at the same time managed to escape the burdens of
obligatory military service.

Some people may argue that during 1725–62, Russia had a
brush with the acquisitive era, while others may legitimately question the acquisitive characterization of the *dvoriane* nobility as a
whole. A fraction of the nobility, which during Peter's times had
been coerced to perform military functions, continued to honor
such commitments. However, most of them were interested not in
service to the state but in tightening their noose around the peasants toiling on their estates. In this endeavor, they succeeded
more than ever before. One by one the serfs were deprived of all
remaining rights. In 1727, even the serf's right to join the army
was repealed. With one stroke he was thus divested of the one and
only avenue of escape from servility.

Thus it is not clear whether the period of palace revolutions
was dominated by the warriors or acquisitors. The source of conflict lies in the fact that the power base of *dvoriane* derived from
their hold on the armed forces, but a sizeable section of the nobility displayed acquisitive mentality: it furthered its own economic
interests without caring for what happened to the serfs. However,
what matters most here is that the source of power was still the
army.

In any case the era of palace revolutions was short-lived. It
came to an end with the reign of Catherine II (1762–96) who also
was catapulted into power by regiments of guards. But after secur-
ing the throne she moved to give new life to royal autocracy. She
did this by pursuing a robust foreign policy as well as by using royal
influence in settling disputes among politically powerful groups.

Despite this, however, Russia did not return to the Petrine
period of impervious despotism where no section of society dared
challenge unrestrained powers of the tzar. Like Peter the Great,
Catherine too has been honored by some historians with the title
of enlightened despot, something for which, it is interesting to
note, she herself yearned. But there was usually a yawning chasm
between her intentions and actions.

She undoubtedly had many enlightened ideas, but few were translated into benign policies, some of which reflected a confused mind and had unintended effects. Towards the plight of the serfs, for instance, she expressed great compunction; yet the serfs had reason to rue her reign. Despite her pangs of conscience, she made generous grants of land to her courtiers, and the result was a further consolidation of serfdom. To her credit, it must be added that some of her reforms were frustrated by the uncooperative bureaucracy of *dvoriane* nobles who were naturally wrapped up in their own interests. And she was too smart, or realistic, to jolt the basic structure of her power, at least as long as it posed no threat to her own dominion.

It is appropriate to say that there was then a sort of stand-off, a kind of unstable equilibrium, between the tzardom and the *dvoriane* aristocracy, with the pendulum of power slightly tilted towards Catherine. In 1917, the year of the Bolshevik revolution that sent Russia topsy-turvy, the same standoff prevailed except that now the *dvoriane's* power base had shifted from their control over vital army positions to their control over large estates and over the bureaucratic machine. For this reason the Russian social order at the dawn of the fateful year of 1917 is commonly described as semi-feudal, signifying a situation where the autocratic state and the landed aristocracy, because of mutual distrust and fear, preferred the *status quo* to progressive change. It was not purely feudal because serfdom, which had been abolished in 1861, as well as the decentralized political authority that is supposed to accompany feudalism, did not exist at the time.

The credit for outlawing serfdom goes to tzar Alexander II (1855–81) who, along with other farsighted Russians, had come to realize that if action to reprieve the serfs did not come from above, from the state, then a volcanic action might come from below, from the servile peasants themselves. Besides, the intelligentsia rightly regarded serfdom as a stigma marring the Russian image in the eyes of Europe.

However, the serf-owning aristocracy was so powerful that its interests, the tzar felt, could not be trampled with impunity. Therefore, when serfdom was abolished in 1861, the nobility was to be generously compensated for the loss of labor services as well as for releasing land that the serfs had formerly cultivated for themselves. The nobility's lands were partitioned and a part ceded to village communes, called *mir*, in which the liberated serfs were free to toil for themselves and make their own production decisions.

However, the reform simply fomented unrest among all classes concerned. The greedy nobility felt cheated despite receiving more than adequate compensation, while the peasantry felt bitter because it could not own the allotted land, quite often barren, until the landowners were recompensed. Instead of making rental and labor payments to the landlords, the peasants now had to pay heavy restitutory taxes to the government: they thus became the serfs of the state. But despite all this ire, both the state and the peasantry were major beneficiaries. While the area under cultivation increased a little, the productivity of farm labor increased many times, and the two combined to pave the way for a degree of industrialization and capitalism.

At the turn of the twentieth century, the heavy weight of taxation on the peasantry was still one of the most cancerous tumors afflicting the Russian polity. Another was a complete absence in government of popular representation for which social consciousness had begun to sprout from the spread of education as well as industrialization. Several clandestine political groups, with disparate philosophies and objectives, had by then come into being. Even though these groups could not have been more diverse, they were all united in their disdain for autocracy, and in their desire for a representative government based on secret ballot and universal suffrage. Countering these groups were the governmental bureaucracy as well as the conservative wing of the nobility with roots struck deep in landed interests.

In 1905, following Russia's trouncing by Japan, simmering embers of unrest erupted into revolutionary violence and a series of political assassinations. However, before the situation got out of hand, the tzar caved in and, in deference to popular sentiment, offered certain concessions. Among other things, he cancelled the peasantry's debt to the state, and proclaimed a bicameral legislative system coupled with a limited suffrage.

It then appears that at the outset of the twentieth century Russia was ripe for a new intellectual age. The warrior era, because of the tzar's unenlightened despotism, had been declining for some time, and the elections of 1906, however undemocratic, seemed to herald a constitutional monarchy and hence a new era of intellectuals. However, this was not to be. The lessons so painfully learned from the 1905 revolution were quickly forgotten by the tzar, who, under the mesmerizing influence of the privileged classes, was ready to dissolve any Russian parliament (or *duma*) of which his ministers did not approve.

Finally, in 1912 was elected a fourth *duma* which was prepared to compromise with the tzar and even rubber-stamp some of his policies. To cap it all, the First World War broke out in 1914, and any drive towards further reforms seemed to be indefinitely stalled. A kind of equilibrium, unstable and vulnerable to any external trauma, had by then emerged between conservative and liberal forces. Revolutionary fervor had subsided, but radicalism was very much alive. It had merely gone underground, from where it marked time to strike back at the political anachronism, which for decades had been standing on shaky grounds.

Such then was the Russian polity at the dawn of 1917, when two revolutions, whose impact no epithets describing brutality and bloodbaths can fully capture, occurred only a few months apart, tore the country to shreds, and reimposed on it the ugly totalitarianism of which the Russian people were undeserving and helpless victims. The warrior era, which was about to witness its own eclipse thus returned with a vehemence reminiscent of the terror of Chingis Khan, only this time the terror sprang from within.

Ever since, Russian society has been living in the agony of the party and state despotism. Theoretically it is ruled by the communist party (formerly the Bolshevik party) of which any countryman can be a member, but in effect the power has revolved around one person, usually the General Secretary of the Party, who only recently has faced hushed challenges to his authority.

The first head of the Soviet Union (as Russia has since come to be called) was Lenin who inaugurated the communist tradition of rule by terror, a tradition that was more than faithfully upheld by his successor—Stalin. Stalin's long reign of twenty-five years constitutes one of the darkest pages in the Russian book of history. Few sections of society escaped the tyranny of his diabolical mind. His was a police state where innocent people would be summarily killed at the dictator's numerous whims. True, economically Russia then developed at an unprecedented rate, but the human cost in terms of life and liberty was incalculable.

After Stalin's death in 1953, a collective body of party leaders ruled for about five years, until Khrushchev maneuvered his way to the top in 1958. The era of one-man rule thus staged a comeback, giving rise to apprehensions of a reversion to the hideous days of Stalin. However, Khrushchev, himself having been reduced to sychophancy in his early career, actually denounced Stalin and his policies. During his reign many relics of Stalin's repression were effaced, and economic centralism and restrictions on society slightly eased.

Khrushchev, however, was abruptly overthrown in 1964, and the principle of collective leadership resurrected. This time the new leaders broke off the venerated tradition of communist Russia, and spared the life of the ousted leader. Since then the principle of collective leadership has been preserved. This is not to say that Brezhnev, the party's General Secretary since 1964, was content to remain the first among equals. He made some attempts to attain dictatorial power, but the alacrity of other party leaders, wary of reversion to Stalinism, successfully thwarted his designs. Politically, not much has changed in the last decade or so, except that in 1977 the Soviet President Podgorny was brusquely removed and his office taken over by Brezhnev.

Today Russian society is a little more relaxed, a little more liberalized, a little more tolerant of dissent than under Stalin's regime, yet the basic commitment of the leaders to "collective dictatorship" or "party dictatorship" remains. They are still devoted to their ideal of state supremacy, even at the expense of individual freedom and fundamental human rights.

That Russia today is languishing in the decadent phase of the warrior era there is little doubt. Whether a particular era is in its progressive or retrogressive phase is determined not by its imposing structures of institutions, nor by its awe-inspiring militaristic colossus, but by the degree to which fundamental human liberties are respected, by the degree of its humanitarianism. On this count, the Russian warrior era today is on the decline and has been so for a long time.

CONCLUDING REMARKS

In the preceding pages I have examined the validity of Sarkar's theory of social cycle in terms of the history of Russia. I argued that the Kievan state, with which the Russian narrative usually begins, evolved as a warrior era, the early appanage period as an intellectual era, the late appanage period up to the middle of the sixteenth century as an acquisitive era that terminated in the social revolution involving the episode of *oprichnina*. This completed one full rotation of the social cycle.

Another cycle began with a period of adjustment following upon the *oprichnina*, and lasted till the conclusion of the "Time of Troubles." The fact that this adjustment took so long is perhaps the reason why the new warrior era, which thereafter ensued, has lasted so long, for the past four centuries. Western civilization, on the other hand, managed to bypass the barbaric and anarchistic phase following its own social revolution. Its transition from the acquisitive age of feudalism to the warrior era of centralized monarchies was much more smooth than was the case with the *oprichnina*, and perhaps for this reason the social cycle moved in the West much more swiftly than it did in Russia.

REFERENCES

[1]   Clarkson, J. D., *A History of Russia* (New York: Random House, 1961).
[2]   Fedotov, G. P., *The Russian Religious Mind* (Cambridge, Mass.: Harvard University Press, 1946).
[3]   Florinsky, M. T., *Russia: A History and an Interpretation* (New York: Macmillan, 1953).
[4]   Pipes, Richard, *Russia Under the Old Regime* (New York: Charles Scribner's Sons, 1974).
[5]   Riasanovsky, N. V., *A History of Russia* (London: Oxford University Press, 1969).
[6]   Vernadsky, George, *A History of Russia* (New Haven: Yale University Press, 1975).
[7]   Wallace, D. M., *Russia* (New York: Henry Holt, 1905).

6

Hindu Civilization

About the time when the pharaohs were busy building their massive pyramids in the valley of the Nile, another ancient society was ready to sprout in the East—in the valley of the Indus. The so-called Indus society, which turns out to be a forerunner of what we call Hindu civilization, dates from about 2500 B.C. Its remains, unearthed at the ancient towns of Harappa and Mohenjodaro, suggest that the Indus society was among the earliest developed societies (dating, some say, as far back as 3000 B.C.); that it reached its zenith some time between 2500 and 2000 B.C., and that in accomplishments it came close to contemporary cultures of Egypt and of Mesopotamia, with which it seems to have had some contact and trade relations.

Around 1500 B.C., the Indus valley was invaded by semi-nomadic tribes of a people called Indo-Aryans, who infiltrated by way of Afghanistan through the flat passes of the Hindu Kush Mountains, which stood between the then India and the Aryan homeland of Central Asia. The culture of native Indians then sank in the deluge of marauding aliens, who transplanted a distinct religion, social norms, and institutions. It is to these Aryans that credit is usually given for giving birth to what is now called Hindu civilization.

We have already seen that, as regards the two societies examined before, the hypothesis of social cycle provides a bond of underlying unity, even though each society emerged with a face of its own, its own destiny, its own mode of expression pointing to surface diversity. With Hindu civilization this surface diversity is even more pronounced, even more muddled and difficult to pene-trate than with civilizations analyzed before. For this is a society where no ecclesiastical organization ever came into prominence. Yet its sublime religion, at once the instrument of salvation for some but bondage for others, has kept its flame aglow down to this day. This is a society where almost from its inception the profes-sions of farming and money-lending have been slighted by the priest, yet this did not preclude the times when some kind of capitalism as well as feudalism prevailed.

Like the Egyptian society, the ancient peoples of India—an area so vast that it has come to be called a subcontinent—also passed through travails, through moments of glory and decay, through barbarian invasions and internal strife. Yet unlike the ancient Egyptian culture that sought eternity in stone, the Hindu culture has survived ravages of man and time, and for this credit goes to the frequent appearance of sages who inspired others through their self-denial. It is because of their cosmic ideas that Hindu society is still alive, even though over the last one thousand years it has had to face one trauma after another.

Although the history of the Indian subcontinent, incorpo-rating the modern nations of India, Pakistan, Bangladesh, Nepal, Burma, and Afghanistan, is more unwieldy than any other, we will find that this one too yields to the ordering of the law of social cycle. Of the Indus society we know hardly enough to test Sarkar's hypothesis. But on the subsequent Indian polity, on its Vedic and post-Vedic age, the ancient scriptures—some of which are mixed with legends and mythology—throw enough light for us to com-mence our historical journey from relatively late, but still ancient, times, going as far back as 1500 B.C.

With any ancient society, the historian of necessity has to rely on archaeological, scriptural, and numismatic evidence, but with Hindu civilization this necessity has gone a bit too far. For the historical record of India, that is, the literature dealing purely with history is missing until as late as the thirteenth century A.D. Not that there is a dearth of written material, only that much of it is ahistorical and tinged with the bias of those who chose to jot down the exploits of their kings and other notables.

Some Indian historians suggest that the Vedas are as much as 12,000 years old. This may be true. However, I have used the evidence offered by Western historians. In any case, for my purposes ancient dates are not terribly important.

THE VEDIC AGE AND THE WARRIOR ERA

The bane of every historian of the subcontinent is the complete lack of chronology for ancient times. However, on the basis of certain reliable criteria such as the evolution of language and literature, the Aryan scriptures, which refer to the times ranging from 1500 to about 600 B.C., have been broadly divided into two categories. The earliest literary works of the Indo-Aryans are collectively known as the Vedas, of which there are four, and of which Rig-Veda is the oldest. The Vedas essentially consist of a *samhita,* or a collection of hymns, prayers, and spells; but certain supplementary literature, embodying the prose Brahmanas and Upanishads, is also regarded by many as parts of the Vedas.

There is a perceptible change in the tone, diction, and contents of the Brahmanas which, though still ancient, belong to the post-Vedic days. On linguistic evidence, Rig-Veda seems to have been composed somewhere between 1500 and 1200 B.C., the later Vedas by 800 B.C., and the Brahmanas and the Upanishads by 600 B.C. The social setting of the first Veda differs significantly from that of later Vedas and Brahmanas, and it is with the Rig-Vedic period that we usually associate the Vedic age.

And what do we find in the Rig-Veda?—none other than the familiar features of an early warrior society; a society of clans, each organized under the leadership of a warlike male or a group of males. The Rig-Veda gives us a glimpse of how the Aryans destroyed the Indus valley inhabitants, variously described as Dasas and Dasyus, how warfare was then frequent among Aryan tribes themselves, and how all this led to the exalted position of tribal chieftains whose principal duty was to defend their citizens. Some of the chieftains were selected while others were elected, but they all had to be men of physical strength and valor—the two assets indispensable for security and defense.

The Aryans worshipped various gods, some of whom were images of a mighty warrior. Their principal god Indra, for example, reminds one of a war hero slaying his enemies. In fact, so deadly and barbaric are some of his deeds that to this day it remains an open question whether Indra was a nature-god or simply a military commander who led the Aryans to sweeping success in battles with the Indus valley people. Besides Indra's battles, frequent mention in the Rig-Veda is made of intra-Aryan wars, such as those pitting King Sudas against a confederacy of ten kings. Matters concerning the kingship and political organization of early Aryans are summarized in these words of R. C. Majumdar, an eminent authority on the history of India:

> The organization of the tribal State was varied in character. Hereditary monarchy was the normal form of government, but sometimes we hear of election of king. In some States there was a sort of oligarchy, several members of the royal family exercising the power in common. . . .
>
> The kingdom was, generally speaking, small in extent. But various passages in the Rigveda indicate a king's supremacy over other kings and his great wealth. . . . The word *samrāt*, which in later days meant an emperor, as well as an expression meaning the ruler of the whole world . . . occur in the Rigveda. In any case, the king was not always a petty tribal chief. Sometimes he occupied a position of great dignity, markedly distinguished from that of the people. . . .
>
> He led the tribe in war and considered the protection of life and property of his subjects as his most sacred duty. [11, p. 45]

The question now arises: did the king and warriors enjoy supreme status in the early Aryan society? The answer is by no means obvious, because the well-known Indian caste system wherein the brahman or priest is accorded the highest social status is itself quite ancient. According to some, it is as old as the Rig-Veda itself. If this were true, then the Vedic times cannot unequivocally be called the warrior era of Hindu civilization.

However, most authorities now believe that the caste system generally developed in the age of the Brahmanas, which came to surface many centuries later. In the Hindu caste system, which is, not surprisingly, a wily concoction of the priestly class, the brahman is placed at the top of the social pyramid, followed by the warrior class, then by the class of artisans and money-lenders, and finally by the class of physical laborers. Over aeons, these classes have become hereditary, although in the beginning they were based purely on merit and profession. Thus, any person of knowledge and wisdom could join the brahman caste, and a person with brahman parentage could move a step or two down along the social ladder if he so deserved.

This is perhaps the most opportune time to draw a line of distinction between Sarkar's conception of the four types of human mind and the four-pronged Hindu caste system. It is of particular relevance here, because it is easy to mistake Sarkar's concepts for the caste designations. In order to avoid confusion, differences between the two ought to be clearly stated.

The difference between an intellectual and a brahman is crystal clear, for a brahman is a Hindu priest, whereas Sarkar's intellectual may be a priest or any person relying on intellect to further his or her interests. The warrior in India has long been called a *kshatriya,* who must be distinguished from Sarkar's warrior, as the latter may be a warrior or any person of high-spiritedness, ready to face problems in a direct fight rather than depend on others. Similarly the artisans and money-lenders in the caste system are called *vaishyas* who must be distinguished from Sarkar's acquisitors—those reflecting a mentality bent on excessive acquisition of wealth. An artisan, or any skilled blue-collar worker, in Sarkar's nomenclature is a warrior, whereas in the caste system he is a *vaishya.* On the definition of a laborer, Sarkar and the caste designation both agree, for to them both a laborer is an unskilled worker.

But while the caste system has despised the laborer, made his torment hereditary, conspired to perpetrate all kinds of atrocities on him, Sarkar cries out against this age-old repression which occurred, and is still occurring, not just in India but in all civilizations. In his view, laborers are the backbone of any economic system, of any social order, yet they are the ones whom other classes have shamelessly exploited all over the world ever since the genesis of Civilization. In any case, Sarkar's classification permits changes in mentality whereby a laborer can turn into a warrior or an intellectual and others can turn into laborers, depending on their actions; but the caste system is inflexible, although it is now slowly easing its grip on Hindu society.

Reverting to our question as to who dominated the early Aryan society, we see that in the Rig-Veda there is seldom any mention of a *kshatriya*. Even brahman does not appear too often. There is only one hymn, out of 1,017, that refers collectively to the brahman, *rajanya* (later *kshatriya*), *vaishya* and Shudra (laborer). From this kind of evidence, Majumdar, among many others concludes that

> it would thus appear that towards the very end of the Rigvedic period the distinction between the four classes had just begun to take shape, foreshadowing the development of the caste system in future. [11, p. 48]

Therefore during the early Vedic times, what we observe are class and not caste distinctions, distinctions which were also common among the early Persians and other contemporary peoples. Since the caste system was as yet undeveloped, there can be no question of the priestly hegemony over the warrior king. It is not that there were no priests, only that they were subordinate to the king. In his interpretation of the early Vedic literature, Charles Drekmeier observes:

> One of the coronation sacrifices (*vājapeya*) included a chariot race in which the king was the victor. This may be a reference to the time when military superiority, as tested in the chariot race, was the basis of kingship. . . .
>
> The position of the king was strengthened by the warfare of the Vedic period. As the military organization, the nucleus of government, grew in influence and defined its sphere of action more broadly, the associations representing the different interests and functions of the community were more closely integrated with the "state" and deprived of the autonomy they had once possessed. [3, p. 21]

Not only was the king superior to his priestly ministers and advisers, the warrior class as a whole stood a notch above the class of priests. The Rig-Veda, a priestly composition, regularly conveys this impression. "In the Rigveda," asserts Drekmeier, "the brahman frequently appears to be of less importance than the rajanya (kshatriya)." [3, p. 21] In other words, the Rig-Vedic period of the Hindu civilization belongs clearly to the warrior age. How long this period was is anybody's guess. It could have lasted from 1500 to 1200 B.C. or to as late as 1000 B.C.

Whether vast empires or great kingdoms were formed during these times cannot be readily determined. The mention in the Rig-Veda of *samrat* or *maharaja* (great ruler) as well as of the horse sacrifice (*ashvamedha*), reflecting the king's sway over vast domains, indeed point to large empires. However, each epoch must be judged from its own standards, and the impressive titles of samrat, etc., may very well reflect the absorption of smallish tribes by large tribes; the resulting kingdoms would be vast by the standards of those times but not of ours. In any case, even the Rig-Veda is not so assuring in this regard. Thus my argument that the Rig-Vedic period is reminiscent of the warrior era derives principally from the mentality of the ruling warrior class and not from the fact that, as with Egypt of the Old Kingdom and the West of the Principate, India was then knit in the fabric of a vast empire ruled centrally by one, or even two or three, monarchs.

In terms of political organization and traits of the rulers, India of those days points to the Egyptian kingdoms of pre-dynastic times. This was an early warrior era and the sway of *dharma* or the moral law was the general rule. True, the king was way above the common people, above the priests, above every other institution, yet he was supposed to govern not only in the interest of security but also of common prosperity and welfare. Such in any case were political ideas or ideals of the times.

Since early Aryan society was a warrior society, women could not but enjoy a high social stature. Even though the family was based on strict patriarchal principles, in which the father exercised absolute authority over his children, the wife enjoyed a high position. None of the latter-day taboos constrained women at those times. Child-marriage was forbidden; *sati,* a practice forcing the widow to immolate herself at her husband's cremation, was nonexistent; interclass marriage was common. Early Aryan society was a kind of uninhibited society where women were freely allowed to mix with men: they did not have to cover their faces with veils. The wife could freely participate in family rites and other religious ceremonies. Even polygamy, which has been the scourge of all medieval societies, was practically absent in the then India. In the words of H. G. Rawlinson:

> Women held a high place in society; the wife was mistress of the house, shared in the sacrifices, and ruled over the slaves and female members of the family. . . .
> The bride was adult, and child marriage was not practiced. Polygamy seems to have been unknown, and marriage was regarded as a sacrament. The bridegroom, taking the bride's hand, repeated the verse (R.V. x. 85), "I clasp thy hand for happiness, that thou mayest reach old age with me thy husband." [18, p. 22]

THE BRAHMANIC AGE AND THE INTELLECTUAL ERA

There is a visible difference between the picture of society painted by the Rig-Veda and that painted by later Vedas as well as Brahmanas. For this reason, the study of the Aryan culture is conveniently divided into the Rig-Vedic period and the subsequent Brahmanic age, which is so called because this caption, better than any other, reflects the social character of post-Rig-Vedic times. It is an age where the priest or the brahman comes to the forefront in society; where the kshatriyas, not to speak of other classes, come out as inferior to the brahmans; where women begin to feel the onus of priestly injunctions; where the caste system begins to take concrete shape. And all this fits only too well with Sarkar's description of the intellectual age.

Historians are often at a loss to explain why in a country like India, where religion has permeated social consciousness for ages, no ecclesiastical organization of the type of the Egyptian or the Roman Catholic Church ever came into being. The point is that it did not have to, because its place was taken by the inexorable caste system which failed to make a dent in other civilizations. The caste system has done in India what ecclesiasticism did in other societies, namely, it preached, and at times managed to ensure, the supremacy of the priestly class over other classes. And in his self-interest, the brahman marshalled all his wit just as his peers did in Egypt as well as in Europe.

During the post-Rig-Vedic period, lasting roughly from 1000 to 600 B.C., the Aryans gradually migrated from their north-western sanctuary in the Punjab towards the East and South until they spread over the whole of northern India, from the foothills of the Himalayas to those of the Vindhyas. Their expansion stemmed mainly from their missionary zeal and from their conquests over the native peoples. For a long time the Vindhya hills provided a line of demarcation between northern, Aryan India and the South inhabited by the Dravidians. But it appears that around 1000 B.C. the Aryans, and their culture, had begun to filter into southern regions as well, and by 400 B.C. they had penetrated the southern-most province of Kerala, with the Indian Ocean kissing its beaches and shores.

However, the ancient history of India, until as late as the illustrious king Ashoka of the third century B.C., is a narrative of its northern wing, as so little is known about the ancient South, where the Aryan colonization was far less sweeping and complete. This does not mean that the Dravidian lands lagged behind while the Aryans in the North basked in splendor, only that ancient southern history remains obscure to this day.

The Aryan progress in the North eventually resulted in large kingdoms, with the older tribes merging into new territorial states. As a result, battles were now fought for bigger stakes, and victory appeared to depend not only on heroism and fortitude but also on the intercession of gods. The priests, and their talent for performing sacrificial rites, were therefore in demand more than ever before. Thus with the rise of kingdoms came the rise of brahmans, who managed to trap the entire society in a web of rituals and dogmas explaining the origin of kingship and of other professions. The process by which all this emerged is succinctly described by R. S. Sharma in these words:

In the later Vedic period smaller communities coalesced into larger units. . . . The rulers no longer depended on uncertain tributes, but probably claimed a portion of agricultural produce. Secure in their regular income they could support a large number of priests, who composed rituals that constitute our only important source for the portrait of later Vedic polity.

Settled life led to the division of the Vedic people into four varnas [castes]. Brāhmans who originally formed one of the 16 classes of priests came at the top, and, in the Vedic ritual tests they composed, claimed both social and political privileges. [22, p. 272]

In some Brāhmanas, the brahman is slighted when compared with a kshatriya, although it occurs very rarely. This may explain the fact that the caste system had not yet become totally hereditary, and that some kings, apparently belonging to the kshatriyan class, were qualified to compose hymns and perform sacrifices. However, the general tone of the Brahmanas is that the priest is the crest of society; that he is the very nucleus of the kshatriyan power, and so while a kshatriya cannot prosper without a brahman, a brahman can. This view at once brings to mind what the Roman Catholic Church later thought of its status in society, and is eloquently expounded by Drekmeier:

The differentiation of Brahma and Kshatra and the question of which constituted the higher authority does, however, have a parallel in European history—the Gelasian theory of the "two swords," first stated in the fifth century. The dispute implicit in the Gelasian doctrine came to a head when, in the eleventh century, the Church claimed exemptions from the controls of the secular power. . . . The brahmans formed no corporate body as such and thus lacked the strength of the hierarchically organized medieval Church; but through the *purohita* (the royal chaplain) the spiritual authority was able to exercise considerable political influence. . . . The *purohita* shared the governing function with the king. According to the *Aitareya Brahmana* the purohita is "half the self" of the king. The sacrifice of the king is not accepted by the gods if the king has no *purohita*. [3, pp. 32–3]

In later Brāhmanas, the kingship was exalted as a divine creation. A hymn in *Shatapatha Brahmana* hailed the kshatriya to be an expression of Prajapati or God. [1, p. 430] But the rank of Prajapati (or Brahma) himself was reserved for the brahman. Above all, while the brahman by birth had a divine status, the king could secure his quasi-divine status only after performing the *Rajasuya* sacrifice in which the priestly role was indispensable. The end result was that the royal power, while bowing to the priesthood, grew at the expense of commoners.

While the kshatriyas were resigned to remain in the shade of brahmans, it is the other two groups that had to bear the brunt of the caste system. However, it appears that the kshatriyas had not handed the supreme status to brahmans on a silver platter. There seemed to have been a long tussle for supremacy between the two upper classes. But the poor vaishyas and Shudras, the artisans, craftsmen, and farmers, who all toiled for the rest of society, were no match for the crafty brahman, and they had to yield even before the battle began. For the shrewd priest had already won over the kings by granting them a semi-divine authority and position.

In order to perpetuate their rule and to preclude revolts of lower classes, the brahmans abused the supremely logical theory of karma and the transmigration of soul. Now the theory of karma, first discernible in the *Shatapatha Brahmana*, says that each and every action begets its own fruit, its own reaction; so our present circumstances are dictated by our past actions, and our future by the present actions. If one believes in transmigration, then this theory suggests that the soul passes from one birth to another until it has enjoyed or, so to say, exhausted, the fruit of all its actions; that is when it attains emancipation and reverts to its pristine state of eternal beatitude.

Whether or not one believes in it, the doctrine of karma cannot be disputed on purely logical grounds. Now what the brahman chose to emphasize was the part which attributes one's birth in a lower caste to one's misdeeds in the past life, while ignoring altogether the fact that the future—and the near future, not just the next life—could be bettered through present actions. The whole setup thus tended to discourage social reforms, for they were equated to subversion of the established, sacred order which God had ordained for the good of everyone in society.

Thus, the brahman on the one hand viciously exploited the lower castes, preyed on them with his silver-tongued blows, yet on the other admonished them not to cry, not to protest, admonished them to be content with servility, for which they were taught to blame none else but they themselves. While ensuring his own luxury and comfort in the present life, the priest advised everyone else to look forward to the next birth or the life beyond. And was there any way to an exultant afterlife other than serving the brahman? "No," said the brahman!

Thus brahmans did what priesthood has done in all civilizations, and in their objectives the caste system was a handy tool, a perfect substitute for ecclesiasticism. In M. W. Pinkham's words:

> The Brāhmanas represent the ideology of a sacerdotal caste which played upon the natural religious instincts of the Hindus. The priests succeeded in changing the early Nature-Worship of the Hindus into a code of intricate artificial ceremonies of sacrifice. . . . These religious leaders unceasingly strove to gain control over the minds of the people. They encouraged a divine halo to be placed upon the priesthood. [16, p. 50]

On the next page, Pinkham continues in the same vein:

> There is a decided difference in the primitive worship of the Rig-Veda and the highly complicated ceremonial of the Brāhmanas. In many instances the Brāhmanas resorted to a fantastic interpretation of the early Vedas in order to make them justify ceremonies in which priests of various classes could officiate. [16, p. 51]

Do these words have a familiar ring from the intellectual eras of civilizations explored before? They do, and no one can deny that. Did the intellectual priest behave everywhere alike? They did, and none can dispute that. Yet most historians today question the underlying unity of civilizations and harp on their superficial diversities.

In the intellectual era, the status of women, of course, could not but decline. The wife in the Rig-Vedic age was free to participate in family rites; but these the priesthood considered its sole prerogative and would not share with anyone else. Women were lumped by the priests in a separate class, different from the male group, yet responsible for certain essential functions of servile nature. Just as it was found necessary to bind the male non-brahman in doctrinal shackles, the same way woman had to be bound, except that for her the shackles had to be of a different metal. Aware of certain physical and psychological differences between men and women, the brahman proceeded to subjugate women on a different, and meaner, plane. While non-brahman males were taught of their inferiority to the brahman owing to their professions, women were taught of their inferiority just because they were women. In Pinkham's explicit words:

> Primarily the priests realized they must control women. In this respect they had much to overcome. There was the early worship of goddesses with which to reckon. Likewise woman's sex-nature, giving her the power of motherhood, had to be reckoned with. Her freedom was a hindrance to the power and domination of the priests. The Brahmans felt that this must be conquered; so with verbal agitation they succeeded in lowering the position of woman. She must be considered an inferior creature without a mind. With heartless cruelty they decided that gradually even religious rights must be taken away from woman.
>
> The priests saw to it that their directions for worship contained a tremendous overemphasis on the physical aspect of womanhood. . . . Also the necessity of male offspring for salvation was stressed emphatically. . . . A son begotten became involved in the idea of salvation. Such desire was one factor which increasingly helped to bring about unfortunate child-marriages, with all the accompanying misery. [16, p. 54]

To be sure there are a few passages in the Brahmanas where the wife is looked upon with great respect. In the *Shatapatha Brahmana,* she is exalted as a "better half" complementing her husband. But this is typical of the deception in which the priesthood in the past tried to soothe its victims in all civilizations: its trick was to puff them up with flattery, but cheat them of their self-identity, as well as wealth, for the sake, of course, of their own good and welfare. Majumdar makes it crystal clear in his remarks about the position of women in the Brahmanic age:

> Theoretically the wife was still accorded a very high position. . . .
> But there are unerring signs that her status and dignity were lowered
> a great deal during this period. Thus many of the religious cere-
> monies, formerly left to the wife, were now performed by priests.
> She was not allowed to attend the political assemblies. A *submissive
> wife* who would keep her mouth shut and dine after her husband is
> now held up as the ideal. [11, pp. 89–90 (italics mine)]

But when it came to sexual indulgence, the brahman took the
lead. No man's wife, not to speak of her daughter, was safe from
priestly excesses once the priest came to ravish her. A hymn in the
Atharva-Veda reserves the right of the brahman to marry any
woman even if previously she has had ten non-brahman husbands
[11, p. 89]. Thus polygamy, and priestly debauchery, were common in the brahmanic period. What it all did to womanhood is not
hard to imagine.

   Until now my account of the brahmanic period has painted
a sorry picture of priestly treachery and oppression. But no age is
without its bright moments, and in this case they shine through
the Upanishads, which rank with the most cosmopolitan works
ever composed. This perhaps illustrates one of those paradoxes
to the Western observer of India where for ages class prejudice
has cohabited with catholicity, heinous customs like child-
marriage and widow-burning with unequalled patience, self-
conceit with self-denial. The Upanishads are also called Vedanta
(the end of the Veda), signifying that they came at the end of the
Vedic period.

   All those tricks by which the brahmans secured their dominion ultimately gave rise to social resentment. Unable to dislodge
the crafty priesthood, many took refuge in asceticism and a life-
style of complete renunciation. The end-product of their vigorous
efforts, of their beatific experiences are the Upanishads in which
has been stored for centuries the sublime knowledge that leads
one to perfect harmony with oneself, to the ultimate goal of all—
unbroken tranquillity of mind. A. L. Basham has captured the
kernel of the Upanishads as well as the cosmic experience of an
ascetic with an understanding that is hard to match:

Gradually plumbing the cosmic mystery, his [the ascetic's] soul entered realms far beyond the comparatively tawdry heavens where the great gods dwelt in light and splendor. Going "from darkness to darkness deeper yet" he solved the mystery beyond all mysteries; he understood, fully and finally, the nature of the universe and of himself, and he reached a realm of truth and bliss, beyond birth and death, joy and sorrow, good and evil. And with this transcendent knowledge came another realization—he was completely, utterly, free. He had found ultimate salvation, the final triumph of the soul. The ascetic who reached the goal of his quest was a conqueror above all conquerors. There was none greater than he in the whole universe. [2, p. 245]

This is the ultimate in spiritual experience, where only ONE remains, either "I," or "Thou," or God. There is no duality, no thought in that super-conscious state, only the human, conscious being, who, prior to this beatitude, was the witness of all those thoughts saying "he or she was a John or a Joan or anyone else." Since no thought then remains to tell the person the existence, or nonexistence, of the universe, there is Oneness, with the human being merged into cosmic consciousness, the microcosm into the macrocosm. Transcendental indeed is the sublime message of the Upanishads, and one wonders how they could have been composed in an earthly environment of the brahmanic age.

BUDDHIST PERIOD AND THE ACQUISITIVE ERA

The intellectual era lasted as long as brahmanism remained unchallenged in society, and since the warrior class would not confront the priest, the priestly wave was eventually swept aside by a tide that ironically had been denigrated in the Vedas for a long time. The Aryan economy of the Rig-Vedic and the brahmanic period had been predominantly an agricultural or a pastoral economy. Money had not yet been invented, and so money-lending as a profession was not widespread, at least in Rig-Vedic times; barter was the general rule, and we catch a glimpse of cow serving as a medium of exchange. There was some amount of trade, and we find that a merchant appears in the Vedas as a *pani*, as a vaishya, and is spoken of in a derogatory way. As Max Weber observes:

In the Vedas the merchant (*pani*) appears only as a wanderer, as a rule from strange tribes, haggling by day, stealing by night, collecting his riches in secret hoards, hated by God because he acts the miser against gods (in sacrifice) and men, especially holy singers and priests. . . . He should give, and give again; when he does, he is "the darling of gods" and men. But the merchant simply does not do this. [25, p. 85]

Thus the merchant in the brahmanic days was ranked below brahmans and kshatriyas, and although theoretically his status has ever since been third-rate, there have been times when he was a respected member of society, eclipsing every other class. One of these times in Indian annals was the Buddhist period—stretching roughly from the seventh century to the fourth century B.C.—which is so called because at the beginning of this period prophet Buddha was born. At the time of his birth, brahmanism permeated Aryan society to the core, but the reason why it had spread in every corner of north India was not just the royal patronage, but also the brahman's eagerness to perform sacrificial rites for rich households and merchants. Materially the economy had been making strides ever since the Aryan tribes had settled down in the Rig-Vedic times.

The forces of wealth had thus been gaining ground long before the seventh century B.C., but it was not until then that they became powerful enough to hold the people in their sway. In the seventh century B.C., the Indian economy, as well as society, crossed an important milestone in that money came in vogue perhaps through contacts with the neighboring Persians. From the coins that have been found, it appears that originally the merchants issued them as silver blanks, with some tiny coded marks punched on one side to guarantee purity and a proper weight. The stimulus that the discovery of coined money gave to the hitherto barter economy is not hard to imagine. It facilitated trade, the growth of industries, money-lending, even instruments of credit, new urban centers and a whole array of new products that could now be bought and sold in the market.

With the advance in trade and industry arose men of considerable means, of fabulous wealth, especially when, as the narrative

of Buddhist times suggests, there was not a speck of state intervention in the free play of market forces. Some sort of capitalism then
prevailed, and it could not but spawn billionaires. I will shortly
provide evidence for all this from celebrated authorities. But for
now, I venture to say that at the time of Buddha's birth around the
seventh or sixth century B.C., Aryan society was well into the acquisitive age.[1]

The historian's main source of information concerning social, economic and political conditions in the post-brahmanic age
is the prodigious Buddhist literature, principally the Jataka, as
well as the contemporary brahmanic works of Sutras, especially
Grihya and Dharma Sutras. Generally, Sutras are assigned to a
period ranging from the seventh century to the second century
B.C. In both the Buddhist and the brahmanic literature, one finds
that the Vedic-age odium of being a merchant or a money-lender,
by the sixth century B.C., had disappeared. In the Buddhist tradition, the brahman is portrayed as inferior to the affluent merchant. This is confirmed by E. W. Hopkins who, commenting on
these times, observes that then "the world of India was one in
which the ancient priestly caste had lost its authority; that nobles
and wealthy merchants were more regarded than Brāhmans." [8,
p. 221] This was particularly true in the eastern part of northern
India, but even in the western part, that old citadel of brahmanism, it appears that brahmans had lost their preeminent position to
men of affluence.

The rich trader, or money-lender, who had been spoken of
so contemptuously in the Rig-Vedic times, was now called by brahmans a *shreshthi*, meaning superior or prominent. And allusion to
this word occurs as early as the brahmanic period. Describing
economic conditions in the intellectual era, V. M. Apte observes
that "rich Vaiśhyas (śreshtins), who had acquired wealth in trade
or agriculture, and who were probably the headmen of guilds, are
often referred to. That money-lending was a flourishing business
is indicated in various ways. *Kusidin* is a designation of the usurer
in Śatapatha Br." [1, pp. 464–5]

What this quote suggests is that the advent of the acquisitive
era had not been so abrupt; rather the intellectual era of priestly

influence had steadily evolved into the acquisitive epoch in which wealth rules the roost. As Weber observes, "even the Atharvaveda contains a prayer for the increase of the money which the merchant takes to market in order to make more money. . . . Indeed, Indra is considered the god of the merchants and the Rigveda permits wealth to gain heaven. Wealth gives even the Shudra influence, for the priest accepts their money." [25, p. 85] Thus, at least in one respect, the priesthood all over the world has been above discrimination: whatever its professed reservations, it has quietly accepted money from all classes. Drekmeier explains how and why the acquisitive era came into being:

> With the development of a money economy in the sixth and fifth centuries (and the resultant phenomena of debt and mortgage foreclosure) and with the expansion of commerce . . . a new distribution of wealth and power took place in India. These changes affected the position of the privileged orders of Aryan society adversely; . . . The priests, whose status was challenged . . . sought to reinforce religious distinctions. . . . The sutra literature undoubtedly represents one attempt of Brahmanism to meet the challenge of new values and beliefs. [3, p. 35]

It is therefore not surprising that in the Sutras brahmans are still assigned the pivotal position in society; they still rank above every other class, even above the king, but, curiously enough, they are not forbidden from professions of the lower castes. No longer is it necessary for them to be confined to priestly activities; trade and agriculture are open to them as never before. From this Hopkins concludes that "at the time of Sutras there were many nominal members of the priestly and royal orders who lived as farmers and traders, perhaps even as usurers." [9, p. 248] Here then is yet another confirmation for Sarkar's claim that in the acquisitive era many intellectuals get infected by the acquisitive mentality. Actually the fact that brahmanism was still alive fits well with Sarkar's depiction of the acquisitive age, for the acquisitors rely on the intellectuals to advance their interests. The influence of wealth in the Aryan society of the time has been forcefully documented by Kosambi:

The existence of new classes in the Gangetic basin of the sixth century [B.C.] is undeniable. . . . Traders had become so wealthy that the most important person in an eastern town was generally the *śreshthi*. . . . The *śreshthi* was actually a financier or banker, sometimes the head of a trade guild. Even absolute, despotic kings treated these śreshthis with respect. . . . However, the prime indicator for the new class is the changed significance of the word *gahapati* (Sanskrit, *grihpati*); literally "lord of the house." . . . It had meant the host and principal sacrificer at any considerable but not royal sacrifice in Vedic and Brahmana literature. Now, for the first time, it came to mean the head of a large patriarchal household of any caste who commanded respect primarily because of his wealth. . . . The *gahapati* . . . could do what he liked with the riches at his disposal. [10, pp. 100–1]

As stated earlier, the economy of the Vedic times was primarily agricultural, although during the brahmanic epoch a number of arts, handicrafts, and industries involving the use of copper and other metals were beginning to flourish. In the Buddhist period, however, industry and trade played a role more important than ever before, although the village economy was still based primarily on farming. Many large cities had by now emerged and they were centers of multifarious crafts and industries, most of which were organized in the from of guilds. We come across organizations as well as whole villages of weavers, jewelers, potters, basket-makers and the like.

According to the Jataka, there were eighteen such guilds, each headed by a president or alderman (*jethaka* in Jataka or *jyeshtha* in Sutras), and some of these chiefs wielded considerable influence with princes and the king. The head of all these guilds had his office in the city of Beneras. In this connection Mrs. Rhys-Davids notes with interest that the office of this supreme head was established at a time when the kingship was elective and the king happened to be the son of a merchant. [19, p. 206] In other words, money had begun to talk in the political sphere as well. And in an acquisitive era, this is not surprising.

Besides *jethaka*, the Jatakas frequently speak of the title of *sethi* (Sanskrit, *shreshthi*), and of the famous *sethi*, Anathapindika, the billionaire follower of Buddha. *Sethis* were usually men of

considerable fortune, and even among them there were gradations—*anusethi* (an executive officer), *maha sethi* (meaning the
chief among billionaires).

Aside from various crafts and industries, trade, both regional and international, played a great role in the Indian economy at that time. Anathapindika himself was a great traveling
merchant who would organize huge caravans to move goods into
different parts of India. Such caravans were not uncommon, and
were organized for both inland and oceanic trade.

The picture of the economic system just above is somewhat
reminiscent of modern-day Western capitalism, where a free market economy coexists with industrial monopolies and administered prices. The principle of private property was respected in
the Buddhist period, and no stigma attached to earning profits
from industrial and commercial activities. There was hardly any
state intervention in the free operation of demand and supply, the
twins that determine the price in a free-market economy. According to Mr. T. W. Rhys-Davids:

> It is only in later times that we hear . . . of any market price being
> fixed by government regulation. In the sixth century B.C. there is
> only an official called the Valuer, whose duty it was to settle the
> prices of goods ordered for the palace—which is a very different
> thing. And there are many instances . . . of the prices of commodi-
> ties fixed, at different times and places, by the haggling of the mar-
> ket. [20, pp. 100–1]

Mrs. Rhys-Davids also affirms this working of a market economy,
unencumbered by state regulation, by observing that "the act of
exchange between producer and consumer, or between either and
a middleman, was both before and during the age when the
Jātaka-book was compiled, a "free" bargain, a transaction unregu-
lated, with one notable exception, by any system of statute-fixed
prices." [19, p. 219] The "notable exception," of course, was one
where prices were fixed for goods purchased by the royalty. In
addition to the market for commodities, there existed a capital
market which dealt with loan-transactions as well as credit instruments, although there were few banking facilities.

There is frequent reference to promissory notes through which merchants would extend credit to each other at rates of interest that are unfortunately not specified, although the Dharma Sutras furnish, for somewhat later days, an interest rate of eighteen percent on loans secured by personal mortgage. In the Jataka, one also catches glimpses of a rudimentary market for futures-contracts or for some kind of speculative activity. How else can one explain the rare mention of a profit rate of 20,000 percent, and the none-too-rare mention of 400 and 200 percent? It should not, therefore, come as a surprise that the distribution of income was extremely inequitable at those times. To be sure, no one then starved, and in general the common people enjoyed a comfortable living standard; but the number of fabulously rich persons, of billionaires, was extremely limited. There were some wealthy kings, but that in monarchical states does not count. In the words of Mr. Rhys-Davids:

> We hear of about a score of monarchs . . . , of a considerable number of wealthy nobles, and some priests, to whom grants had been made of the tithe arising out of certain parishes or counties or who had inherited similar grants from their forefathers; of about a dozen millionaire merchants . . . and of a considerable number of lesser merchants and middlemen, all in the few towns. [20, p. 102]

Thus there were only a dozen traders who were millionaires, and if we compare the exorbitant price levels of today with the generally low prices of Buddhist times, these millionaires were no less affluent than modern-day Sheikhs as well as billionaires in the United States and other nations. And since we are all aware of the tremendous social, political, and economic clout that men of affluence exercise in the world today, it is not hard to envisage the kind of influence that the billionaire merchants must have had in Buddhist times. In this regard, Webber's words speak for themselves:

> Caravan trade was typically organized by caravan leaders and the guilds . . . rivaled the knighthood and priesthood in power. The king became financially dependent on the guilds with no means of controlling them other than playing them off against one another

or bribery. Even in the epics the king, after a defeat, expresses his concern about them (excepting his relatives and the priests). . . . Now the three genteel estates were those of the secular and priestly noble and the trader. They were often considered peers, they often intermarried, they had concourse with princes on equal footing.

The merchants financed the wars of the princes and had them mortgage or lease-prerogatives to them as individuals or to their guild. . . . Even rich artisans, i.e. those who participated in trade, trafficked with the prince. . . . It was a time in which people of all classes, even the Shudra, were able to obtain political power.

The rising patrimonial prince with his disciplined army and officialdom was increasingly embarrassed by the power of the guilds and his financial dependence on them. We learn that a *vanik* (trader) denied a war loan to a king with the comment that the *dharma* of princes was not to conduct war, but to protect peace and peaceful prosperity of the citizens. [25, pp. 87–88]

From all these accounts, it is clear that the forces of money then held the reins. Acquisitors had the edge not just in social and economic affairs but also in the realm of politics and administration. Some of the guilds and caravans had their own armies, which come to the rescue of many a king hard-pressed at times of war. Thus the Buddhist period, stretching roughly from the seventh to the fourth century B.C., belongs to the acquisitive era of Hindu civilization. If Sarkar's theory holds water, it is now the turn of a revolution to occur, a revolution that must precede the onset of another warrior age.

Before proceeding to examine the storms that blew the acquisitive era aside, let us see how women fared in the new social order. Did they gain or lose in terms of social respect for their rights? There is little evidence available one way or the other. All one can say is that womanhood certainly did not benefit from the new arrangement of power. The Sutra literature continues to exclude women from many religious and social functions. In one respect, at least, their position had changed for the worse. They were now increasingly looked upon as property, to be enjoyed either by the owner or by others [9, p. 247]: no longer did the brahman have a monopoly over debauchery.

CHANDRAGUPTA MAURYA AND THE
SOCIAL REVOLUTION

The political map of India during the Buddhist period reflects a situation of decentralization along with certain developments that foreshadow subsequent centralization. In the seventh century B.C., a number of monarchical states are known to have existed by the side of a few republics or oligarchies; the number of important states is put at sixteen, but most likely there were many more. Some scholars argue that republics in India existed as early as Vedic times, but the evidence on this is far less than conclusive.

The Buddhist period, however, suggests that monarchy was not the only form of government, either in the North or in the South. Indeed, at the time of Buddha's birth it was not even the dominant form of government. Buddhist literature mentions eight oligarchies, and the remaining eight were perhaps ruled by kings. These republican governments functioned something like the present-day democratic systems: Not surprisingly, their strings were pulled by the magic spell of money. Hopkins [7], for instance, notes that among the thirty-six members of a republic's legislative council, twenty-one were *vaishyas*.

Of all the kingdoms, those at Kosala and Magadha seem to have been the most powerful. Some of the kings were related by matrimonial alliances, but that did not preclude sporadic warfare among them. During the early part of the fifth (or sixth) century B.C., the kingdoms of Kosala and Magadha were locked in a bitter struggle for supremacy over north India, a struggle that was sanguinary and indecisive for a long time, but in which Ajatashatru, the Magdhan king and a contemporary of Buddha, eventually won out. Thus was paved the way for the subsequent Mauryan empire, with a vastness that in India has never been equalled again.

This was a period of great unrest in the Indian polity. Ajatashatru himself had ascended the throne after murdering his father, and while the former was peacefully succeeded by his son Udayi, Udayi and his descendants of three generations were not so fortunate: each had to pay for the royal privilege in terms of his life. All this, according to the Buddhist tradition, alarmed the people so much that they elected as their king a minister named Shishunaga who thus founded a new dynasty. The fifth (or sixth) century B.C. coins seem to support this view. By then the kings were stamping their own marks on the coins, and some of the Magadhan coins reveal signs of having been hammered several times, suggesting violent dynastic changes, indicating that the new ruler attempted to replace the marks of the deposed king with marks of his own [10, p. 125]. It is in such heavy weather that Shishunaga had come to power with a promise to restore order and peace.

However, the scourge of conspiracies and assassinations eventually caught up even with the new dynasty, because Shishunaga's successor fell victim to another usurper named Mahapadma Nanda, of whom the literature reveals little. The new king, seemingly carrying forward the tradition that Ajatashatru had inaugurated, extended his domains far and wide. The truth of so many episodes of patricide, to which the Buddhist tradition has given prominence, is not possible to ascertain, but what seems fairly certain is that Mahapadma Nanda came to the throne through conspiracy and a palace revolution. At this point all records seem to contradict each other, and when the curtain lifts again we find an India threatened by Alexander's invasion, which took place in 326 B.C.

Unfortunately for the historian, Alexander stopped at the outskirts of the Magdhan empire, otherwise the Greek accounts might have shed more light on the then Nanda king who is hidden from us by the veil of history. Alexander, having conquered parts of the Punjab, did want to cross swords with the Nanda monarch, but his army, fatigued mentally and physically from years of warring campaigns, refused to advance any further. From those paltry Greek records we learn that the reigning Magadhan king, because of his avarice and wickedness, was extremely unpopular; that he was the son of a barber—allegedly belonging to the lowest caste—who had removed the royal family, and usurped the throne.

This narrative, which accords with the evidence of contemporary brahmanic works called the Purnas, suggests that the

Nanda dynasty was of obscure origin, and that it endured for only two generations—Mahapadma Nanda and his son Dhana Nanda, who was evidently contemporary with Alexander. Dhana means riches, so that the last Magadhan king was either very rich or possessed an acquisitive mentality. Later, the Chinese pilgrim Hiuen Tsang also alluded to the Nanda king as a man of fabulous wealth.

Such were the political conditions when Alexander invaded India, a goodly part of which then constituted the Magadhan empire. Still no paramount power then dominated the Indian political scene. In the Punjab and Sind, the two provinces invaded by Alexander, there were several independent kings along with some republics. And such political decentralization was the general rule. The Greek visitor Megasthenes later wrote that at the time of Alexander's invasion India was divided into 118 distinct nations or tribes. And constant warfare bedeviled them all. Thus India around Alexander's days was plagued by internal dissensions and the oppression of the Nanda king, who like many other rulers of the time, represented the influence of money. These are symptoms of a laborer era of restiveness and anarchy, and the country was ripe for a revolution that would end this state of turmoil.

It turns out that a revolution did occur at this time. It was engineered by a certain Chandragupta Maurya, a warrior of humble origin, and his brahman adviser Chanakya, both of whom seem to have been earlier humiliated by the king Dhana Nanda. The revolution at that time was by no means an easy task. The Punjab and Sind were then occupied by Alexander's governors, whereas the Magadhan king was bolstered by a powerful army. It took the combination of the martial genius of Chandragupta and the shrewdness of Chanakya to overthrow not only the Nanda monarch but also the Greek governors. What followed this momentous event is a vast empire, along with the demise of many small states and the sway of money. A new warrior age was then born, and that is why the rebellion of 324 B.C., master-minded by Chanakya and executed by Chandragupta, qualifies as the laborer revolution of Hindu civilization.

THE MAURYAN AGE AND THE NEW WARRIOR ERA

There is little doubt that, after the overthrow of the Nanda king, the turbulence in which much of India was caught during the last days of the acquisitive era gave way to peace. Within a few years, Chandragupta's military genius unified all of northern India, including the modern nations of Pakistan and Afghanistan, under one centralized rule extending from the Bay of Bengal to the Arabian Sea. But whether this political and administrative centralization propelled India immediately into a new warrior epoch is open to question. For it is not altogether clear whether the scepter was then held by Chadragupta or by his influential minister Chanakya (who is also known by the names of Kautilya and Vishnugupta). Was the apparent ruler also the real ruler?

About Chandragupta's innate courage and other martial qualities, there is no dispute. But some scholars contend that he had to live in the shadow of his Machiavellian adviser Chanakya, whereas others argue that the latter, after removing Dhana Nanda, renounced everything to become an ascetic. A sixth-century A.D. play, *Mudra Rakhasa* (or "The Minister's Seal"), portrays Chandragupta as Chanakya's tool. [13, p. 4] If this were true, then following the social revolution, the Hindu civilization really moved into an intellectual age, where persons of intellect reign in the name of the apparent ruler. Even if true, it is not unusual, because in the confusion of the laborer revolution, society may drift into conditions conflicting with the warrior era, but this cannot last long: After the termination of the acquisitive age, it is the warrior's turn to become preeminent.

Indeed, this is what seems to have transpired following the deposition of the Nanda dynasty, because within a few years of Chandragupta's demise (or abdication), which occurred twenty-four years after his coronation, we hear of no personality as strong as Chanakya holding the hands of the Mauryan king. Thus the new warrior age of political and administrative centralization, which, as subsequently argued, lasted about two centuries, followed either immediately upon the dethronement of Dhana Nanda around 324 B.C. or a little later. It is worth stating at this point that

Chanakya's role as a king-maker is disputed by the Buddhist literature. It is the brahmanical tradition of the Puranas which assigns a
place of pride to him, who was a brahman himself. It is also possible that Chanakya remained active as long as conditions were uncertain, but, after the dust settled, he chose to retire from politics
and become a hermit during Chandragupta's lifetime.

Chandragupta Maurya must at least be credited with laying
the foundation of the new warrior age where his successors were
the absolute rulers—untrammelled by any backstage authority—
of an immense empire. Before I proceed further with my analysis,
it may be noted that the Rig-Vedic as well as the Mauryan period
are two different species belonging to the same genus. They both
belong to the warrior era, but, in some respects, are highlighted
by far-too-diverse features. True, in both periods, Aryan society
was ruled directly by men of warrior mentality, by men of fortitude and physical strength, by men of the warrior class. But in
Rig-Vedic times, India was politically decentralized, as it was divided into disparate tribes frequently at war with each other.

Somewhat similar political, though not social and economic,
conditions also prevailed around the pre-Mauran times which, as is
now clear, constituted the degenerative phase of the acquisitive
age. Is there then a contradiction? Not really, because during the
Rig-Vedic days Aryan society was in the embryo of the warrior
age, one that emerges when a laboring community first evolves
into civilized existence, or when a paleolithic society first matures
into a neolithic organization marked by tribes and agriculture. In
terms of political conditions, the acquisitive era is not far from the
rudimentary warrior society in that political power in both systems is exercised by local elements.

Obviously, it cannot be expected that at the very first stage
of social evolution, through which all ancient societies had to pass,
great kingdoms were born, or the entire area, in which a race or
community subsisted, was centrally governed by one ruler. But
once civilization had come into being, once vast empires had been
established, usually during warrior but also during intellectual
eras, any subsequent division of that empire into a multitude of
distinct units might then be called political decentralization. Thus

the numerous states that dotted the map of India during the Buddhist period or at the time of Alexander's invasion are reminiscent
of such decentralization, and it is on this, together with some
other characteristics no less important, that my analysis of the
acquisitive era was based.

In any case, the tribal form of the warrior society, in which
the Rig-Vedic Aryans were organized, was centralized in relation
to their early laboring, paleolithic subsistence. Exactly when the
Aryans surged out of their paleolithic phase, has not yet been
determined. Nor is this information essential to my analysis, because at the time they left their original home of Central Asia and
colonized northwest India, their polity was well into the rudimentary form of the warrior age. However, the Rig-Vedic warrior era
stands out in sharp contrast to the Mauryan warrior age, even
though in both cases the warrior class had gained the upper hand.
For with the latter, in contrast with the former, the government,
power structure, and administration were highly centralized.

If the Rig-Vedic period was the rudimentary warrior era,
the Mauryan polity was the full-blooded warrior age. All it shows
is that in the past twelve hundred years of a steadily expanding
Aryan umbrella over the native peoples, India had come a long
way. The rise of the Mauryan empire was a logical development in
a civilization that had yet to find its efflorescence, its zenith, its
fullest expression. While during the Mauryan days the Hindu civilization failed to scale the peak, it came very close indeed. The
peak was to be reached during the subsequent Gupta period,
which too, as I shall argue later, turned out to be another species
belonging to the warrior genus.

Around 300 B.C., Chandragupta was succeeded by his son
Bindusara, known in the Greek tradition as Amitraghata or
"slayer of foes"—a title reflecting his many conquests. He seems
to have annexed many parts of the Deccan (southern India) to the
already vast domains to which he was heir. Other than this, his
reign appears to be lackluster, and one reason may be that he has
been historically overshadowed by his illustrious father and by his
son and successor, the celebrated king Ashoka, who is the cyno-
sure not only of the Mauryan age but also perhaps among kings of

all times. When he came to the throne around 273 B.C., Ashoka showed few signs of the brilliance and compassion that subsequently distinguished his administration. In fact, soon after his accession, he made war against the southern kingdom of Kalinga, but the war turned out to be bloodier than he could stand.

After hundreds and thousands of soldiers were killed and mutilated, Ashoka could no longer ignore the horrors and pangs of conscience. He vowed to shun war forever, and to work for a social order from which the sentiment of aggression would be exorcised. For all his humanitarian deeds which followed from this, for all the monuments that have survived to reveal his benevolence, Ashoka has been acclaimed by H. G. Wells as the greatest king of them all. In any case, from Ashoka's times, southern India also begins to share the spotlight of history, as his empire extended to all but a smallish southern extremity of the subcontinent.

After the Kalinga war, Ashoka was converted to Buddhism, which during his long reign prospered as never before. And while he was not the one to persecute other religions, they, especially brahmanism, suffered from benign neglect. Therefore the formerly influential brahman class, the intellectuals who had ruled society during the brahmanic age and then enjoyed a status second only to acquisitors during the Buddhist period, were now overshadowed. The king was absolute and all-powerful, but to his credit he never misused his power. Rather Ashoka called upon his officers to be as considerate to the general public as he was himself. And he did not just give them lectures, but also set an example to them by leading a virtuous life.

Much about Ashoka's reign has come down to us from his inscriptions engraved in the form of Rock Edicts. In the Fourth Pillar Edict, for example, he says, "Just as one entrusts one's child to an experienced nurse, and is confident that the experienced nurse is able to care for the child satisfactorily, so my *rajukas* [officers] have been appointed for the welfare and happiness of the country people." [24, pp. 120–3] Without doubt, India was then in the benevolent phase of the warrior age, and, not surprisingly, in many respects Aryan society surpassed what it had accomplished thus far. New heights were achieved in art, architecture, education, economic prosperity, and the efficiency of justice and administration.

While brahmanism had declined in the Mauryan period, the acquisitors too could not remain unscathed. Economically, the Mauryan age was one of complete antithesis to the spirit of capitalism that had prevailed earlier. In Buddhist India, we hardly hear of any reference to state intervention in the operation either of markets or of the craft and merchant guilds. But now the tables were completely turned. The Mauryan state regulated the economy much as the socialist nations do it today. Merchants and other wealthy persons were heavily taxed, as were people in general. Many industries were nationalized or operated under the state monopoly, and their profits accrued to the royal treasury. Price-fixing by merchants was subject to severe penalties. Thus even though India was then richer than ever before, its economy functioned under the watchful eyes of the state. Gone were the Buddhist days where a market economy coexisted with price-fixing by merchants as well as the guilds. Needless to say, mercenary armies of traders were now barred.

While both intellectuals and acquisitives gave ground, the warriors recaptured the pivotal place they had lost owing to their intellectual poverty ever since brahmanic times. The Mauryan kings maintained a huge army, which made constant demands on the state treasury: hence the state monopoly of some industries and the multitude of taxes. It was not a force of militia but a standing army of some 600,000 men, ready at the command of their emperor to march for further conquests (as with Chandragupta and Bindusara) or to quell the germs of rebellion. Actually the warrior class had been gaining ground ever since the Nanda dynasty, but until Chandragupta's rise, its supremacy in society was open to question, because in order to finance their wars the kings were pitifully dependent on affluent merchants.

With the decline of brahmanism and the steady rise of Buddhism, the status of woman changed for the better, for while the brahmans had emphasized her innate inferiority and excluded her from religious rites, Buddhism stood for the opposite. The Buddhist order admitted women as nuns and laid stress on their education. There are clear signs that the Mauryan period was adorned by many highly educated women, commanding respect in society and the household. Some were even admitted to military training. Megasthenes tells of the female bodyguards who attended on Chandragupta, especially on his hunting expeditions. They were capable of handling chariots, horses, all kinds of weapons, and even elephants. All in all, the Mauryan period paints a much more luminous picture of womanhood than the preceding intellectual and the acquisitive age.

The new warrior era began to decline soon after Ashoka's death around 232 B.C., because his successors lacked his charisma and forceful personality which had managed to knit disparate polities of India into one fabric, despite his avowed renunciation of force and violence. The empire, somewhat truncated, as well as the Mauryan dynasty, lingered till 185 B.C., when the last of the Mauryan kings was overthrown and slain by his own commander Pushyamitra. The Sunga dynasty, of which Pushyamitra was the founder, then came to power, and although the new monarch was by birth a brahman, he was by temperament a warrior who was able to hold on to the bulk of the Mauryan empire. In any case, brahmanism was back in the saddle, and it was not much later, perhaps soon after Pushyamitra's demise, that another intellectual era came into being.

SUNGAS, KANVAS, ANDHRAS, AND THE NEW INTELLECTUAL ERA

Pushyamitra spent much of his life in warfare, in which he had his ups and downs. While he suffered some reverses at the hands of a King Kharavela of Kalinga, he successfully defended the bulk of his empire from attacks by a Greek intruder named Menander. The northwestern part of India, including the Punjab, had already been lost to the Greeks, and Pushyamitra was unable to make any impression there. Still, his domain was then the largest in India, although he had to beware of powerful neighboring kingdoms which were on the prowl to grab remains of the Mauryan empire. During his reign the sacrificial rite of horse sacrifice—through which he proclaimed his supremacy over northern and central India—staged a comeback, indicating the revival of brahmanism and the decline of Buddhism, which does not permit any violence, much less animal sacrifice. Yet there is little evidence that Pushyamitra was just a figurehead and a plaything of the brahmans. Therefore the direct rule of the warrior era seemed to have continued until 149 B.C., when he died and was succeeded by his son Agnimitra.

Not much is known about Pushyamitra's successors, some of whom succumbed to swords of their assassins. It is quite possible, nay very likely, that they were weaklings and mere tools in the hands of their brahman ministers. Because this much we know— that Devabhuti, a debauchee and the last of the Sunga kings, was murdered at the orders of his brahman minister Vasudeva, who then seems to have placed a puppet on the throne. On this matter historians disagree, and the Puranas deserve the blame. On the one hand, the latter record that Vasudeva founded the Kanva dynasty which ruled for forty-five years until 27 B.C., when its last ruler was overthrown by a king of the Andhra or Satavahana dynasty; on the other they suggest that the Andhra king destroyed the Kanvas as well as remnants of the Sungas. The truth seems to be that the Kanvas were the real rulers but that they ruled in the name of the Sunga kings. E. J. Rapson confirms this view:

> We may conclude, then, that the Çungas [Sungas] were a military power, and that they became puppets in the hands of their Brahman counsellors. [17, p. 522]

It then appears certain that after Pushyamitra's demise around 149 B.C., a new intellectual era came into being, because the Sunga kings, too feeble or licentious to reign themselves, were overshadowed by their brahman ministers. As usual in an intellectual era, there was now some diffusion of governmental authority, because neither politically nor administratively was India now as much centralized as the Mauryan state. As stated earlier, although the Sungas (and Kanvas) held the bulk of the former Mauryan empire, they had to contend with other powerful kingdoms. Consequently, they were more dependent on their officers than the Mauryan kings. Also brahmanism now flourished as much as it had in the post-Rig-Vedic age, and continued to do so even when the Kanvas were overthrown by the Andhras, because the Andhras too claimed brahmanical parentage. Although this by itself does not prove anything, as Sarkar's definitions of mental attitude are not based on familial descent, it does suggest that brahmans as a class could not but have prospered. As Kosambi observes:

> Official (not monastic) caves at the important Nānaghāt pass . . . record full details of the innumerable donations as *yajna* [sacrificial] fees made over to brahmins by the Sātavāhana kings: cattle by the thousand, elephant, chariot, horses, coined money, and so on. [10, p. 184]

The Indian narrative at the dawn of the first century A.D. is highly muddled and not amenable to clear analysis. For, in addition to the confusion caused by contradictions of the Puranas and by a deficient chronology, the picture is complicated by foreign invaders of diverse origin. Soon after Ashoka's death, the Greeks had captured Kabul and the Punjab but were then stopped there by Pushyamitra. However, around 65 B.C. the Greek sovereigns of the Punjab were overcome by the Sakas, again a tribe alien to India and migrating from central Asia. One Saka tribe, which ruled over extensive domains southwest of the Punjab, was rapidly Indianized, assuming Aryan names as Rudradaman, and came into violent contact, despite matrimonial alliances, with the neighboring Andhras.

But this is not all. Around the first century A.D., another alien tribe, the Kushans, seized some Indian territories from the Greeks as well as the Sakas. Thus at the end of the first century A.D., about half of the subcontinent was ruled by aliens. Who governed there, whether the warrior or the intellectual, is not clear. The issue depends on how deeply the foreign sovereigns affected social and political institutions of their subjects, and in view of the great paucity of in-depth records, the answer cannot be given with any precision.

If we limit our discussion to the Northeast and the South, it seems that the intellectual era, which reappeared after Pushyamitra's demise, continued when the Andhras, around 27 B.C., demolished the Kanvas and remnants of the Sungas. This is because the literature of the time portrays a brahmanism that matches, nay excels, the brahmanic sway of the age of Brahmanas. On linguistic evidence, the celebrated law book, *Manu-Smriti,* that absolute champion of the brahmanic supremacy in society, seems to have been written in the first or the second century A.D. [22, p. 16] This is, at best, indirect testimony, for ideally we should examine the sociopolitical life in the vast Andhra domains and see who really wielded the scepter. But since such data are scanty, we must have recourse to circumstantial evidence.

In this case, however, it turns out that the indirect testimony may more than make up for the lack of on-the-spot inquiry. So vehement is the support of *Manu-Smriti* for the supremacy of brahmans, the very fact that it was permitted by the royalty suggests that it contains a grain of truth. The brahman in this work claims precedence in every imaginable respect, although adequate space is allocated to qualifications on which this precedence may rest. Not surprisingly, the caste system became more rigid around the first century than ever before. Even in the *Shatapatha Brahmana,* the Shudra's duty was to serve the other three classes, but "Manu," according to Drekmeier, "holds that he was created expressly for the service of the brahman." [3, p. 86] Similarly, Manu insists that high administrative offices ought to be reserved for the brahmans. In *Manu-Smriti,* Drekmeier continues,

> brahman superiority is described and justified in the most extravagant terms. *Even the gods depend on the brahmans.* Though the prosperity of the community rests on the king, the king's welfare, in turn, depends on the brahman class—the spiritual power is the source of the temporal power. To anger the priest is to seek destruction. [3, p. 231 (italics mine)]

In terms of legal concepts also, the brahman claims impunity. While he is not totally above the law, the severest sentence for him, even for rape, murder or treason, is banishment, and that too only from his homeland, not from his property and possessions.

Thus even though the brahman did not claim wholesale immunity from the arm of the law, he did claim it from harsh penalties including capital punishment—a privilege, of course, denied to other castes.

As far as woman is concerned, *Manu-Smriti* treats her no better than it treats the Shudra. Every now and then it provides her with some sops, not only to maintain a semblance of objectivity and compassion towards the so-called weaker sex, but also to keep her from rising against brahmanism.

If all these prerogatives were in fact granted to the brahmans, then in parts of India unoccupied by the foreigners, there is no doubt that the intellectuals were predominant. We do not have any conclusive testimony regarding actual living conditions, but the testimony of *Manu-Smriti* is indisputable. Since, as is practically certain, it was compiled around the first or second century A.D., I conclude that the new intellectual era, which began around 149 B.C. at the time of Pushyamitra's death, continued into the second century A.D. The existence at the time of somewhat decentralized administrative and political system all over the subcontinent, of empires composed of feudatory kingdoms also tends to confirm this view.

THIRD-CENTURY INDIA AND THE NEW ACQUISITIVE ERA

Within a few years after 27 B.C. when the Andhras came to prominence, their word prevailed not only over the Deccan and the south-Indian peninsula but also over Magadha and central India. It is only towards the end of the first century A.D. that the tranquillity of such vast domains was perturbed by winds of violence which the invading Greeks and Sakas had brought with them. It is then that the Andhras had to cede some territories southwest of the Punjab to the victorious Sakas. However, before long the celebrated Andhra king Gautamiputra Satkarni came to the throne, and around 106 A.D. he avenged his precursor's humiliation and recaptured the lost areas.

Gautamiputra, like the other Andhras, boasted of a brahmanic descent, but by his actions and attitude he was a first-rate warrior. Through extensive campaigns of conquest, it is said that he extended his domains from sea to sea. He regarded himself as the defender of Hindu faiths, both brahmanic and Buddhist, against foreign onslaughts. After a splendid reign of about twenty-five years, he was succeeded by his son Pulumayi, and it is he who had to cross swords with the Sakan king Rudradaman of whom I have spoken before.

Intermittent conflicts with foreign powers ultimately proved fatal to the extensive Andhra empire which, at the end of the second century A.D., splintered into myriad principalities, each ruled by a petty prince. We hear of the Abhiras, the Ikshvakus, the Bodhis, the Chutus, the Brihatphalayanas, the Pallavas, the Vakatakas, among many others, who all rose on the debris of the Andhra empire. At just about the same time, perhaps half a century before, the vast empire of the Kushans had also split into small kingdoms. Thus at the end of the second century, the entire subcontinent was divided into numerous political units. Such a decentralization is reminiscent only of an acquisitive age. That is why I venture to say that the third century India belongs to a new acquisitive era, which might have begun as early as the middle of the second century.

This is the only point that I have in support of this argument. For the historical narrative of the first and second century is sketchy, but that of the third century is even sketchier. With little data to stand upon, I do not want to hazard any conjectures regarding socioeconomic conditions of the time. One thing seems certain though. As the third century progresses, politically India becomes more and more divided; the average size of the kingdoms grows smaller and smaller, with each kingdom constantly at its neighbor's throat, ready to mutilate it, but unable to do so owing to internal dissensions. In other words, during the third century the new acquisitive age was moving towards anarchy, thus paving the way for a new revolution.

SAMUDRA GUPTA AND ANOTHER SOCIAL REVOLUTION

At the dawn of the fourth century, a certain Chandra Gupta, who was a petty chieftain somewhere in Bihar, married a daughter of the powerful Lichchavi clan, and in the process acquired the principality of Magadha. Upon his coronation in 320 A.D., he greatly enlarged his kingdom, extending it to all of Bihar and part of Bengal, and proclaimed a new era called the Gupta era. Thus, with Chandra Gupta's accession, there began the reverse, cyclical process of the decentralized polity moving back towards political unification. However, Chandra Gupta could not finish what he had started, for he died in 330 A.D., and the mighty task of unification fell on rugged shoulders of his son Samudra Gupta, who through his military genius conquered far and wide, and thus put an end to the acquisitive age. He, therefore, gets credit for engineering another laborer revolution.

THE GUPTAS AND ANOTHER WARRIOR ERA

Samudra Gupta's manifold military expeditions and conquests have moved Vincent Smith to call him the Napoleon of India. He uprooted so many principalities and kinglets that his campaigns give an idea of numerous fragments into which India was divided at the time of his accession. But when he breathed his last around 380 A.D., these fragments were once again welded into an empire that was the largest since Ashoka. About half of the subcontinent then was either part of Samudra Gupta's kingdom or paid him tribute. Simultaneously, in the Deccan there emerged another large and powerful state, that of the Vakatakas, with whom the Guptas had friendly relations. Thus about three-fourths of India during the Gupta period was unified under the centralized rule of two dynasties, of whom the Vakatakas were clearly overshadowed by the Gupta sovereigns.

The Gupta kings, like their Mauryan counterparts, have been occasionally accused of being despotic rulers. Smith implies this in his narrative. Describing Samudra Gupta's capital city, he asserts that "the real capital of an Oriental despotism is the seat of the despot's court for the time being." [23, p. 310] Now the Gupta kings were admittedly strong, unquestioned masters of their vast domains, and echos of their forceful rule can be heard in *Narada-Smriti*, the law book written during their times. But they were also absolute champions of brahmanism which, as we have learned before, had already experienced a resurgence. Their autocratic impulse, if any, was tempered by their brahman ministers, variously called *mantrins* or *amatyas,* whose offices seem to have been hereditary for several generations. In addition to their ministers, the Gupta kings were advised by a council (*mantri mandalam*), which was a deliberative body, headed by a minister called *mantri mukhya.* This council exerted some influence in administrative decisions, and Drekmeier goes as far as to assert that "there is little reason to believe that the king dared act without consultation, or that he could controvert the decision of a cabinet constituting the best minds in his kingdom." [3, p. 184] Thus, the view that the Guptas were Oriental despots must be discarded. If anything, they gave free rein to talented persons in the interest of efficient administration.

Brahmanism was now as strong as ever, although Buddhism was allowed to flourish. In fact, the Gupta period reveals itself mainly from the work of a Chinese monk, Fa-hsien, who came to India to study Buddhism. Prerogatives claimed for brahmans in *Manu-Smriti* were recorded in *Narada-Smriti* verbatim with one prominent exception.

Whereas Manu exalts the brahman above every other caste —even above the king—Narada, while still placing the brahman on the crest of the social hierarchy, is a champion of monarchical absolutism. While Manu proclaims the king to be subordinate to the sacred law or *dharma,* by which he means the brahmanic interpretation of the Vedas, Narada, according to Drekmeier, insists "that the king be obeyed whether right or wrong in his actions, though he doubts that it is possible for the king to be wrong." [3, p. 232] Drekmeier further observes that "the *Naradasmriti* is the only political treatise in which an unrestricted absolutism can be found: a ruler must be obeyed irrespective of his worth and competence if the social order is to be preserved." [3, p. 251]

Why do the two Smritis differ so radically on the matter of royal prerogative, even though regarding the brahman's social primacy they fully concur? The reason lies in the different political environment in which the two books were written. *Manu-Smriti,* scholars believe, was written during the first or the second century when India was divided into large kingdoms, when the monarchs were feeble and therefore very probably under the control of their brahman ministers. *Narada-Smriti,* on the other hand, was written during the Gupta period, and it could not possibly ignore the vigor with which the king welded his empire and managed his administration: it could not but be infected by his majestic vivacity and grandeur.

Without doubt the Gupta period belongs to the benevolent warrior age. The apparent ruler was now the real, and magnanimous, ruler. And is it a coincidence that this epoch has been enshrined by historians, of both Indian and Western origin, as India's Golden Age? Is it a mere coincidence that this golden era, much like Egypt's and England's, also blossomed during a warrior age? Not according to Sarkar's theory of social cycle!

In almost every sphere—in art, literature, drama, poetry, science, economic prosperity, music, crime-prevention—the Gupta period surpasses the preceding eras, even the Ashokan days. For while the tranquillity and prosperity of the Mauryan times are now preserved, the Mauryan system of extreme administrative centralization is not. Individual initiative is now given the fullest expression, and the culmination is a civilization that in India has been excelled neither before nor since.

In order to attract individual talent to government, especially to local administration, the Gupta sovereigns unwittingly planted the germs of feudalism, which was to unfold in the future. Like Charlemagne, who reigned in Europe some three centuries later, the Gupta rulers made grants of land to learned scholars and to administrative officials in lieu of cash payments, and in due course the local lords became hereditary owners. I will dwell more on this in the ensuing discussion.

The Gupta empire, and peace, lasted from the beginning of the fourth century to about the end of the fifth, when under the onus of the Huna *Völkerwanderung* it cracked into large pieces. But soon the Hunas were repulsed by either Yasodharman or by

Narasimha Gupta, who is popularly known as Baladitya. Thus the empire seems to have survived well into the middle of the sixth century, although its energy, under the Huna shock waves, had been all but spent.

For the next half-century, India was ruled by provincial governors and feudal chiefs, but the warrior era was to make at least one more attempt at a comeback—this time at the hands of one Harsha Vardhana, who came to the throne around 606 and ruled until 647. Within six years, he reconquered much that was part of the Gupta empire, although he had to accept defeat from the powerful southern kingdom of the Chalukyas. Harsha, a man of considerable vigor and energy, provided efficient administration for his people; but he died without an heir, and upon his death his empire faded away.

The next six centuries are again obscure, and my arguments that follow are partly based on known facts and partly on inference. The history of India constantly plays hide-and-seek with the scholar, but following Harsha's death it hides for a really long time. For this reason, I am not sure exactly when the third warrior era of the Aryan society came to an end. It could have passed away with Harsha, for towards the end of the seventh century we begin to hear of the rise of new dynasties with brahmanical parentage, and the brahmans could not but have prospered. Only vigorous rulers like the Guptas and Harsha could keep the brahmans under control; and since following Harsha, there were few monarchs of that calibre, the priesthood, the brahman ministers, and other administrative officers must have thrived. Yet we also hear of new and powerful dynasties rising in the eighth century—in Kashmir and Bengal, as well as the Deccan—with few officials prominent behind the scenes.

Some accounts of ministerial sway over the kings come to light from narratives of the ninth and tenth centuries. Especially is this true of Kashmir, whose history a learned brahman named Kalhana has preserved in the metrical chronicle called *Rajatarangini*. It turns out that in Kashmir's case the ninth and tenth centuries unambiguously belong to the intellectual age.

With other kingdoms, since the historical record is deficient I have to rely on secondary evidence.

NINTH- AND TENTH-CENTURY INDIA AND ANOTHER INTELLECTUAL ERA

Kashmir is pertinent to Indian history from ancient times. It was a part of Ashoka's empire, and later it paid homage to Harsha. But on its own it came into historical limelight only with the beginning of the eighth century, when a king named Lalitaditya extended his dominion far beyond its normal mountainous frontier. In a series of brilliant military expeditions, he defeated the Tibetans, Bhutias, and Turks settled along the Indus, and the king of Kanauj, which had been Harsha's capital and for which major dynasties were vying at the time. His son Jayapida, reputed to have single-handedly killed a lion, extended his influence still further. He won victories over Nepal and also over the rebellious Kanauj. Thus towards the end of the eighth century, Kashmir's word prevailed over substantial territories of northwest and central India.

However, at the dawn of the ninth century, Jayapida seems to have incurred the ire of brahmans, who conspired to have him overthrown. Puppet kings were then placed on the throne, first by the maternal uncle of the deposed king and later on by a minister named Sura. In the tenth century, a minister named Prabhakara was at the helm for a short time. From him the role of the king-maker passed into the hands of a powerful political organization called Tantrin infantry; but power was soon concentrated in another minister, Parvagupta, who eventually became so prominent that he usurped the throne for himself. In the second half of the tenth century, a queen named Didda ruled as regent for her son, but she also relied on a number of ministers.

Thus during the ninth and tenth centuries, the real authority was exercised either by the ministers or by an assembly of the brahmans, while the kings were mere puppets whose strings were pulled by others. The history of Kashmir, with its extensive influence on vast territories, thus provides an argument for regarding these two centuries of the Hindu civilization as belonging to the intellectual age.

Another argument derives from the annals of the Pala dynasty, which rose to supremacy in Bengal during the second half of the eighth century. Soon, through several military campaigns, it ruled over all of the northeast, central and some parts of northwest India. The Palas were at their zenith during the reign of Dharmapala, who reigned from 770 to 810. Their vast domain lasted till the end of the ninth century, after which much of it was annexed by Pratihara-dynasty kings. The Palas were not graced by the presence of a Kalhana, or else we might have known at first hand who really held the sceptre—the kings or their chief ministers, who all seem to have come from a prominent brahman family. In this connection, U.N. Ghoshal asserts that "making due allowance for evident exaggeration in claims of these ministers, we may conclude that they exercised a commanding influence on the early Palas." [5, p. 242] In the neighboring and contemporary kingdom of Assam, too, there are clear indications that some prominent officials (called elders) could not be ignored even in matters as important as the succession to the throne [5, p. 243].

The story of north and central India of the time remains incomplete if no reference is made to the Pratihara dynasty which came to prominence in the second half of the ninth century, mainly at the expense of the Palas. The Pratihara kingdom was large enough to be called an empire, but the Pratiharas too boasted of brahmanic descent, and brahmans, especially those well versed in the Puranas, could not but flourish. A pointed example of the priestly sway is that the commoners were by law required to pay the priests a regular tax (*brahmanavimsati*), which is reminiscent of the tithe collected by the Catholic Church during the Middle Ages [10, p. 176]. At the same time the idea of *Manu-Smriti* that the king is below the sacred law (*dharma*) was resurrected in jurisprudence. It found its most assertive exponent in Medhatithi, who affirms that the kingship, deriving its sanction from the people, is subservient to the fundamental law expounded by the Dharma-Shastras (law books), which, of course, can be explained by none else but the brahman.

In the South, the eighth to tenth centuries witnessed the rise of the Rashtrakutas, who also at times dominated the kingdoms of the North. This dynasty, though blessed with some mighty warriors, generously patronized religion. During their times, brahmanism uprooted Buddhism, and developed faster than ever since Buddha's birth. Much of this was accomplished by an ascetic brahman named Shankaracharya whose wit, erudition and eloquence no contemporary could match. Almost single-handedly he shook the foundations of Buddhism around 800 A.D., and ultimately helped it vanish from the land of its birth. This was the zenith of brahmanic renaissance, and it supports my view that, despite the full-blooded warriors that the Rashtrakutas produced, even the southern part of ninth- and tenth-century India reveals brahmanic dominion and hence the intellectual age. The ostentatious temples that were then built only serve to reinforce my argument.

FEUDALISM AND ANOTHER ACQUISITIVE ERA

I have already mentioned that by making generous grants of land to learned scholars and administrative officials, the Guptas had planted seeds that later were to sprout as some kind of feudalism. Such gifts of land had also carried with them the administrative and fiscal responsibilities of villages in their jurisdiction. Subsequently, around Harsha's times, the landlords were also granted judicial privileges, thus turning the village into a self-sustaining system, much like the latter-day manorial economy of feudal Europe. If we define feudalism as a decentralized political system where big landlords, by virtue of their landed wealth, become local nuclei of power, attracting local loyalties, then a full-fledged feudalism was on the rise in India after the demise of Harsha and his empire.

But this was not to be, for during the eighth to tenth centuries powerful new dynasties, as we have seen before, arose one by one to preserve a semblance of centralized authority: the Kashmiris, the Palas, the Pratiharas and the Rashtrakutas appeared almost contemporaneously to organize, as it were, the subcontinent into semi-centralized bastions of intellectual-dominated communities. True, the typical monarch of the time had his own feudatory kings paying him homage and tribute, but he was not as yet greatly dependent on his vassals.

Political decentralization and powerful landed magnates really emerged towards the end of the tenth century. By this time warfare among the kingdoms of the post-Harsha intellectual era had so emasculated the social fiber that there was no king powerful enough to tame his vassals. There is one exception, of course, and that refers to the Chola dynasty which assembled a large kingdom in the South during the eleventh to thirteenth centuries; but the Chola empire covered less than one fifth of the subcontinent, which is an area as vast as Europe minus Russia. The rest of India, however, was split into numerous warring principalities which, if any one cared to count, ran into hundreds —perhaps thousands.

Thus feudalism in India really emerged at the dawn of the eleventh century, and, not surprisingly, it is at this time of deafening internal dissensions that regular incursions from the aliens— this time the Muslims—began and struck deep into the heart of India. The eleventh, twelfth, and the thirteenth centuries, throughout which centrifugal forces were supreme, thus belong to the acquisitive age. K. M. Munshi observes that during this period "a king, instead of being the only source of power, was no more than the first among the equals, the head of interrelated overlordships, never in a position to overrule the wishes of his feudal lords." [14, p. xiii] In the same vein, B. P. Mazumdar contends that[2]

> the period between 1030 and 1194 A.D. may be regarded as the heyday of feudal anarchy . . . [because] the feudatories acquired so much power and influence that it became necessary for the King to watch their movement and conduct very carefully. [12, p. 11].

Actually the Muslim invasions had begun as far back as the eighth century when the Arabs conquered the Sind, but that merely turned out to be a forewarning of the protracted conflict which commenced with the eleventh century. Lured by tales of India's fabulous wealth, many Muslim warriors then invaded the subcontinent, but it was not until the fateful year of 1192, when Muhammad of Ghur trounced Prithvi Raj Chauhan, that the Muslims gained a permanent foothold on Indian soil. Soon afterwards, in 1206, Qutabddin Aibak established a sultanate in Delhi and started the Muslim rule. But the acquisitive era continued, because the centralized Muslim rule made but a small dent in torrents of political decentralization that had bedeviled India for the past two centuries.

Even after deadly exposure to the ruthless adversary, who plundered countless villages and temples without remorse, the remaining Hindu kinglets were too myopic and vain to unite. It is not that they were wanting in valor and resources, only that, wrapped up in their own petty little feuds, they would not present a united front. Even as the muslims were steadily expanding their stranglehold, the Chalukyas and the Cholas were battling it out in the Deccan.

THE ACQUISITIVE-CUM-LABORER ERA AND THE SOCIAL REVOLUTION

The political scene of thirteenth-century India brings to mind the degenerate phase of the acquisitive era, which is marked by lawlessness and total anarchy. In the South the Chola empire, during the first quarter of the thirteenth century, had broken into numerous petty states constantly at loggerheads with each other. In the North the Delhi Sultanate was a hotbed of conspiracies, which were prompted by the absence of any law of succession and by the unmitigated resistance of the Indian people, whom the Muslims called infidels or Hindus. Nowhere in India could a civilized society then exist, much less prosper. The Delhi sultanate, in the first half of the thirteenth century, was tyrannized by the famous group of "forty slaves" attached to the court. On top of this, the sultan's authority was constantly challenged by his provincial governors and the Hindu chieftains. Even when the kings were powerful, as with Iltmush and Balban, they had to fight to hold on to their territories. Chief interests of the sultanate were plunder and conquests, of which Hindus were the hapless but resisting victims. Therefore, as far as the Hindu civilization is concerned, the thirteenth century belongs to a laborer era where brutality and the law of the jungle prevailed everywhere in India.

If civilized life is to continue, such a state of affairs cannot endure long. But among the Hindu kings, reeling under disunity amongst themselves, there was then no one potent and wise enough to stem torrents of anarchy. The burden of putting an end to this lawlessness, therefore, had to fall on the shoulders of a Muslim ruler. In 1296, a powerful military commander named Alauddin Khilgi rose to the sultanate and soon established his *imperium* all over India, thereby putting an end to the acquisitive-cum-laborer forces of decentralization and anarchy. He also abolished private property, thereby smashing the power base of the feudal lords. In other words, his warrior prowess brought about yet another laborer revolution in Indian history.

KHILGIS, TUGHLUQS, MUGHALS, AND THE MUSLIM WARRIOR ERA

To be sure, the Khilgi dynasty was perhaps no less barbarous than the so-called Slave Sultanate of the thirteenth century; but now much of India, for the first time since the Guptas, was unified under one central command from Delhi, although the South was held in mere feudatory relationship. Until Alauddin's accession, the Muslim religion represented by Ulemas had played some role in administrative affairs. In theory, though not in reality, the Muslim domains in India were extensions of the eastern Caliphate. Alauddin was the first Indian ruler to shake off this theoretical vassalage and assert independence from the orthodox church. As a result, the Hindus got some reprieve from religious policies which the earlier sultans had followed.

In 1320 the Khilgis were superseded by the Tughluq dynasty, of which Muhammad Bin was the most colorful, as well as eccentric, ruler. During his reign, the vast Muslim empire began to break down and a number of military states, such as the Bahmani and the Vijaynagar kingdoms in the South, came into being.

In 1398, remnants of the Tughluq empire were plundered by Timur the Lame, and in the ensuing carnage his successors established a Sayyid dynasty. Thus throughout the fourteenth century India was either centrally ruled or organized into a few militaristic states, which were all despotically governed, with perhaps the one exception of Vijaynagar. But even there, the king and his military had the upper hand, for in those days of the survival of the fittest the non-warrior classes had no chance of coming into prominence.

The fragmentation that had once again begun in India during the reign of Muhammad Tughluq continued during the fifteenth century, but still large pockets of centralized rule existed. In the South, the Vijaynagar kingdom continued to flourish, although the Bahmani domains were broken up into five provinces. In the North, the Sayyids were replaced by the Lodis who quickly began to expand their kingdom, so much so that by the end of the fifteenth century their rule extended from the Indus to the western fringes of Bengal. Simultaneously there existed some other good-sized kingdoms—Mewar, Gondwana, Gujrat, Malwa, and Bengal—all organized on a war footing, distrustful of their neighbors. Thus the warrior era continued, with India of the time resembling contemporary Europe which, by the end of the fifteenth century, was also divided into centralized nation-states.

This system of about a dozen centralized kingdoms continued well into the sixteenth century, until a Mughal ruler, Akbar the Great, by virtue of his military genius, conquered the whole of northern India and organized it into an efficiently managed empire. The reader may have been searching for the benevolent phase of what we may call the Muslim warrior age. Well, it arrived during Akbar's times, which surpassed the Sultanate period in all those achievements that reflect the flowering of a civilization.

The reason why the facet of benevolence appeared so late in the Muslim warrior era is that at the onset of the foreign rule the Muslims and Hindus were too suspicious of each other to live in harmony, which is a prerequisite for social efflorescence. And the early sultans did little to soothe the Hindu panic or the mutual phobia that naturally arises when two disparate cultures run into violent collision. However, Akbar was made of a different mettle. He introduced a policy of toleration for all religions, and thus paved the way for a long reign of creativity and prosperity.

THE MUGHAL-MARATHA INTELLECTUAL ERA

Akbar's cosmopolitan attitude towards all faiths was devoutly followed by his son and successor Jahangir, but during the former's reign one also discerns the germination of forces that were soon to lead the Muslim warrior era into an intellectual age. Akbar was unquestionably the master of the state as well as of the church, but his catholicity aroused the ire of the orthodox or Sunni section of the Muslims. They discovered an eloquent champion in the person of a saint named Mujaddid Sarhindi, but, despite his great influence on some nobles, he was unable to bring either Akbar or Jahangir round to his view. Nevertheless, in Jahangir's times the intellectual era reappeared but in an altogether unexpected way. The real power during his rule rested with his queen Nur Jahan and her brother Asaf Khan, whom she appointed as Prime Minister. And the sister and brother combined to dictate all policies and administrative affairs. But these early warnings of the new intellectual epoch vanished with Jahangir's demise, because during the reign of his successor, Shah Jahan, the despotic and direct warrior rule staged a resounding comeback.

Meanwhile during the half-century (1605–58) reign of Jahangir and Shah Jahan, the orthodox Muslim faith had been steadily gaining ground, and when Aurangzeb succeeded Shah Jahan in 1658, the writ was there for all to see. Most autocratic of all the Mughal rulers, Aurangzeb took instructions from Sarhindi's son, Khwaja Muhammad Masum, as well as from his grandson, Khwaja Muhammad Saifuddin. Their influence was visible in almost all his activities and policies, whether towards the unorthodox or Shia Muslims, or towards the Hindus. Mark Naidis remarks:

Aurangzeb's religious bigotry seemed to grow with the years. As early as 1667 he imposed a discriminatory tax on Hindu traders. In 1669 he issued a general order to demolish all the temples and schools of the Hindus. . . . The climax of this policy came in 1679 when Aurangzeb revived the poll tax on unbelievers. [15, p. 78]

But Aurangzeb's fanaticism, as Mohammad Yasin states, was inspired by Mujaddid Sarhindi's teachings as well as by leaders of the Sunni Muslims:

The Puritan in Aurangzeb was not a sudden outburst or an accident but the logical consequence of the long cultivated reactionary tendencies. It will not be an exaggeration to say that Aurangzeb's *state policy* was prompted by the *voice of Sarhindi* from behind the scene. His dictates and orders were approved and counter-signed by the religious heads of the Sunni sect. [26, p. 171 (italics mine)]

It is not that the Muslim religion and its emissaries, the Ulemas, had never wielded any influence in state policies before. But Balban, Alauddin Khilgi, Muhammad Bin Tughluq, among many other sultans, had made it sure that the Ulema influence was kept under control. Seldom were Indian political affairs so positively subordinated to wishes of the Sunnis, and, as S. A. Rizvi [21, p. 292] argues, there were many other orthodox saints and scholars, besides Sarhindi's children, who dictated state policy in Aurangzeb's times. Thus the intellectual era, those roots are discernible even in Jahangir's days, came into full swing with the accession of Aurangzeb.

After his death in 1707, the indirect intellectual dominion continued and showed up in two ways. First, his successors were mostly weaklings and therefore tools in the hands of their ministers (*wazirs*). Second, Aurangzeb's myopic policy of contempt for the non-Muslim sentiments had sown seeds of rebellion among his subjects—Sikhs, Jats, Rajputs, Marathas—and within thirty years after his demise, his empire, which was vast enough to rival Ashoka's, split into several pieces. On the ruins arose the paramount Maratha power which a great warrior named Shivaji had molded into a force that could not be ignored even during Aurangzeb's reign.

Thus Indian history in the eighteenth century is mainly a history of declining fortunes of the Mughals and rising fortunes of the Marathas, and in both cases apparent rulers were swayed by their intellectual ministers. Hence the title of this section: the Mughal-Maratha Intellectual Era. While the Mughals were in the grip of their wazir, the Marathas were in the grip of their brahman minister, Peshwa. The Maratha king (Raja), the descendant of Shivaji, was so overshadowed by the Peshwas throughout the eighteenth century that they have often been likened to the mayors who had kept the Merovingian king under their thumb during the early intellectual era of Western civilization (see Chapter 4). In short much of the seventeenth century and all of the eighteenth belong to the intellectual age.

THE BRITISH PERIOD AND ANOTHER ACQUISITIVE ERA

The Maratha dominion in India lasted, with inevitable vicissitudes, until the end of the eighteenth century, when another power rose to primacy in an unexpected way. In the context of Western civilization, we have already seen how, during the fifteenth century of adventure on the high seas, a new route to India had been discovered. Following this emerged the Portuguese, Dutch, French and English companies to conduct trade with India. Gradually all four companies were embroiled in the Indian politics so as to win favorable trading rights. Each tried to outdo the other, and, if necessary, to fight it out with gunboats and soldiers.

In this quadrilateral struggle, lasting well over two centuries, eventually the British East India Company won out, so much so that in 1765 it obtained the right to administer the states of Orissa, Bihar, and Bengal from the Mughal emperor. Thus was paved the way for the British umbrella to spread quickly over India. Within the short span of the next four decades, the English annexed—or obtained tribute from—many Hindu and Muslim territories, including those of the Peshwa, and became the paramount Indian power. By the onset of the nineteenth century, therefore, the

British could not be challenged by anyone, save the powerful Sikh state of Punjab ruled by Ranjit Singh, with whom they judiciously avoided collision. After the Sikh ruler's death though, the Punjab fell on evil days, and in 1849 met the fate that had befallen many other provinces.

Usually the victorious nation superimposes upon the vanquished its own phase of civilization; this, for instance, was India's experience with the Aryans as well as the Muslims, both of whom transmitted to it their own warrior age. The British, around 1800, were not as yet in the acquisitive era, as their mercantile concerns were subordinated by their Prime Minister and the House of Lords to the landed interests (see Chapter 4), but they were virtually knocking on its doors. The acquisitive era actually arrived in England during the second half of the nineteenth century, but in India it arrived in the first half. This is because, until 1858, the economic, social, and political affairs of the bulk of the subcontinent were managed, or mismanaged, under the watchful eye of the British parliament, by "servants" of the East India Company which was controlled by London's capitalist merchants.

As far as Indian society is concerned, these voracious capitalists inflicted upon it the worst kind of acquisitive exploitation. While itself wary of the English merchants, the English parliament could not care less if they ran amuck with an alien land and reduced its peasantry and craftsmen to abject poverty. By one trick or another, by imposing extortionate land taxes, or by destroying indigenous handicrafts and industries, the Company and its officers working in India enriched themselves beyond imagination.

The tax revenue, which was previously collected by the Muslim and Hindu landowners (*zamindars*), was now mostly expropriated by the Company's officers in India and then remitted to England. In itself, this would not have increased the exploitation of Indian workers, except that the system now functioned in two new, and detrimental, ways. First the taxes, though not necessarily raised in some cases, were so ruthlessly collected that the tax revenue increased many times. As a result, many peasants, and even *zamindars,* were forced either to sell their land to the village money-lender or get into heavy debt. Thus the British acquisitive

domination over India germinated the prominence of Indian acquisitors, of usurers who charged confiscatory interest rates, followed dubious accounting practices, and proved, with little let-up
so far, to be the scourge of the rural sector of which three-fourths
of India today is composed.

Second, prior to the British conquest, the *zamindars*, spending their incomes within India, provided a demand for Indian
industries. With the transmission of this income now to England,
that source of demand disappeared, and so did India's vast industrial wealth. And if any industrial base remained, British commercial policy, designed to convert India into a source of cheap raw
materials for English manufacturers, took care of it. Prohibitive
tariffs barred Indian silk and cotton products from British markets, while no, or nominal, duties were imposed on English ex-
ports to India. In Michael Edwardes' words:

> In the first half of the nineteenth century . . . India was to lose the
> proud position of supremacy in the trade and industry of the world
> which she had been occupying for well-nigh two thousand years, and
> was gradually transformed into a plantation for the production of raw
> materials, and a dumping ground for the cheap manufactured goods
> from the West. [4, p. 225]

Such policies continued with little change even after 1858 when, in
the wake of widespread mutiny in India, the Indian administrative
affairs passed directly into the hands of the English parliament.
The end-product of all this was that the Indian economy became
increasingly agricultural and rural; urbanization declined, many
agricultural workers became landless, and the usurer emerged
with a parasitic role unknown in India before. Never has the
Indian peasant been under such thraldom to the village money-
lender as he is today, and for this he has to be grateful to the
British occupation.

Eventually, the British self-interest gave rise to that extreme inequity of income distribution which comes to prevail
during every acquisitive age. After the Indian mutiny of 1857,
the British felt the need for a class of natives allied to their cause.
The village *zamindars*, and also some Indian industrialists, were

granted concessions and carefully pampered. As as result, another group of wealthy landlords and capitalists arose in India; along with them arose the impoverished agricultural and industrial workers. When the subcontinent attained independence from the British yoke in 1947, and got partitioned into India and Pakistan, this system, wherein the affluence of the few mocked at the penury of the masses, remained.

Yet the British contact was not wholly damaging to Hindu civilization. India was divested of many of the heinous practices that had afflicted Hindu society for a very long time. *Sati,* or widow-burning, was then abolished; brahmans could no longer claim precedence over the arm of the law. Above all, the British system of education created an unprecedented sentiment of nationalism, of which Mahatma Gandhi, Muhammad Ali Jinnah, Subhash Chandra Bose and Jawaharlal Nehru were among the most prominent leaders. Eventually these stirrings of nationalism convinced the British of the injustice of their occupation and the fact that it was doomed, and they decided to grant the subcontinent its long-cherished independence. The peaceful manner in which they consented to let go of their vast Indian empire is an act of self-denial which is a credit to the English people and their democratic institutions. According to Sir Percival Griffiths:

> To that great act of abdication there is no historical parallel. . . . This final act has released India from all the inhibitions of subjection, purged Britain from the racial pride of domination, and established between the two countries a bond of friendship which may well prove stronger and more enduring than the political tie which it has replaced. [6, p. 488]

Even after the British departure, the Hindu civilization,[3] now confined to territories outside the area of Pakistan, continued to move through the acquisitive age. Its leaders could have then choked the acquisitive dominion, but they frittered away all the goodwill and esteem they had earned as a vanguard of the nationalist movement. In a country as illiterate as the then India, with numerous latent tendencies towards fragmentation, with an income distribution as inequitable as can be, they chose the system of British parliamentary democracy. The inevitable happened: soon, the forces of money took over; smuggling, profiteering, black-marketing, tax evasion and overbearing bureaucratic corruption came to permeate each and every pore of Indian life. The greed of acquisitors impeded whatever half-hearted efforts the Indian leaders made to lift the masses out of the morass of poverty.

From the year of Independence to the fateful year of 1977, the Congress party, the spearhead of nationalistic fervor, remained in power. Not that there was then no other political party, only that there were too many, and consequently too feeble to provide effective opposition. The first Prime Minister of modern India was the charismatic Pandit Nehru, the next one Lalbahadur Shastri. He was followed by Mrs. Indira Gandhi (no relationship with Mahatma Gandhi); and now Morarji Desai, belonging to the Janta party, holds the reins.

The acquisitive forces of political decentralization let loose with India's adoption of the parliamentary system came to a head in June 1975 when Mrs. Gandhi was convicted of illegal practices during the preceding election. The opposition parties called for her resignation; general strikes were threatened and, above all, the police and the military were allegedly incited towards rebellion. In response, Mrs. Gandhi proclaimed a state of emergency, assumed wide executive powers, and then unleashed a reign of terror in the public mind. To inculcate a new sense of discipline, she sent many smugglers and black-marketeers, along with political opponents and numerous innocent people, to prison. The Indian Constitution was also then amended to perpetuate her new status. The press was gagged, and the police given extraordinary powers. And all this was done in order to serve the people—the people whose fundamental rights were trampled.

But sooner or later every abuser of power has to pay the price. Mrs. Gandhi had to pay it sooner than expected. When power goes to a person's head, all perception of reality is lost. Just as Mrs. Gandhi felt the the public was solidly behind her draconian measures, she called a new election. But this time her party (the Congress party) had to contend with a united opposition, whose leaders had been jailed during the emergency. To the surprise of all political pundits, Mrs. Gandhi suffered a landslide defeat at the polls; and this is how Morarji Desai, the opposition (Janta party) candidate, was catapulted into power in March 1977: Mrs. Ghandi's fall is thus the latest warning to dictators everywhere that tyranny is its own nemesis.

How are we to evaluate the fateful event, the emergency of June 1975? I have chosen to dwell at length on this event, because it occurred at a time when India was, and is, passing through the degenerate phase of the acquisitive age. The change of government in 1977 was healthy, but it cannot undo ill-effects of the last two centuries of acquisitive exploitation. Only a revolution of ideas can.

India is now fast moving towards a social revolution, one that will put an end to its acquisitive, or the present acquisitive-cum-laborer, age. By my calculations this revolution should occur by the year 2000. The present acquisitive era began in India when the British defeated the Peshwa in 1803 and removed the last intellectual bastion out of their way. This means that the preceding intellectual era, starting as early as 1605 when Jahangir came to the throne, lasted about two hundred years. The acquisitive era should also last that long. In other words, it will terminate in a laborer revolution towards the end of this century, and then pave the way for another warrior era of centralized authority and social discipline.

It is in this light that the import of the 1975 emergency ought to be seen. The centralization ushered in by Mrs. Gandhi was a harbinger of the centralization that is yet to come; but the coming centralization, being in the early phase of the warrior era, will be benevolent. It will bring lasting relief and prosperity to the impoverished masses. What Mrs. Gandhi did reflects the desperate act of an acquisitor trying to maintain her exploitative hold on society. The centralization she introduced did improve the country's economic condition; it did bring smuggling and black-marketing under control. But all the healthy effects of her actions were more than offset by her brazen disregard for human rights, by her attempts to crush all dissent. Consequently, she had to go.

If there is one lesson of the Emergency, it is that India badly needs social discipline and centralized political authority, one that despite its wide executive powers rules with compassion, and feels for the impoverished masses. India today needs a benevolent warrior at the top—another Ashoka, or Samudra Gupta, or Akbar. Is this all possible in the present age? No! But the new warrior era is not far off.

The current Indian milieu has a parallel with final days of the acquisitive era around Buddhist times. Then, as now, money ruled the roost. Dhana Nanda was then a powerful, but corrupt, ruler commanding a powerful army. He could have unified the whole of India under the aegis of a just and efficient government. He did not! Sure enough, a Chanakya and a Chandragupta Maurya emerged from the grass roots to wrest the initiative and ultimately bring an end to the acquisitive age. Ever since Independence, the Indian leaders, especially the late Nehru and Mrs Gandhi, have had the same opportunity. At times, they have had the charisma to smother the torrents of corruption, to relieve the masses of their penury, to do the maximum good to the maximum number of people. They did not. They frittered their moments away, and now the disorderly trend is irreversible. It will move apace until it is met by the powerful shock of the laborer revolution, whereupon, as stated above, a new warrior age will be born.

SUMMARY

An interpretation of Hindu civilization in accordance with Sarkar's theory of social cycle was the objective of this narrative, and the objective has been fulfilled. When enough evidence was available, whether archaelogical, numismatic, scriptural, or inscriptional, the hypothesis of social cycle was shown to be clearly valid. And even when at times Indian history drew a blank, Sarkar's theory found support from secondary evidence. Going through the Hindu civilization, we found that the Vedic age, traceable as far back as 1500 B.C., belongs to the warrior era, the subsequent brahmanic age to the intellectual era, and the ensuing Buddhist period to the acquisitive era, which terminated in the social revolution engineered by Chanakya and Chandragupta Maurya. Then came another warrior era of the Mauryan period, followed by another intellectual age of the Sungas, Kanvas, and the Andhras, then by another acquisitive era of the pre-Gupta times, culminating in another laborer revolution brought about by Samudra Gupta.

Following this event, another social cycle began with the warrior era of the Gupta period, the intellectual era of the brahman chief ministers, the acquisitive era of feudalism, culminating in the laborer revolution of Alauddin Khilgi. Thus began the Muslim warrior era, followed first by the Mughal-Maratha intellectual era, and then by the acquisitive era under the British domination. That is where Hindu society, more properly Indian society, now stands. By the year 2000, it will be engulfed by another social revolution, paving the way for another warrior age.

NOTES

1. The year, and even century, of Buddha's birth is a matter of controversy among historians. See Majumdar [11] and Smith [23], for example.

2. The quote from Mazumdar says nothing about feudalism in the thirteenth century, but as subsequently argued, the acquisitive era then degenerated into the laborer age.

3. Actually it is a misnomer to regard modern Indian society as Hindu civilization, because even after the germination of Pakistan, which siphoned off a majority of the Muslim community of the subcontinent, a sizeable section preferred to remain in the modern Indian state. Therefore, modern Indian society is, and has long been, a Hindu-Muslim society, with the Muslim minority accounting for as many as ninety million people.

REFERENCES

[1] Apte, V. M., "Social and Economic Conditions," in *The History and Culture of the Indian People, Vol. I*, ed. R. C. Majumdar (Bombay: Bhartiya Vidya Bahvan, 1951), Ch. XXIII.

[2] Basham, A. L., *The Wonder That Was India* (London: Sidgwick & Jackson, 1954).

[3] Drekmeier, Charles, *Kingship and Community in Early India* (Standord: Stanford University Press, 1962).

[4] Edwardes, Michael, *A History of India* (New York: Farrar, Straus & Cudahy, 1961).

[5] Ghoshal, U. N., "Political Theory, Administrative Organisation, Law and Legal Institutions," in *The History and Culture of the Indian People, Vol. 4*, ed. R. C. Majumdar (Bombay, Bhartiya Vidya Bahvan, 1955) Ch. X.

[6] Griffiths, Percival, *The British Impact on India* (Archon Books, 1965).

[7] Hopkins, E. W., "The Social and Military Position of the Ruling Caste in Ancient India," *Journal of the American Oriental Society*, XIII (1889), pp. 57–322.

[8] ——, "The Period of the Sutras, Epics, and Law-Books," in *The Cambridge History of India*, Vol. I, ed. E. J. Rapson (London: Cambridge University Press, 1935) Ch. IX.

[9] ———, "Family Life and Social Customs as They Appear in the Sutras," in *The Cambridge History of India,* Vol. I, Ch. X.

[10] Kosambi, D. D., *The Culture and Civilization of Ancient India in Historical Outline* (London: Routledge & Kegan Paul, 1970).

[11] Majumdar, R. C., *Ancient India* (Delhi: Motilal Banarsidas, 1960).

[12] Mazumdar, B. P., *The Socio Economic History of Northern India: 1030–1194* A.D. (Calcutta: Firma K. L. Mukhopadhyay, 1960).

[13] Mookerji, R. K., "The Foundation of the Mauryan Empire," in *A Comprehensive History of India,* Vol. II, ed. K. A. N. Sastri (Bombay: Oriental Longmans, 1957) Ch. I.

[14] Munshi, K. M., Foreword to *History and Culture of the Indian People,* Vol. V, ed. R. C. Majumdar (Bombay: Bhartiya Vidya Bahvan, 1957).

[15] Naidis, Mark, *India: A Short Introductory History* (New York: The Macmillan Co., 1966).

[16] Pinkham, M. W., *Woman in Sacred Scripture of Hinduism* (New York: Columbia University Press, 1941).

[17] Rapson, E. J., "Indian Native States After the Period of the Mauryan Empire," in *The Cambridge History of India,* Vol. I, Ch. XXI.

[18] Rawlinson, H. G., *India: A Short Cultural History* (New York: Frederick A. Praeger, 1952).

[19] Rhys-Davids, C. A. F., "Economic Conditions According to Early Buddhist Literature," in *The Cambridge History of India,* Vol. I.

[20] Rhys-Davids, T. W., *Buddhist India* (New York: G. P. Putnam's Sons, 1903).

[21] Rizvi, S. A., "Islam in India," in *A Cultural History of India,* ed. A. L. Basham (London: Oxford University Press, 1962).

[22] Sharma, R. S., *Political Ideas and Institutions in Ancient India* (Delhi: Motilal Banarsidass, 2nd edition, 1968).

[23] Smith, V. A., *The Early History of India,* 4th edition, revised by S. M. Edwardes (London: Oxford University Press, 1962).

[24] Thomas, F. W., "Notes on the Edicts of Asoka," *Journal of the Royal Asiatic Society of Great Britain and Ireland,* 1916.

[25] Webber, Max, *The Religion of India* (Glencoe: The Free Press, 1958).

[26] Yasin, Mohammad, *A Social History of Islamic India* (Lucknow: The Upper India Publishing House, 1958).

7

The Downfall of
Totalitarian Communism

I have argued before that for the last four centuries Russian society has been moving through the warrior era, of which extreme political and administrative centralization is the chief characteristic. During this rather long period, the Russian polity has gone through radical changes, through several economic, political, and cultural upheavals, but its total commitment to the supremacy of the state over everything else remains. Even the plastic surgery to its face since the Bolshevik Revolution has made no dent in its absolutist tradition.

I will now argue that the new intellectual era in Russian society has been long overdue, and that the transition could come any time, perhaps in the next twenty-five to fifty years, perhaps in another century. But come it must. And the current Soviet repression of intellectuals is simply a harbinger of the new age. The contemporary Russian system may be called totalitarian communism—totalitarian, because it is autocratic, and exalts the ruler and the state over every other institution; communism, because whenever it suits its purpose, it draws upon, or reinterprets, the communist thought of Marx. In the new era, however, the present setup will give way to the rule by intellectuals, by those who concoct new dogmas and govern society indirectly in the name of the apparent ruler. There will be totalitarianism no more; nor will Marxism survive in its present form. Hence the title: The Downfall of Totalitarian Communism.

In order to chart the future course of Russian society, it is first necessary to understand how it has evolved ever since the revolution of 1917;[1] how, and why, in spite of its transmutation, it has maintained some links with the past which officially is so patently denounced; how the transmutation itself has generated conditions that will invariably give rise to an intellectual-inspired social evolution or revolution.

RUSSIA UNDER LENIN, STALIN, AND KHRUSHCHEV

After the Bolsheviks took over the reins of government, Russia, having already been battered by the First World War, slipped into a state of enhanced agony and turmoil. Lenin had expected that the revolutionary spark in Russia would quickly ignite fires in neighboring capitalist countries—such as Germany—which would then help the Russian movement to stand on its own feet, even though the Russian semi-feudal structure was not yet ripe for a successful revolution. According to Marx, capitalism must precede socialism and communism, so that a successful revolution was by implication ruled out in an underindustrialized country like Russia. Therefore, the fact that the disciples of Marx first came to power in an underdeveloped country made a big difference to the future development of Marxist ideology as well as to Russian society.

The Bolsheviks had expected help from industrial countries; they got unmasked hostility instead. Far from triggering revolutions elsewhere in Europe, communists in Russia were confronted with enemies at home and abroad, with civil war as well as economic catastrophe. All this could not but spawn anarchy and help the autocratic forces to regain their stranglehold over society.

In the first blush of revolution, the Bolsheviks displayed great zeal in giving effect to the Marxian vision of an egalitarian society, including worker control over industry, decentralization in government, and eliminating inequalities in income distribution. Peasants were allowed to seize lands from the aristocracy, workers to take over and run factories; salaries of managers, government officers and technicians were curtailed to bring them more in line with factory wage rates. Thus, for a few months it appeared that Marx's humanism would be taken out of his writings and translated into reality. But all these visions were cut short when the anticipated help from the West failed to materialize, when the communist leaders had to fight for their own survival, when the infant revolution continued to face rough weather.

To that life-and-death struggle, the Bolsheviks responded by replacing worker control over industry with centralized decision-making by the government. Former tsarist managers and bureaucrats were recalled into government and industry, with their high salaries and other privileges partially restored. Economically, the results were even more catastrophic than before. While the workers were disenchanted without the incentive to work, the inexperienced government provided faulty guidance. The inevitable happened: by 1921 the entire economy was in a shambles, with the peasantry and the workers standing on the verge of revolt.

In the face of mounting opposition, Lenin relented and introduced the New Economic Policy (NEP), in which capitalism was partially restored. The government retained control over heavy industry, banking and finance, transportation, and communication; but light industry, agriculture and trade were left to private enterprise, where the forces of demand and supply could determine the allocation of resources. Not that Lenin had given up his ideal of a centralized economic and political system, only that he had relented to gain time, regroup his demoralized forces, and design a coordinated attack on those he considered inimical to his cause.

The NEP met with instant success. The limited revival of the private sector, along with government control in areas involving heavy investment which private enterprise could not afford, enabled the entire economy to move apace. Within five years, the country recovered from the economic dislocations caused by wars and the government's meddling with private life. The communists also realized, more than ever before, that their revolutionary fervor was not contagious to other countries; that the revolution could be safeguarded and extended only by first erecting an imposing industrial structure within Russia; that for the sake of speedy industrialization, the state had to take over the task of saving and investing, and thus completely demolish the private economy; and that the state itself would have to become absolute and autocratic in order to transform the Russian economic weakling into an industrial giant.

Thus when the crunch came the communists threw Marxian humanism down the drain and decided to build apace an industrial state regardless of how it afflicted other walks of life. Perhaps the outcome would have been quite different had Lenin not prematurely died and the communist party not taken over by Stalin who proved to be the apogee of absolutism. Once Stalin maneuvered his way to the top by erasing all opposition within the party, any serious debate on economic planning ceased altogether. Stalinist communism is quite divorced from the Marxian version and devoid of any concern for the people. It may be simply defined as a strategy to achieve rapid industrialization through draconian means. It has very little to do with Marxism proper; yet Stalin did not officially abandon the Marxian doctrines. He drew upon them to sanctify his economic, religious, and social policies, or simply reinterpreted them to stifle the dissenting view, if any.

Thus when it came to capital accumulation, regarded by every communist as indispensable for industrialization and growth, Stalin cited Marx, who too had stressed the role of capital goods in this regard. This is how Stalin justified his extreme emphasis on investment in the capital-goods sector, while neglecting the consumer-goods sector as much as possible. But as regards the Marxian egalitarian view of minimizing wage differentials, he dismissed it by simply begging the question—by suggesting that in the absence of private ownership, income inequalities were impossible. In practice several groups, especially some military officers, were accorded highly favorable treatment. Similarly, Marxian prophecy of "dictatorship of the proletariat" was read as the dictatorship of the communist party, and, eventually, as the dictatorship of the party chieftain himself.

The Stalinist strategy for rapid industrialization involved two major steps: first, peasant labor, which constituted the majority of the labor force, was transformed into industrial and urban labor; second, industrial labor was heavily employed in the production of capital goods. The state also took over the function of price-fixing and in the process extorted the maximum amount of investment from peasants as well as industrial workers. While low prices were set for farm products, so that the agricultural surplus accrued to the state, high prices were set for industrial consumer goods, of which the production was also monopolized by the state. Thus both peasants and industrial workers were squeezed to the utmost to generate the maximum investible surplus, which year after year was plowed back into heavy industry. The result was a phenomenal rate of industrialization and growth, coupled with ubiquitous productive inefficiency and social tension.

It should not be forgotten that this success story conceals in its wake the incalculable cost paid by millions of human lives. There is a decided difference between Marxian humanitarian communism and Stalin's ruthless version rooted in the aggrandizement of the state which, I venture to say, has nothing to do with proletarian welfare. Whatever Stalin did was rooted in egomania, in his desire to tower over everything else in society. His own glory lay in glorifying the state, in exalting nationalism, even though this idea was also at variance with the internationalism of Marx. The Marxian view regarding the international brotherhood of workers was, of course, used to advantage when Stalin needed sanction for Soviet imperialism over Eastern Europe.

Even today (1977) the Soviet leaders preach Marxism whenever their dominion is threatened by their subjects in the satellite states. The evolution of Russian society under Stalin is thus a lengthy tale of atrocities, hypocrisy and brazen propaganda unleashed to mask its ugly totalitarian face behind the cosmetics of socialism. Since Stalin's death in 1953, life in Russia has eased somewhat, but its leadership is still committed to the dictatorship of the sovereign or a body of sovereigns.

Even the Soviet constitution adopted in 1938 is a cosmetic document, a sham designed to dupe the Russian people and the gullible in other parts of the world. In theory it seems little different from the constitutions of democratic nations in Europe, but in practice it is openly flouted. Thus it duly provides for universal suffrage to all adults, a bicameral legislature called the Supreme Soviet, an executive and administrative body elected by the Supreme Soviet and called the Council of Ministers, as well as a bill of rights guaranteeing the citizens some human rights such as the freedom of speech, of assembly, of religion, and of the press. The Supreme Soviet, consisting of a thousand elected members of the two chambers, is given broad legislative powers; when out of session, it is represented by the Presidium, a body of thirty-seven members enjoying the same powers as the Supreme Soviet.

The Soviet constitution, however, was, and still is, a façade designed to mask the dictatorship of the leader (or leaders) of the one and only Communist Party. How perfidious this system is is apparent not from what the Constitution emphasizes but from what it fails to emphasize. In its 146 Articles the Party is mentioned only once, much like a minor addendum to the main text. Yet the sway of the Party on Soviet life belies this impression. The constitution would have us believe that the Party is a nonentity in the Soviet system, yet ever since the 1917 Revolution the Party's decrees and regulations have been the gospel, carrying the solid force of law.[2] The day-to-day administration is in the hands of a vast bureaucracy headed by the Council of Ministers, but all its operations are overseen by thousands of Party members who debate, decide and then execute various policies dealing with all aspects of life.

Heading the Party hierarchy is its Political Bureau (Politburo), which now consists of sixteen members; in theory it is responsible to its Central Committee, but the reverse has really been the case. Membership of the 426-man Central Committee is formally bestowed by the Party Congress, which in turn is composed of members selected from lower echelons on the basis of a series of indirect elections. Thus ultimately power rests with the Politburo chieftain, who is also called the Party Secretary or the General Secretary. The command of the General Secretary, the boss of all bosses, filters into the bureaucracy as well as the rest of society through the arteries of a body called the Secretariat, which has far fewer members than the 426-man Central Committee.

In such a monolithic setup, society can be free from oppression only if its sovereign is a benevolent ruler; but the Soviet leadership until today has been anything but benevolent. With perhaps the singular exception of Lenin, all the party Secretaries have been self-centered, caring nothing for the empyrean humanism of Marx, although every repressive act has been committed by them in his name.

By Stalin's death, the Soviet-style communism had spread its tentacles over all facets of Russian life. The economy, by then completely collectivized and organized under state capitalism, had grown at an astonishing rate, but moral and social fiber lay prostrate and bleeding. It was against a background of police brutality that Khrushchev succeeded Stalin, and within a few years returned to the now familiar one-man rule. Already the economy had shown signs of strain. Much of the unemployed labor and other natural resources by then had been fully utilized, and further development could come only from economic reforms, reduced bureaucratic meddling, and new technology. Under the brutal prodding of the state, the economy had grown enormously, but it was far from efficient.

With individual initiative choked by centralized decision-making, it is not surprising that after attaining near full employment in the 1950s the economic engine had come to a screeching halt. It is in this perspective that Khrushchev, at first imperceptibly and then systematically, began to dismantle the authoritarian machine that Stalin had designed. Khrushchev's total denunciation of Stalinism, his efforts to loosen the reins on the economy, failures of Soviet agriculture, and his abortive skirmish with the United States over the Cuban affair were among the reasons that brought about his downfall in 1964.

The Soviet leadership since then has been a collective leadership of sorts; it has been spearheaded by the Party Secretary, Brezhnev, and the Head of the Government, Premier Kosygin. While Lenin and Stalin were children of the Revolution, Khrushchev was a child of civil war and of the early phase of Stalinist communism. The new leaders, however, have been raised in an atmosphere more settled than the early atmosphere of intrigue and bloodshed that attended the Revolution. Consequently, the influence of ideology has declined while that of government bureaucrats has gone nowhere but up. All this has served to erode the charismatic appeal of the Party Secretary. No longer is his office combined with the office of the Premier in one and the same person.

CONTEMPORARY SOVIET SOCIETY

As a result of many economic, political, and social changes during more than half a century of communist rule, contemporary Soviet polity differs radically from old tzarist Russia or from Russia at the time of the Revolution. The only surviving link is provided by the absolutist heritage, and even there some fissures are beginning to appear. The Communist Party of the Soviet Union (CPSU) was virtually a homogeneous unit at the dawn of 1917. Inspired by a revolutionary fervor, by the egalitarian ideology of Marx, it was solidly united behind Lenin, a gifted political leader with a rare magnetism over his followers. He was at once the chief ideologist, the founder of the Bolshevik movement, and above all a keen administrator of the economy and the state.

Stalin was less charismatic but he continued to embody various Party and state functions in his person, as one opponent after another, thanks to the secret police and the purges, disappeared. Khrushchev, the least charismatic of the first three main rulers of the Soviet Union, condemned Stalinism, but then attempted to impose his own authoritarian rule over the Party and the state. But, as Brezinski [1] observes, no longer was the leader able to provide a "fusion of leadership functions." Since Khrushchev the division of such functions has continued with the leadership. No longer is the Party chief the top ideologist and the top administrator or technician. The typical leader now is simply the bureaucrat who has been a witness to Stalin's scourge but not its victim. With him the formal commitment to Marxist ideology is the least, and power lust the highest.

The change in aspirations of the top leadership is simply a mirror image of the change in lower Party echelons as well as in the rank-and-file members. The Party is no longer a homogeneous entity of ideologists and propagandists, but a medley of conflicting interests that inevitably arise in an industrially advanced society. Whereas in the aftermath of the Revolution, the rigid class structure of tsarist Russia was destroyed, massive industrialization ever since has produced a tremendous growth of administrative and technical personnel, which, together with the Party leadership, has for some time become the new leading class. Scientists, engineers, artists, professors, and other intellectuals have joined the ranks of the new elite in increasing numbers. Russian society today, therefore, is remarkably different from what it was just three decades ago. Its aristocracy is steeped as much in materialism as anywhere else in the world.

Russia today presents a striking contrast of a highly educated society enduring a dictatorial regime. The commitment of the Soviet leadership to public education has been admirable and total, and as a result almost everyone is literate today. But the growth of education, correlated as it is with industrialization, has also given rise to Party heterogeneity and new tensions in society. Without well-educated social and physical scientists, the industrial machine will grind to a halt. However, the intelligentsia are not so amenable to Party indoctrination, and this makes them suspect in the eyes of the Party, which can ill afford to do without them yet cannot let them move to the top. The relatively dull Party stalwart increasingly feels inferior to the intellectuals, yet must accept their membership to fathom the functioning of an increasingly complex socioeconomic system.

This dilemma has been partly solved by a device called *nomenklatura*, which is the nomenclature or classified list of those considered suitable for sensitive positions. It is through this system that the top leadership, up to the Party Secretary, maintains its privileged status in society. *Nomenklatura* exists at practically every stratum of Soviet life—from the topmost posts to lower-level appointments. By restricting their hiring to those on the secret roster, the Party bosses make sure that potential trouble makers are shut out from the inner circle. They thus have a vested interest in keeping those with initiative, drive and intelligence out of the seat of power. For these reasons, the current Soviet leadership has been often called a self-perpetuating oligarchy, interested in promoting the dullards in society: "A new generation of clerks" is how Brezinski puts it [1, p.8].

The composition of the Party has thus radically changed with the advance of education and industrialization. The intellectuals conforming to the Party doctrines, which exalt nationalism, the absolute supremacy of the Party and state, and ideological formalism, have been allowed to join the Party ranks in increasing numbers. This growing trend towards intellectualization of the Party, combined with increased political stability and economic prosperity, has considerably diminished the role of ideology in the formulation of policy. It is this erosion of ideological formalism that may explain in part the growing materialism now creeping into society at all levels, especially at the top. In the process even the formal adherence to Marxian ideals has been evaporating into thin air.

Nothing illustrates the divorce of the Soviet regime from Marxian egalitarianism better than this materialistic bent of the new elite which, according to Hedrick Smith, constitutes "a sizable chunk of Soviet society—well over a million and, counting relatives, probably several million" [2, p.35]. As mentioned earlier, apart from the Party chiefs and bureaucrats, the new elite includes the conformist members of the intelligentsia, including senior social and physical scientists, artists, writers, and so on. It also includes army and naval officers. (In spite of the Party's unquestioned dominion, the military has a great say in the Soviet polity.)

Not surprisingly, only the elite have access to privileges and luxuries—automobiles, television, lush apartments and villas, education in prestigious schools, foreign travel—that are denied to the general public. In fact the Soviet system at the top of the social pyramid is as inequitable as any other in the world: all this shamelessly goes on in the name of Marxism. (Brezhnev prides. himself on his motley collection of foreign luxury cars—Rolls-Royce, Lincoln, Mercedes, Cadillac.)

I have dwelt at length on the corruption and materialism of the Soviet regime to argue that Russian society is now languishing through the degenerate phase of the warrior age. It now displays the marks of a society in transition from one era to another. Even though the intellectuals are steadily gaining in importance, it may still be called a warrior society—or more properly a warrior-dominated society in flux. Some might argue that Russia is now in the intellectual era, because the Soviet leaders have displayed some intellectual qualities since the Revolution. Have they not subdued the warriors—the military, the secret police (KGB), etc. —through extensive indoctrination into the Party ideology? Yes, they have.

Ever since the Revolution, the military has had to submit to the Party ideologist, especially in Stalin's days when army officers too feared the secret police. Even today the military has to bear with constant meddling from the Party. Yet contemporary Russian society cannot be called an intellectual society, for its absolutist linkage with the tsarist regime remains. The Soviet approach seems little different from that of Peter the Great, who imposed modernization and Western culture on Russia at great human cost and repression. It is only in the last decade of modern Russian history that the government has begun to resemble a government by consensus. Otherwise, it has been ruled by one autocrat after another, be it the Tzar or the Party Secretary. In this light, the change that has occurred since Khrushchev's fall is certainly remarkable, yet it falls short of a move into the intellectual age. Extreme centralization in politics as well as administration continues with few signs of abatement.

Even the military, subdued by Lenin and Stalin, has shown signs of resurgence. Since Khrushchev's fall its influence and command over national resources have been on a steady rise. The secret police too has waxed again. Actually, the fact that it is hard to pin a label on contemporary Russian society in terms of Sarkar's concepts is precisely why Russia may now be said to be passing through the degenerate phase of the warrior age. While the intellectuals are on the rise, they are not yet at the helm. At the same time, the Russian leaders display a mixture of warrior and intellectual mentality. On the one hand they are committed to their dictatorial rule, on the other they have trapped their people in the web of rigid rules and dogmas. Their corruption, worldliness and brazen disregard for human rights, coupled with the continued sway of the military, are clear symptoms of a warrior society gasping for a fresh breath of life.

FUTURE RUSSIAN SOCIETY: THE NEW INTELLECTUAL ERA

Despite the hazards of forecasting the future course of Russia, and despite a dismal past record in this connection, the Soviet future continues to fascinate the scholars of communism. They have not been deterred by the fact that almost all such predictions have failed; nor is it going to deter me. Some of this predicting, however, has derived from revolutionary euphoria or wishful thinking. In the aftermath of the Bolshevik Revolution, the Marxists foresaw the spread of their fervor all over the capitalist world. They have been sobered by subsequent events, but the diehard and orthodox communists still believe that communism is the wave of the future; that world revolution is inevitable.

If the predictive record of the Marxists has been poor, that of the anti-Marxists is even poorer. That the Soviet experiment is doomed to failure has been prophesied again and again by Western observers. Among the latest of such prophets of communism's doom is Michel Garder, who had predicted the collapse of the Soviet colossus by 1970. Most scholars today believe that the apocalyptic visions of an imminent, or even the near future, demise of Soviet communism rely more on hopes than on careful analysis; that although the system will probably undergo some change in line with current trends, its basic features, such as the one-party system, state capitalism, ideological formalism, etc., will, in some form or the other, remain.[3] In part, and only in part, I tend to agree with this view, although admittedly such a broad generalization about the Soviet future leaves little room for disagreement. But the Soviet polity, I believe, will not only reflect the picture now in the making but also some radically new features that are predictable from the application of the theory of social cycle.

Currently the Russian people are under the dominance of what we may call pseudo-warriors, i.e., those exhibiting partly warrior and partly intellectual mentality. As described earlier, their dominion rests on ideological deception, on extensive political indoctrination of the citizenry by what has been often called the *apparatchiki*—career politicians or those trained in the Soviet version of Marxism. At the same time, the Soviet leaders are champions of social discipline and of the absolute supremacy of the state. Thus they are a mixed breed. The fact that Russia today is being ruled by pseudo-warriors is not surprising, because it is now, and has been for several generations, lingering through the terminal phase of its warrior age. Its leadership, in Toynbee's terms, is a dominant minority, one interested only in self-perpetuity and personal gain at the expense of other classes. The change in Russia, in terms of the law of social cycle, has then been long overdue, and as suggested earlier, the new intellectual era could emerge at any time in the near future. It still might take many more generations, but most likely the Russian body social will soon cast off the thraldom of pseudo-warriors and advance into a society ruled by intellectuals. That in any case is the decree of the theory of social cycle.

The group next in line of succession to power, the intellectual class, has been subjected to intermittent persecution for more than three hundred years—more so in the Soviet than in the tsarist regime. This is then a fitting prognostic of a new society that is bound to emerge in the fullness of time, because usually the section that struggles against the dominant clique in one era inherits power in the next. The law of social cycle is rooted in human evolution, and if evolution is inevitable, so is the social change in accordance with this law.

Let us then briefly examine the history of social repression in the annals of modern Russia. In the times of the tsar, the group that suffered most comprised the servile laborer toiling on estates owned by the bureaucracy and the militaristic nobility. In other words, the serfs were repressed the most, and this was nothing unusual because the physical workers bear the brunt of persecution in almost all phases of the social cycle. Only slightly less persecuted were the intellectuals—the churchmen or writers, or both. During the seventeenth century, there was a general belief among prelates that the Russian Church had done everything but lead the people, that the country's misfortunes mostly stemmed from ecclesiastical apathy and inertia, and that religious reforms were badly needed. This sentiment found its champion in Nikon, the Patriarch from 1653 to 1656, who introduced many changes in the religious ritual.

However, the reforms did not go well with the conservative churchmen, and before long an anti-Nikonian movement came into being. The affairs of religion, ironically, seldom preclude the use of force: the tsar took harsh measures against the protesters, who came to be known as Old Ritualists. Their leader, Avvakum, was burned alive, along with many others. Incredible as it may seem, thousands of protesters, out of despair, immolated themselves on flaming pyres. And brutalities against the Old Ritualists continued during the eighteenth century. The government was particularly fond of burning the leaders at the stake, although the last quarter of the eighteenth century witnessed a measure of religious tolerance.

Unfortunately, the reprieve to the dissenters was short, as in the middle of the nineteenth century the government resumed its repressive policy, which persisted in one form or another until 1905 when some constitutional reforms guaranteed the freedom of worship and faith.

Stronger tremors, however, were yet to come. From the seventeenth century to the nineteenth, the dissenters of all persuasions had been repressed, but at least religion was still alive; its need, despite murmurs of atheism, was not yet questioned. As a matter of fact, the Church, in some respects, was still robust, ready to assume moral leadership in society. Its prestige had been restored in the nineteenth century by a number of illustrious leaders who commanded great esteem from the public by living up to pure and lofty ideals. The world-renowned saint and author, Leo Tolstoy, was only one among them.

After the revolution of 1917 the Church encountered something that it had never faced before—disintegration. Marx, the mentor of all communists, regarded religion as the "opium of the people," something that exploits humanity and should be done away with. Following the revolution all monasteries and theological academies were ordered closed and the Church property nationalized. Many bishops were arrested, and in 1918–19 about twenty-eight lost their lives for what they believed; another fifty were murdered between 1923 and 1926. In spite of such persecution and the state's unrelenting antireligious propaganda, religion has survived in communist Russia. A sizeable minority still believes in God and patronizes what few churches that remain. At present the government is a little more tolerant of religious sentiment; there is freedom of worship but nothing more. While atheistic ideas are part of the school curricula, the religious faithful are not permitted to preach and proselytize.

Let us now turn to the issue of governmental persecution of the intellectuals—scientists, literary writers, university professors and the like. For over two-and-a-half centuries, Russian literature has been subject to censorship. That is, both under tzardom and communism, those errant writers who failed to toe the official line were, and are still, shown the light by censorship boards either through endless literary criticism or through the threat of physical punishment, or both. A system of censorship unfolded in tsarist Russia as early as the eighteenth century, by which time a Russian intelligentsia had matured enough to become noticeable.

At first the responsibility for correcting the wayward writer rested with the Church, but following the French revolution in 1789, the government itself stepped in. By 1863 this task was taken over by the top state organ—the ministry of the interior. Censorship in the eighteenth century mainly afflicted those intellectuals and writers who were infected with "liberal" Western thought that seemed to undermine the imperial government. Some writers, such as Radischev and Novikov, who would not care for "enlightenment," were awarded long prison sentences. At times, however, punishment involved only reprimands, fines, excommunication, and the outright banning of books and journals.

Censorship has continued under Soviet rule, except that in tsarist Russia it was overt, vested in a ministry of the government, whereas in communist Russia it is covert, hidden under euphemisms. The Soviet constitution provides for a free press, and officially there is no censor. Its place has been taken by a governing body called Glavlit which is the chief administrator for publications and literary works. At the same time the leaders of the Soviet Union, from top to bottom, are personally involved with censoring any material deemed objectionable to "proletarian welfare."

Censorship in communist Russia has been much more stifling and pervasive than it ever was during tsarist times. Not only is there now a list of topics that cannot be discussed, the Soviet writer must write what he is told; he must conform to the official style of the so-called Socialist Realism. Whether he believes it or not, he must demonstrate the inherent superiority of all socialist institutions over their counterparts in the West; and this he must accomplish in a way that sounds logical and appealing to the rational mind.

Prior to Stalin's Great Purge of the 1930s, when thousands of Party workers were killed, the intelligentsia in the Soviet polity had a somewhat checkered career. During the civil war, they met the same fate as the former elite, and were treated with contempt. Despite their services to the economy and the war effort, they were scorned as bourgeois specialists, and forced to live on subsistence. The situation changed for the better during the period of NEP, and those loyal to the Revolution could expect advancement and improved living conditions. However, after Lenin's death, the radical Marxists took over again, and that spelled disaster for the intellectuals. The bourgeois specialists were accused of being reactionaries, of showing partiality for capitalism, of impeding industrialization. Some were simply purged, while others were removed from sensitive positions.

But then came the Great Purge which at one stroke swept the radical Marxists aside. Surprisingly enough, the old bourgeois specialists now returned but only as mute sheep, ready to obey Stalin's whims and commands. Gone were the days of even the phantom autonomy they had enjoyed in their work only a decade before. The Party now demanded their full loyalty, a total commitment to the cause of socialism: in that atmosphere of terror, any dissenting voice was out of the question.

After Stalin's death, some dissenting voices made a whispering return. They were particularly encouraged by Khrushchev's scathing denunciation of Stalinism, and the writers now obtained a degree of literary freedom unthinkable just before. Following Khrushchev's fall, however, the Soviet leadership restored Stalin's image to a degree, and met the writers' demands for increased autonomy with repression—not like the old-style terror but terrifying enough. Since then the nonconformism of the so-called dissidents has become a political issue both in Russia as well as in the West, which has often reacted with shock and dismay at the Soviet contempt for the fundamental rights of its citizens. Actually the most amazing phenomenon of post-Stalin Russia is not that the intellectual dissent has been silenced, but the fact that such dissent has been grudgingly permitted by the authorities.

This is yet another sign that Russia is now slowly veering away from the customary communist penchant for bloodshed, and evolving towards a somewhat pluralistic society with some tolerance for opposition as long as it remains within bounds and does not undermine the establishment.

Despite the heavy hand with which the authorities have struck down the nonconformist writers, the intellectual dissent has displayed the fortitude and resilience of the Soviet religion. Many young writers, who prefer to publish of their own free will, have been tried since 1966 and convicted of anti-Soviet activity. They have been deprived of their jobs, occasionally sent to jail and quite often banished to lunatic asylums. But the underground press, known as Samizdat, continues to breathe. The 1974 exile of Solzhenitsyn, the maltreatment of Andrei Sakharov, and the recent arrests of Yuri Orlov and Alexander Ginzburg are only the latest episodes in the continued saga of Soviet dissidents against the official tyranny.

The crux of the discussion thus far is that churchmen and the intelligentsia have been the prey of persecution for much of the new warrior era that has prevailed in Russia for the last four centuries. This phenomenon has a certain parallel with the intermittent Roman oppression of Christianity during the first three centuries following the birth of Christ. Who could have then imagined that the Christian leaders would one day hold the vast Roman state in their sway? Yet intellectuals in the West inherited the power of the warriors just as inevitably as the Roman Empire declined. The social cycle in Russia has been moving at a tortoise pace at least in comparison to that in India and in the Western world, and it is for this reason that despite occasionally savage repression of the intellectuals the warrior era still lingers in Russian society.

But now its days are numbered, and nothing manifests this more than the fact that the self-conceit and materialism of the Soviet leadership are pitted against the dedication, sacrifices and self-denial of such intellectual giants as the Nobel Prize winners, Solzhenitsyn and Sakharov. Sooner or later the change has to come, but it will not be easy. The entrenched Soviet establishment will not surrender to the progressive forces, unless and until it is left with no choice. For this reason the struggling dissidents of Russia need, and deserve, all moral as well as material support from the enemies of repression.

The Western world, especially the U.S., is now doing an admirable job of stirring up the question of human rights in the Soviet Union, and this should be zealously pursued in the future as well. Those who want to see the Soviet leadership humanized must help those spirited enough to confront the Soviet authoritarian machine. It is not easy, or possible, to visualize the exact process that will spur the Russian society into an intellectual era, but since such movement is inevitable, the strengthening of dissidents will hasten the demise of the present regime.

Will the new era arrive peacefully or under the pall of violence? Or in Sarkar's terms, will there be an intellectual evolution or revolution? Posing this question is easier than answering it. Current informed opinion is not helpful either, as it is itself divided between those suggesting that any future transformation will be but gradual and others arguing that because of the self-conceit of the Soviet leadership no change can occur in Russia without convulsions. It is my belief that the change in Russia will be swift and violent, but not necessarily revolutionary, as some features of the future Russian polity have already surfaced. And this is not unusual, because the outer shell of government and administration of the warrior era remains more or less unchanged in the intellectual era. But while the political structure remains intact, the balance of power swings visibly in the direction of the intellectuals who govern in the name of the apparent ruler.

Let us now apply this principle to Soviet evolution. Ever since the Revolution, the country has been ruled by the Party Secretary, who in the person of Lenin or Stalin was also the top ideologist and the top administrator. As mentioned earlier, such leadership functions have been increasingly differentiated ever since Stalin's death. Today the Party Secretary is neither the top ideologist nor the head of administration. But he is still the most powerful figure in the state—the first among equals. He is the chairman of the Politburo and of the Party Secretariat, two bodies that are the command and nerve centers of the Party, and ultimately of Russian society. In the forthcoming intellectual era, however, this will no longer be the case.

The Party Secretary, the real as well as apparent ruler thus far, will have to defer to the Head of the Government—the Soviet Prime Minister. Not that there will be any basic alteration in the present Constitution or the system of government; only that the Party which has been supreme so far will lose much of its influence. The Constitution which has been good only in theory until now will assume a more positive role, and the Supreme Soviet will assert itself in governance.

The Soviet polity will be dominated by the intelligentsia, and the Prime Minister will be adept in oratory as well as in the art of balancing diverse interests of various groups which have already come into being. In terms of politics, the future Soviet society will be reminiscent of the British parliamentary system that developed immediately after the Glorious Revolution. There will be some surface differences of course. For instance, the Soviet party system will perhaps continue to remain monolithic as opposed to the two-party system of England. But in most respects the Soviet polity will display the features of the British intellectual era of the eighteenth century. Thus the Party Secretary, much like the British king, will enjoy high privileges and public esteem but only nominal political influence. Similarly, the Soviet Prime Minister, like his early British counterpart, will be an efficient "manager," displaying intellectual qualities. He might even come directly from the ranks of the intelligentsia.

The early British parliamentary setup, though far from democratic, was less centralized than the warrior regimes of the Tudors, Stuarts, and Oliver Cromwell. By the same token, the Soviet intellectual era will not be democratic, at least by present-day Western standards, but it will certainly be more decentralized than the present regime. The Head of the Government or of the Council of Ministers will be somewhat more responsible to the Supreme Soviet and ultimately to the general public. In addition to the political process, the administration will also become more diffused in all spheres; centralized economic decision-making will give way to greater autonomy at the entrepreneurial level. No longer will the Party *apparat* be allowed to meddle so extensively with the people; no longer will the intellectual community be subject to so vast an instrument of censorship, harassment and persecution. But the freedom of thought, press and speech will not approach modern Western standards.

Those losing the most from the change will be the present Party cadre of pseudo-warriors and the genuine warrior groups such as the secret police and the military. No longer will there be so great an allocation of scarce resources for heavy industry as well as the military establishment. The Soviet consumer will see a rise in his general standard of living; but the intelligentsia will be the biggest beneficiary, and, in comparison, the lot of the industrial worker and the peasant will improve only slightly.

Another distinguishing feature of Russian society will be an extensive recasting of the Marxist-Leninist ideology. The dominion of the Prime Minister will be justified by novel and, as always, self-serving interpretations which will demolish the spirit and substance of Marxism if not its outer forms. It is precisely this kind of work in which intellectuals are particularly proficient. No one should be surprised if in the future Soviet scholars find some kind of backdoor support for private property as well as the profit motive. In short, the new state in Russia will not be totalitarian; nor will it adhere to its present interpretation of Marxian Communism. Verily, there will be a downfall of totalitarian communism, which will be replaced by a decentralized structure, although the degree of decentralization will not approach that prevailing in the West today. This will also come one day, as it must, but not in the near future.

It is possible that my scenario of the Soviet future outlined above may never materialize in its entirety. This will not be the first failure either, for many predictions made before in this regard have come to naught. My prophecies may not then come true in all details, yet one thing is certain: Soviet society is now evolving toward a new era which will be highlighted by the dominance of the intellectuals. Therefore the present regime of pseudo-warriors is doomed to extinction in the near future.

Why is Russian society now ripe for a new intellectual era any more than it was at the outset of the twentieth century? After all, the present regime is no more oppressive of its people than the tsarist state. Is it not then possible that, given Russia's long absolutist tradition, totalitarian communism may continue to endure as far as one can peer into the future? My answer is no. It is true that Russia at the dawn of the twentieth century displayed all the symptoms of internal decay, yet a new society was beyond its reach, simply because a broad intellectual base had not been prepared. Russian intellectuals, to be sure, had been struggling for a long time, yet they were in a stark minority amidst a populace that was overwhelmingly illiterate.

Neither the Church nor the intelligentsia had the ability to lead the groping society. The result was that even though an emaciated tsarist structure crumbled under the first wave of Bolshevik assault, the absolutist inheritance survived and later recoiled on the citizens with a vengeance.

The complexion of Russian society is drastically different today. Since nearly all are literate, the foundation on which the government of the intellectuals may stand is there. When the latent rift between the subjects and the state erupts into an open protest on a large scale—and for this we may not have to wait long—the resulting change will lead Russia into the intellectual age. This is simply inevitable.

NOTES

1. I have spoken of this in Chapter 5, but will now discuss it in greater detail.

2. In 1977 a new, amended Constitution was introduced, but the emendations only confirm one's faith in the duplicity of the Soviet regime. The new Constitution merely puts the old wine in a new bottle, adding some sweeteners in the process. It now addresses itself directly to the question of the Party's ultimate command in society; also, the Russians now have more phantom rights than before, but they are openly asked to submit to the state. In addition, Brezhnev is now the Party Secretary as well as President of the country.

3. See the excellent discussion on the Soviet future in various articles compiled in [1].

REFERENCES

[1]   Brezinski, Zbigniew, *Dilemmas of Change in Soviet Politics* (New York: Columbia University Press, 1969).

[2]   Smith, Hedrick, *The Russians* (New York: Ballantine Books, 1976).

8

The Downfall of Capitalism

In the foregoing pages I have argued that ever since the second half of the nineteenth century, Western society has been moving through the acquisitive age in which men of affluence hold the reins. The dominion of the ruling class then stems from its control over wealth as well as the means of production, while all other classes—the warriors, the intellectuals, the laborers—readily submit to the affluent elite. It is in this era that the system of government is extremely decentralized and, as a consequence, crime flourishes, families break down, prostitution soars, and extreme individualism comes to permeate the social order. Such a socio-economic system prevailed in the West in the second half of the Middle Ages and is generally called feudalism; today it prevails again and is called capitalism.

It should be clear by now that, despite overwhelming surface disparities, feudalism and capitalism have many features in common; that the demise of capitalism is as inevitable as the demise of feudalism; that it will be first brought down by a social revolution at a not-too-distant future, and then replaced by a new centralized, but benevolent, rule of people with warrior mentality. Such a vision of capitalism flows logically from an application of the law of social cycle to the future of Western society.

In prophesying the doom of capitalism, I, of course, am not alone. A large body of literature, based on the writings of Marx and Lenin, has sought to demonstrate that capitalism is its own foe; that it is an economic order riddled with self-demolishing contradictions. Such a prognosis has been generally unpopular with Western intellectuals, not only because it has been disproved by history but also because Marx's own analysis has been found wanting in logical perfection. Yet the doomsaying for capitalism has not been a favorite pastime of Marxists alone. Many non-Marxists, such as Joseph Schumpeter, Robert Heilbroner, and Toynbee among others, have also foreseen the end of capitalism, though not in a violent revolution.

That capitalism is eventually doomed to extinction, even its most ardent supporters would admit. Many would argue that by gradual evolution itself the facial features of capitalism will be altered, if not transformed. However, I believe that the social revolution will occur in the next twenty-five to fifty years. Thus it should occur in our own lifetime, or certainly in the lifetime of our children.

SOCIAL EVOLUTION OF THE UNITED STATES

Before I elaborate on the conclusions presented above, it is necessary to see how capitalism has evolved, especially in the United States of America, which is among the youngest offshoots of Western civilization. The United States is currently the nerve-center of capitalism, and its history deserves a separate treatment. For this reason, I ignored its analysis in Chapter 4 and postponed it to this chapter.

In terms of Sarkar's thesis U.S. history presents few complications. It is easy to see that right from the influx of Europeans to the North American continent, the U.S. has been moving through the acquisitive age. This is not to suggest that capitalism has always prevailed in U.S. society, only that right from its inception the forces of wealth have been predominant. Prior to the American Civil War (1861–65), the landed proprietors of great wealth were in command of society and government, but since then the supreme social status has belonged to owners of financial capital and of industries. Thus in one form or another, the affluent have dominated U.S. society right from its birth, and this signifies the long continuance of nothing else but the acquisitive age.

Although it is customary to commence U.S. history from 1492, the fateful year in which Columbus discovered America, American settlements really began with 1607 when an English merchant company arrived at Jamestown and founded the colony of Virginia. Another colony was settled in 1620 at Plymouth—this time by the Pilgrims who left England to avoid the persecution of James I and the Anglican Church. These two experiments were merely the beginning of what turned out to be a steady stream of immigrants sailing from Europe, especially England, to America. Within a span of another century, thirteen-odd English colonies were established along the Atlantic coast of North America. In addition, Spain and France occupied the remaining areas of what today is the U.S. mainland.

Europeans came to settle in the colonies for a wide variety of reasons. Some groups such as the Pilgrims, Puritans, Quakers, Roman Catholics, and Huguenots came for the sake of freedom in their religious practices. Others like the English merchants were lured by trade and good economic prospects. Most of the early settlers in the English colonies were determined to assert religious and economic freedom. Having suffered much at home, they were not inclined to accept monarchy or any other autocratic government in the colonies. They had come as private groups of people, and, except in the earliest years, they did not regard themselves as agents of the British king or of anyone else who could command them from home. For all these reasons, the system of government that developed in the colonies was from the earliest much more representative than the British counterpart. Even as England chafed under the autocracy of Stuart kings, the colonists enjoyed some form of representative government.

The basic structure of each colonial government resembled the British archetype. Each colony was headed by a governor, appointed either by the king or, as in Maryland, Delaware, and Pennsylvania, by private proprietors who, in hopes of high profits, had decided to attempt settlement in the New World. The governor was advised by an appointed council and a lower house, which was elected in general elections by those who satisfied certain property qualifications. In theory, therefore, each colonial government could have been an autocracy dominated by the governor or the proprietor, but in practice real power gradually passed to elected legislators, who were either owners of vast estates, or, as in New England, wealthy merchants. Several reasons were responsible for this shift of power.

Most of the proprietors who obtained charters from the king had grandiose visions of royal prerogatives and authority. They had hoped to impose on their colonies the same social stratification as characterized England, where land was scarce and a landed magnate was a man of influence and prestige in society. Conditions however, were entirely different in America, which was one vast expanse of unmolested land. Any repressive system based on the relationship between landlords and landless peasants was simply doomed to failure in the New World, because if a person disliked living under one proprietor, he could move elsewhere. It is not then surprising that as economic enterprises most proprietorships proved to be colossal failures. Hence, in most colonies, one by one the proprietors relinquished their claims to the royal authority.

While the proprietors were patently unsuccessful in establishing political oligarchy, the governors did not have much luck either. In principle they had veto power over all legislation enacted by their legislative assemblies, but in practice they could do little but treat the assemblymen with deference. This is because the assemblymen came to control the allocation of revenues; even the governor's salary depended upon their appropriations. Thus the power of the purse generally prevailed over the threat of veto, and the colonists deftly employed it to run their affairs: they were masters in their own land.

Another experiment at some kind of centralized government was made in Massachusetts, which was founded in 1629. This was an attempt to establish a theocracy—a government based on religious tenets. Massachusetts had been settled early by a group of English Puritans, men imbued with evangelical zeal, who, having been deprived of their visions in the mother country, now hoped to build a Christian commonwealth on the new soil. It is not that the Puritans displayed tolerance for other faiths, only that they sought to found a society of like-minded, God-fearing people. In their system, the civil authority was supposed to submit to dictates of the Church.

The Puritan regime did prevail for a while, but it was doomed to failure for same reasons that subverted the proprietors' attempts to found an oligarchy. As the colonists moved from coastal areas to the interior, some of the early religious zeal waned, and economic concerns in the harsh, unfamiliar environment began to take precedence. As the economy grew over time, religious matters were subordinated to mundane affairs. Even though religion and the clergy continued to have some sway, by the eighteenth century the theocratic experiment in Massachusetts died under the unrelenting onslaught of improving economic conditions.

A similar fate awaited the later theocratic experiments in Rhode Island and Pennsylvania. There too economic concerns eventually prevailed over the sagging currents of religion, resulting in some kind of democratic government. The crux of my argument so far is that all attempts to found warrior or intellectual varieties of relatively centralized governments eventually failed in colonial America. By the eighteenth century, representative governments were established in all English colonies with varying, but mostly nominal, degrees of intervention by the Church in secular affairs.

Colonial American society is quite often pictured as a homogeneous entity with few of the class conflicts that bedeviled contemporary Europe. This was perhaps true of the early settlements, but as the abundance of natural resources led to considerable economic growth, social stratification resulted from differing economic fortunes. Early settlers tended to have an advantage over latecomers, as the former occupied the best and well-located tracts of land. In any case, even though few aristocratic families migrated from England to American colonies, and even though most colonists brought with them little wealth, a native aristocracy, based on wealth differentials, did develop by the eighteenth century.

In America, unlike contemporary England, capital and labor were extremely scarce, but land and natural resources abundant.

In England wealth belonged to capitalists, in America to owners of vast estates, especially those in the Middle and Southern colonies. It is mainly in New England, which throve on trade and commerce, that wealthy merchants appeared, and there, unlike contemporary Europe, no stigma was attached to income derived from interest and profit.

Regardless of the source of wealth, those who owned it commanded great esteem and influence even in colonial America. The office that an ordinary American then coveted most was the governor's council, which was composed mainly of the richest men in the land. Appointed for life, the councilmen participated in the making of laws as well as in executive decisions. In the fullness of time, the governors and their councils were overshadowed by the elected legislative assemblies, but the assemblymen too were far from men of humble means. This sway of opulence in early American life emerges strikingly in the words of Charles A. and Mary R. Beard:

> In each colony the representative assembly, by whatever process instituted, was elected by the property owners. The qualifications imposed on voters were often modified but in every change the power of property . . . was expressly recognized. In the South, where agriculture was the great economic interest, land was the basis of suffrage; Virginia, for example, required the elector in town or country to be a freeholder, an owner of land—a farm or a town lot of a stated size. Where agriculture and trade divided the honors, politics reflected the fact; in Massachusetts, for instance, the suffrage was conferred upon all men who owned real estate yielding forty shillings a year income, or possessed other property to the value of £40. [1, pp. 109–10]

Thus, right from the beginning American society has evolved in terms of the acquisitive age, and although religion also played a strong role in early settlements, its influence was soon swept aside by the rising tide of economic growth and prosperity. Does this in any way contradict my conclusion reached in Chapter 4 that the eighteenth century of Western civilization belongs to the intellectual age? In other words, does the acquisitive era of eighteenth-century American society, an offspring of western Europe, nullify the result already obtained? It does not.

One reason concerns the population. The U.S. population, though growing at astronomical rates, was for a long time just a fraction of the population of England and France. It is only after 1850 that America overtook either in this regard. Another reason concerns the U.S. influence in Western society in which England and France were dominant until the end of the nineteenth century. It is not until the turn of the twentieth century that the United States assumed leadership of the Western world. The industrial revolution had originated in England, but by the late nineteenth century America had far surpassed every European nation in industrial might. Capitalism had its roots in the British soil, but it is in America that it attained its biggest triumphs, its full bloom.

Thus it is only towards the end of the nineteenth century that America began to affix its stamp on the West, and by then the leading nations of western Europe, such as England and France, had moved into the acquisitive age. Thus the fact that America, even in its formative phase, had begun with the acquisitive era, while its European parents were moving through the intellectual age, does not in any way impair the validity of the law of social cycle for Western civilization. The United States then was not what it is today.

Going back to U.S. history, the thirteen American colonies, strewn along the Atlantic coast, remained under the formal dominion of Britain until 1775, when a series of British policies designed to squeeze more taxes out of the colonies led to their revolt. Out of that revolutionary turmoil, an American nation was born. It is then that the democratic forces got a new shot in the arm, but the hegemony of wealth continued.

The independent country made a fresh start by adopting a new constitution, which on the whole has served it well to this day. Three different branches of government—legislative, executive, and judicial—were established, with each serving as a check on the potential abuse of power by the other two. Within a few years, a Bill of Rights guaranteeing some fundamental rights to all people, not just the citizens, was added to the original Constitution. In this bill, the acquisitive imprint can be clearly seen. While it contained some human rights such as the freedom of worship, speech, the press, and petition among others, it ignored the fundamental human right to work and employment. Yet the unlimited right to private property was duly included.

Even though the U.S. Constitution did not then establish a democracy based on universal suffrage, as voting rights still derived from property qualifications, it was nevertheless the first experiment in history to ensure a rule of law and not of men and institutions. In practice, of course, the intent of this noble document was frequently flouted, for its enforcement was still left to men; yet it was more humanitarian than any other set of principles guiding contemporary governments. True, it was unable to abolish slavery of the black people, but slavery had been a relic of pre-independence times. Ultimately, however, the Constitution did play a role in its abolition.

True, it was not without a frightful civil war (1861–65) that Abraham Lincoln, a man of courage and boundless love for humanity, could finally exorcise the curse of slavery from the nation; yet it is under the auspices of the Constitution that Lincoln, born of ordinary parentage, could in the first place become the U.S. President. Thus the U.S. Constitution is a magnificent document that can take credit for many admirable achievements, but it has also been often abused by men of acquisitive mentality.

One notable instance of this abuse immediately comes to mind. Until the Civil War, wealth derived mainly from land and natural resources. While the manufacturing sector had been far from backward, agriculture was the dominant sector of production all this time. This fact, of course, had been reflected in politics, as the political arena, with but few exceptions, was a playground for landed magnates as late as the middle of the nineteenth century. Following the Civil War, however, the roles were gradually reversed. Although agriculture continued to grow, it failed to keep up with manufacturing, which became the dominant sector of the economy. This was not a sudden development, but a product of decades of rapid industrialization and capital accumulation.

Politics too could not but reflect this gradual shift of economic power from landlords to businessmen and merchants. At the outset, there was only one political party—that of the Federalists—which was dominated by landed interests with no effective opposition. The birth of the modern system of two parties, each with distinctive programs, styles and policies, is a later development which reached its culmination in 1854, when the Democratic Party, formed earlier in 1825, was opposed by the Republican Party. However, while both political parties differed from each other in significant ways, they both gradually came into the hands of big capitalists, financiers and merchants. And it is this group of acquisitors that used the Constitution to its own advantage, and has been using it to this day.

Following the Civil War, Congress (the U.S. legislative assembly) passed the first Civil Rights Act as the Fourteenth Amendment to the Constitution. Ostensibly, American blacks were to be major beneficiaries of this law, which granted them citizenship and equal rights and forbade any state government from taking away life, liberty, or property of any person without due process of law. However, for several decades the Fourteenth Amendment did little to protect civil rights of American blacks, who were forced to live in misery, squalor, and poverty—hardly better than slavery. Instead, the Amendment became a handy tool in the hands of the rich for self-enrichment. Most state courts ruled that corporations were persons and therefore entitled to protection under the due process clause. Each time a state government passed legislation to curb the antisocial practices of a corporation, the federal courts would step in and proclaim the state regulations unconstitutional as they flouted the "due process" clause of the Amendment. State governments thus became helpless before the might of giant enterprises.

Unencumbered by any state intervention, and with the federal government at their beck and call, corporations throve in America as never before. The economy grew at an unprecedented rate, while small businesses were gobbled up by a few giants. The wheeling and dealing that went on among businessmen towards the end of the nineteenth century have earned them the label of Robber Barons, men who, according to Fite and Reese, "built poor railroads, turned out shoddy products, cheated honest investors, sweated labor, and exploited the country's natural resources for their own wealth and satisfaction." [2, p. 355]

Almost every major industry became a monopoly. The economy might not have grown as fast without these swindlers, but there were certainly distressing side-effects of this concentration of economic power on so vast a scale—a malady the U.S. society has never since been able to shake off. So outrageous were their practices that by 1889 the whole country was up in arms. In response the Congress passed the Sherman Antitrust Act, which barred any person or corporation from conspiring to form monopolies or to stifle competition in any way. This, however, turned out to be a carrot dangled by the business-dominated Congress before an aroused public. As with the Fourteenth Amendment, this Act too was eventually used by businessmen to their own advantage.

For the next few decades, the Sherman Act was interpreted by the courts in a way that emasculated the labor unions. Their strikes were ruled as anticompetitive practices. Thus a law meant to soothe the public ire became an antilabor and eventually an antipublic law.

What businessmen detest most is competition among themselves, for competition increases uncertainty and trims profits. They are also, in general, wary of governmental intervention and regulations, lest their profits are adversely affected. Regulation, of course, is welcome to them if it cuts competition and ensures a steady and high return. Towards the end of the nineteenth century, while most industries became concentrated in the hands of a few barons, the railroads continued to be competitive. In fact, the competition there was so intense that they themselves demanded regulation from Congress, which, of course, was quick to oblige them.

In response to moans of businessmen, Congress in 1887 established the Interstate Commerce Commission (ICC) to regulate the railroads in the public interest. Thus one might say that from the Civil War down to the fateful year of 1929, the year of the greatest economic depression, the acquisitive era in the U.S. was on the rise. Capitalists flourished on all fronts: on the one hand, feeble antitrust laws like the Sherman Act provided the smokescreen under which monopolies, oligopolies and trusts could flourish while labor unions remained on the leash; on the other, various regulatory commissions such as the ICC were instituted to eliminate competition among oligopolies, which seemed unable to collude and thus act in unison as a monopoly.

One by one, competition, the bane of exuberant profits, was smothered in virtually all industries. Since then the covert collusion between the government and big business has steadily increased, as the latter can earn monopoly profits with the blessing of various regulatory agencies. These agencies are composed of hirelings of the very industries they are supposed to regulate. A nice racket thus goes on day after day under the watchful eyes of the government.

That capitalism is subject to unique internal traumas had been fathomed by Marx long before other economists began to diagnose this malady, whose symptoms were discernible as early as the first quarter of the nineteenth century. U.S. capitalism was in its infancy when it had its first bout with economic depression in 1819; it weathered that storm, only to be hit by it again in 1837. Thus during the first half of the nineteenth century, it encountered two economic crises; during the second half, however, it encountered five (in 1854, 1857, 1873, 1884, and 1893).

The twentieth century opened with brighter prospects, but the jinx of depression would not let go of the economy. After giving a mild foretaste of its impending assault in 1907, 1921, and 1927, the jinx struck with a vengeance on October 24, 1929—the day of the Great Crash. On that day, the bottom fell out of stock prices on the New York Stock Exchange. The downward spiral of security prices that then began quickly engulfed the entire American economy, and eventually the entire capitalist world. The economic catastrophe of the Great Depression cannot be easily pictured. Within three years, there were 85,000 business failures in America, and twelve million people, equal to 25 percent of the labor force, became unemployed. The brunt of the layoffs, of course, fell on the blacks who had been exploited ever since colonial times.

The economic blight spread overnight to other troubled nations linked with American economy through international commerce. The entire capitalist world then stood on the verge of collapse. The apocalyptic Marxian vision of the demise of capitalism seemed closer to fruition than ever before. But then came a brilliant economist, John Maynard Keynes, and the Second World War. Keynes prescribed the medicine, while the war served to show that it would work. Under the enormous government expenditures occasioned by the war, unemployment slowly disappeared, and, for a while, gave way to shortages of labor. Keynes had recommended massive doses of government spending to combat unemployment, and the war proved him right. Ever since, Keynesian economic theory has been guiding the capitalist world.

Under the watchful eyes of Keynesian policies, capitalism seemed to be operating smoothly for a full quarter of a century following the Second World War. There were mild relapses occasionally but no duplication of the 1929 tragedy. But just when the war against economic crises seemed to have been won, another intractable problem, potentially more dangerous than large-scale unemployment, cropped up and has persisted since 1969—namely the coexistence of inflation with a high level of unemployment. This problem eluded Keynes, for there is supposed to be a tradeoff between unemployment and inflation in the Keynesian system: both cannot rise or decline at the same time. As yet there is no consensus among economists—and there hardly ever is—as to how the new challenge should be met. Not that the problem has faded away, just that it admits of no simple, and politically feasible, solution.

On top of all these troubles, the capitalist colossus was in 1973 jolted by an international cartel called the Organization of Petroleum Exporting Countries (OPEC). There was a fourfold rise in oil prices as a result, and capitalism tottered once again.

The recession of 1973–75 was the steepest since the Great Crash, but more than that it was accompanied by an unprecedented double-digit inflation. Keynesian remedies were applied again, and as a consequence the worst seems to be over. But since no fundamental reform has been undertaken, the crisis is still simmering, ready to erupt any moment again.

THE IDEOLOGICAL PILLARS OF CAPITALISM

No socioeconomic system can last long unless it rests on an appealing ideological structure. In this regard, capitalism is no exception. And, as with every exploitative system, its ideological thread is sound in theory but tenuous in practice. Capitalism is defined as a social, economic and political system where the means of production—industries, banks, natural resources, etc.—are owned by private corporations and individuals, where the political system operates in the interests of such owners, and where the distribution of national income is determined by them. It is quite often associated with the free enterprise system, which may be defined as one where capitalists, the owners of the means of production, are free to maximize their profits.

This freedom in profit maximization is central to capitalism, for during the modern warrior and intellectual eras, when state dominance and the Christian paternalistic ethic worked to ridicule income from interest and profits, the prevailing economic systems were called mercantilism and "physiocratism." Industries and commerce existed even during those days, although not on so vast a scale; merchants did own financial capital, but the state did not permit them a free hand in earning profits. Hence economists do not refer to those systems as capitalism: aggrandizement of state income and power was then the chief concern of scholars. Thus the word "free" in the free enterprise system refers really to the capitalist's freedom to maximize the return from his investment, and not, as many would have us believe, to the free operation of a market economy. The latter definition is only a special case of my definition, one that applies when perfect competition among businessmen prevails.

The days of competition have long been gone, but capitalism continues to be called the free enterprise system. This is because while competition is there no more, the capitalist's ability to maximize his profits has soared more than ever before.

I have already noted that in an acquisitive era intellectuals come forward to offer theories justifying the dominion of acquisitors. To the majority of intellectuals, it matters little how specious their justification is as long as it is catchy and acceptable to the system. Only a few advocate genuine reform and concern for the exploited, much to the dislike of the ruling class. It is in this broad perspective that the economic theory of capitalism propounded by Adam Smith, the father of Economics, ought to be viewed.

The period between 1500 to 1700 is traditionally associated with mercantilism, which apparently overlapped with the modern warrior age. It may be recalled from Chapter 4 that it is during this period that the foundation for modern-day capitalism was laid. Yet the activities of merchants and industrialists were curbed by myriad state regulations. Even though many merchants and other special interest groups made a fortune from these regulations, the real driving force behind capitalism—the acquisitive instinct or the profit motive—was sanctioned neither by the state nor by the Church. Since the Church had submitted to the king, the responsibility for restraining the merchants from unbridled pursuit of self-interest fell on the crown. However, the state regulations continued to derive from medieval ideology—the Christian paternalistic ethic.

Following the Glorious Revolution of 1688, dogmas exalting the power of state gave way to those exalting individualism and ultimately the acquisitive instinct. All this intellectual ferment occurred during the intellectual era in which income from land commanded more moral and social prestige than income from usury and profit. Thus when Adam Smith wrote his masterpiece, *The Wealth of Nations,* in 1776, merchants and capitalists, though not as unencumbered by state regulations as during the preceding warrior era, were still not completely free to pursue their quest for profits. Smith's contemporaries sought refuge in the argument that human beings are moved primarily by selfish and egoistic motives; all human actions are rooted in self-preservation, and hence in egoism and self-interest. Selfishness and avarice, therefore, are not vices but virtues for hard work and economic prosperity. By implication then, the state should keep its intervention in human activities to the minimum so that individual and social welfare is at the maximum.

This sanctification of greed and acquisitive behavior that had found support from the intellectuals—many of whom were employed by great trading enterprises—was readily embraced by the capitalists. But its excessive stress on individualism produced apprehensions of anarchy in quite a few minds. It is Smith's brilliant contribution that tended to calm their fears. His carefully thought-out analysis of the capitalist system, blessed with keen competition, removed from the doctrine of individualism many flaws that had worked to impede its general acceptance.

Smith argues that, left to themselves, capitalists and workers are guided by self-interest to put their capital and labor to uses where they are the most productive. The mechanism which ensures this is the "invisible hand" of a free market where producers compete for consumers' money in an egocentric search for profits, and where consumers seek to obtain the best-quality product at the cheapest price. In quest of profit maximization, the producers are impelled to employ labor only in those goods for which there is demand, and to use productive techniques that are the most efficient so that unit costs are minimized. In a free market economy, therefore, everyone is happy: while the producers earn maximum return, consumers are satisfied with a high-quality product available at the lowest price ensured by maximum productive efficiency. All this is the miracle performed by the "invisible hand" in spite of, or rather because of, relentless human greed and acquisitive behavior.

Smith thus assailed the mercantilist regulations that had worked to perpetuate monopolies and further the interests of various groups. For monopolies destroy operation of the free market that ensures maximum social welfare. His work, therefore, was on the one hand a scathing denunciation of mercantilism, and on the other an eloquent plea for free enterprise or *laissez-faire*.

However, the free-enterprise system that Smith had in mind con-doned the capitalist's search for profit, but only in an environment characterized by keen competition among businessmen.

Not only would a free operation of the forces of demand and supply for goods lead to maximum economic efficiency, it would also, according to Smith, ensure a high rate of economic growth and hence a rising standard of living. But growth depends on capital accumulation, which in turn depends on the adequacy of profits. This is then another line of defense for acquisitive and self-serving behavior, for it ensures continued economic progress of society. Thus growth and efficiency are the two pillars on which Smith erected his eloquent defense of the free enterprise system unencumbered by any state interference. Although his prognosis relied on calculating instincts of individuals, it was also a moral indictment of mercantilism, which now stood exposed as a culprit impeding maximum social welfare. It is perhaps for this reason that his thought left its mark on writings for generations to come. Businessmen and laborers alike found passages in his work to support their own concerns.

The doctrine of *laissez-faire,* first propounded rigorously by Adam Smith and later refined by his disciples such as David Ricardo and J.B. Say, among others, is now known as the classical theory of economics. With this "liberal" economic ideology went a political creed that slighted the state or government as a neces-sary evil—evil because of its encroachments on individual lib-erty, but necessary for an escape from anarchy. To government, Smith assigned three basic functions: justice, national defense, and the provision of certain public goods that are too unprof-itable to be ever provided by private enterprise. This is a very general list of state functions, and although he denounced the state patronage of economic interests in any form, his political ideas were seized by businessmen, and their hired intellectuals, to justify government paternalism whenever they themselves were the beneficiaries. [6, pp. 52–4]

At the time Smith wrote his book, capitalism was still in embryo. His vision of a competitive system where the consumer is sovereign, and where the powerless producer is scrambling to satisfy market demand and preferences did, to an extent, reflect economic reality. But by the late nineteenth century, capitalism had grown into adolescence. All over the capitalist world, but especially in Germany and America, industrial colossi had sprung up to undermine the market mechanism that is supposed to generate maximum social welfare. While the forces of demand were free to operate, those of supply had been effectively constrained. But all this failed to deter a new breed of economists from erecting an even nobler defense of the free-enterprise system.

At precisely the time when the process of industrial concentration was under way, some economists, notably Jevons, Walras and Marshall, among others, set out to clothe the classical economic ideology with an elaborate mathematical apparatus, while maintaining the assumption of perfect competition. Theirs is the so-called neoclassical economic analysis, but in their basic theme of espousing *laissez-faire* they differ little from their precursors. Thus while the economic reality of capitalism had been drastically altered, economic theory emerged with a new make-up applied to the old face. Even as the Robber Barons were soaking away national wealth in their coffers, the neoclassical economists recommended "hands-off" economic policies by the government, lest the giant corporations be inhibited from acting in the public interest.

While foundations of the neoclassical economic theory were laid during the late nineteenth century, its progress and refinements continued well into the twentieth century and in fact they have continued, with brief interruptions, down to this day. In America a new generation of neoclassical economists began to recognize some of the flaws in capitalism—namely the absence of perfect competition, under-production of socially desirable goods such as roads, parks, armies, etc., undesirable social externalities such as air pollution and a squalid environment, and, above all, the economic depressions.

But while such afflictions of capitalism were explicitly recognized, most economists reared in the neoclassical tradition continued to regard them as aberrations tending to correct themselves. There were some who saw the need for serious governmental intervention to cure these socio-economic ills, but they were in a stark minority. As a result, economic theory was ill-prepared to prescribe medicine for any economic cataclysm such as the one that beset the world in 1929. In short, the neoclassical economists had undying faith in the ability of capitalism to pull itself out of any crisis as long as the state abstained from rendering help. For, in their view, official intervention could only make matters worse.

The Great Crash of 1929, therefore, caught the economists napping in their idealized world. It was not supposed to last that long—not when the entire conventional wisdom was dead set against it. The entire capitalist world was then frightened not of any natural calamity, nor of any war on which the public wrath could be easily focused, but of the man-made calamity with no avenue of escape in sight. Before the medicine could be prescribed, the malady had to be properly diagnosed; venerated dogmas had to be discarded.

It was Keynes who set out to reshape and fundamentally reorganize economic theory to bring it in line with reality, which clamored for speedy treatment. In contrast to the major neoclassical concern with micro-economics, i.e., with the economic behavior of individual economic units such as businessmen, consumers, etc., he addressed himself to the question of macro-economics, i.e., with the analysis of the entire economy.

Keynesian economics is an antithesis of the neoclassical ideology, for the government is now cast in the role of a constant watchdog indispensable to continued economic health. The appeal of Keynesian theory lay in the fact that not only did it properly diagnose the economic ills, but it also advocated policies well within the reach of governments. For this reason its spread was swift and decisive, and, in spite of stubborn initial resistance from doctrinaire economists who detested any state intervention on purely ideological grounds, Keynesian thought soon displaced the ideas of his predecessors. Today it has become the orthodoxy to which challenges from other quarters are often posed. The most notable challenge was posed in the 1960s by the Nobel Laureate Milton Friedman, who is credited with pioneering a whole new approach, called the monetarist approach, to the question of economic fluctuations under capitalism.

At present the majority opinion of economists is represented by the views of another Nobel Laureate, Paul Samuelson, whose varied contributions are marked by mathematical rigor and elegance. He has been instrumental in integrating Keynesian and neoclassical economics in what he calls "the neoclassical synthesis." The Keynesian prognosis can be fruitfully used to maintain full employment, and the neoclassical ideology can be the beacon light for free operation of markets within the Keynesian framework. Thus under capitalism, the society can thrive on both fronts—full employment along with a high degree of productive efficiency [7].

It is hard to believe that the views of Friedman and Samuelson have attained so much popularity in an economic milieu dominated by industrial giants that glaringly defy the requirements of perfect competition on which neoclassical thought is based. The same kind of gulf that separated economic theory from reality on the eve of the Great Depression is very much in evidence today, and displays few signs of abatement.

Not only is the neoclassical world downright unrealistic, it is also heartless, with little concern for those for whom the labor-market finds no use. It is not my intention, however, to dwell at length on the inhuman aspects of capitalism, for volumes have already been written from this viewpoint, and I can do no better than wholeheartedly agree with them. For decades capitalism has been indicted for the fact that it rewards the affluent, the gifted, the intelligent, the privileged, but penalizes the weak, the handicapped, the poor. In a word, the system is cruel. What I wish to stress now, and in a short while, is that most critics of capitalism are no different in mentality from its proponents; that they are hardly in a position to throw stones at others, for they themselves live in the glasshouses of materialism; that those who decry the profit mentality today, themselves exhibit acquisitive behavior—in short they are the intellectual acquisitors or capitalists.[1]

CAPITALISM AND FEUDALISM

I have said it before that capitalism has much in common with feudalism which prevailed in Western society from about 900 to

1400 A.D., and I say this again in the full knowledge that surface disparities between the two systems are overwhelming. If capitalism is confined to an economic setup where the owners of capital are in charge of hiring factors, producing goods, and determining the distribution of national income, then the two systems could not have been more apart. But that would be too narrow a definition of business-dominated society, one that does it ill-justice. Capitalism, as stated before, is not only an economic order, but also a sociopolitical order that goes with it. For without the social sanction of the capitalist's unlimited property rights, the business world would not last another day.

If we look only at modes of production, the disparities between capitalism and feudalism boggle the mind. While capitalism presents the picture of a highly industrialized, technically advanced society capable of assailing the moon, its predecessor was, in comparison, an economic pygmy organized in a series of small, self-sufficient rural communities. But if we look for the power-base of the ruling class, the similarities in the two systems could not be more striking. Similarly, the social and political philosophy underlying the two systems reveals greater unity than has been hitherto recognized.

As far as the mentality of the ruling class is concerned, capitalism and feudalism are both alike. Then, as now, wealth reigned supreme. Under feudalism the rich ruled because of their control over vast estates, which then comprised wealth; today the rich rule because of their control over stocks, bonds and other capital assets. Feudalism was marred by constant feuds among landed magnates over land, capitalism has been marred by industrial warfare in which big corporations have been constantly preying on smaller corporations. In late medieval Europe, wealth was concentrated in the hands of landlords—dukes, barons, earls, margraves; today it is concentrated in the hands of capitalists—corporation presidents, vice-presidents, executives. Feudalism was barbaric and oppressive of peasants and serfs, capitalism has been cruel and oppressive of underdeveloped countries, blacks, and unskilled workers. And in both cases, exploitation is based on economic deprivation and inequities.

In terms of social and political philosophy, the ideas of individualism permeated the feudal order much as they do now. Then, as now, the main function of the sovereign authority was to administer the law, not to make it or shape it out of his own whims. In theory, the ruler's capricious behavior was then as much a social anathema as it is today. The dominion of landlords was then justified by the Christian paternalistic ethic in the name of a God-created order; today the dominion of capitalists is justified by the neoclassical ideology in the name of economic growth and productive efficiency. People then used to argue in terms of theology, hence the intellectuals, in the guise of the clergy and other writers, provided a theological defense for the feudal order. Today the intellectuals speak in terms of logic; hence the defense of capitalism also derives from logical arguments. Thus in both systems, the intellectuals can be seen to have been sold out to acquisitors.

In terms of ordinary life, too, there are many similarities. High prostitution and crime rates were as much the scourge of feudalism as they are today of capitalism. Then, as now, family bonds had become loose; then, as now, political authority and administration were highly decentralized. In the feudal order, the knights fought the wars of their overlord; today their place has been taken by army lieutenants, captains and generals. In short, then as now, the acquisitive mentality ruled the roost. It is for reasons such as these that I regard feudalism and capitalism as two different branches of the same family-tree called the acquisitive age.

SOCIAL REVOLUTION AND THE ECLIPSE OF CAPITALISM

The reader may have noted an obvious difference between the two systems compared above: while feudalism has come and gone, capitalism remains, and seemingly in good health. But while it continues to survive, I believe that capitalism is now gasping for breath, with the end coming in twenty-five to fifty years. It has been in its declining phase ever since the 1930s, when the neoclassical ideology of *laissez-faire* gave ground to the Keynesian thinking. It is then that interventionist sentiment began to find favor with governments in the capitalist world, and today that sentiment has resulted in a bureaucratic monster which is exceedingly difficult to contain. Prior to the Great Crash, state interference with the system had been minimal, and that too was contrived to shield unruly businesses from close public scrutiny, or to curb competition among feuding corporations. But when Keynes demonstrated the need for constant governmental watch on the economic system to keep it from collapsing, the influence of capitalists began to decline. Their loss, of course, was a gain for intellectual capitalists, and today it is the latter breed that holds the reins.

The acquisitive era begins when the forces of wealth take over the social and economic levers of society and generate a decentralized political system; it reaches its peak when the acquisitive dominion is absolute and unchallenged; and its decline commences the moment the political machinery is taken over by intellectual acquisitors. Scrutinizing Western history, we find that capitalists had reached the top of the social hierarchy by the 1860s, at least in England and the United States. By then the odium of earning income from interest and profits, which were denounced earlier by the Christian paternalistic ethnic, had disappeared. But now the same old odium has returned. The profit mentality is now again under fire; motives of businessmen are being constantly questioned, while high incomes from other sources fail to invite so much publicity and condemnation. This whole atmosphere is reminiscent of the physiocratic era when Christian paternalism was used to glorify income from sources other than usury and profits.

It is then clear that time does not now favor the genuine capitalists. To be sure, they have not yet been trounced—their influence in fact is second only to that of intellectual capitalists—but they are retreating. They are still fighting, spending millions of dollars to refurbish their image, but it is a rearguard action designed to delay doomsday as long as possible. Thus it is noteworthy that the acquisitive era begins to decline the moment the political apparatus slips out of acquisitive hands.

Symptoms of this decline are now all there if anyone cares to see. The horrifying crime rate, the breakdown of family ties and the concomitant plight of the elderly, the appalling divorce rate, the scandalous tolerance of pornography and prostitution, the rising tide of drug-abuse and alcoholism, the commercialization of art, sport and practically everything else, the insensitivity of the employed to the unemployed, the insensitivity of the bureaucratic colossus are all symptoms of the malaise that now bedevils capitalism. These are all symptoms that appear in an acquisitive era only towards its end. The apologists of capitalism assert that the system is still healthy, that never in history has there been so much prosperity, and that, despite the enormous concentration of wealth in a few hands, never has a system provided so much comfort and happiness for so many citizens.

This is precisely where they err. To them materialism is all that matters; but at bottom it is this super-materialism, especially the materialism and hypocrisy of capitalists, that is squarely to blame for all the social ills. Leaders of the Western world today inspire neither confidence nor respect; all they inspire is envy— envy for their luxurious life, envy for the ease with which they dupe the general public, envy for the light or no sentence they receive for their known excesses. Is there any wonder that the masses emulate them and attempt to attain the same comforts by any means? Is there any wonder that the crime rate is high? The real culprits go scot-free for all their known and unknown crimes, but the poverty-stricken people, who are simply following in the footsteps of their leaders, get all the blame.

Even on the material front, some, though not all, claims of capitalism are hollow. America, for instance, with a six per cent share of the global population, consumes at least thirty per cent of the natural resources of the entire world; yet within its borders there is considerable poverty, especially among the blacks and other minorities. If this is the best that capitalism can do after annually gobbling up one-third of the world's resources, one wonders what all this fuss regarding economic prosperity is about.

Currently the West is passing through the acquisitive-cum-laborer phase of its social cycle. This is because the people, under the contagion of their leaders' greed, are gradually acquiring the selfish mentality. The masses understandably try to attain comforts that capitalists have, but in so doing they have to work long hours. Both the husband and wife in a family have to strain to keep up with creeping inflation. Consequently, the warrior and intellectual interests of pure adventure and art find little time for self-expression. Thus, infected by the capitalist's acquisition disease, the masses are being forced into selfish behavior. This, and this alone, is at the bottom of the present malaise in capitalist countries. And the malaise is going to get worse in the next few decades. Eventually it will invite rebellion from the masses, even if, in the unlikely event, the capitalist economies continue to function well.

If my calculations are correct, then the current acquisitive era began in the West around the 1860s, reached its peak by the late 1930s, and has been going downhill ever since. From historical experience, the periods of up-trend and down-trend of an era are roughly equal. If the up-trend of capitalism lasted for about seventy to eighty years, its decline will roughly take the same number of years, which means that the social revolution, that will dethrone the acquisitors, should occur by the year 2010, give or take one decade.

Those entrenched in the seat of power have the most to fear from my prophecy, but I do not think they will believe it. But then never have they believed this in all past revolutions. A careful study of the major revolutions of the world—the French Revolution, the Bolshevik Revolution, Mao's Revolution, etc.— reveals one common cause. They were all provoked by the excesses of an overbearing bureaucracy insensitive to plight of the masses. The same bureaucratic behemoth, thanks to the constant meddling of intellectual capitalists, now threatens to undermine the stability of the Western world. The behemoth is still growing, and will continue to do so in the near future, eventually compelling the masses to rise in arms, and to sweep it aside along with its progenitors.

Who will bring this revolution about? Who will be in its vanguard? According to the theory of social cycle, every acquisitive era ends up in a social revolution which is engineered by a group of disgruntled intellectuals and warriors. Today in Western society, the intellectual class is mostly composed of secular intellectuals—the writer, the teacher, the white-collar worker, the lawyer, the physician, the politician—although some of them have joined the ranks of capitalists. The warrior class comprises the army officer, the policeman, the firefighter and the skilled blue-collar worker. The semi-skilled and unskilled workers belong to the laborer class. Despite occasional murmurs, the nonacquisitive classes today support the system in which they live. Those who wish to see the system uprooted are today called extremists; they are decidedly in the minority, but their ranks are gradually swelling. The laborers today, as in most epochs, are the most oppressed and exploited by the capitalist order, but their feeble voices of protest go unheeded because the intellectual and warrior groups enjoy adequate standards of living.

The aristocracy, composed of intellectual and genuine capitalists, does not today inspire revolt among warriors and intellectuals, only envy for its fabulous wealth to which everyone else aspires. Within two decades, this situation will change under the burden of creeping economic troubles that now confront the capitalist countries. While capitalists will be able to maintain their conspicuous consumption, the living standard of non-capitalist classes will progressively decline. Some of the warriors and intellectuals will become as impoverished as laborers are today. It is out of this impoverished group of warriors and intellectuals that revolutionaries will be born. It is they who will be in the vanguard of the social revolution.

Will this revolution be peaceful or violent? Will it blaze a trail of terror or be marked by an orderly transfer of power? The answer depends on what the ruling class does between now and the next two decades; how it copes with impending economic dilemmas; how it shares sacrifices that will determine the fate of all concerned. True, the storms that are now in the making are among the most tempestuous that capitalism will ever face. The crippling energy shortages that now loom in the horizon pose a challenge no less catastrophic than the Second World War, in which the acquisitive forces came out with flying colors.

But if the ruling class sets an example by making all the sacrifices that are well within its reach, if it shows sympathy and compassion for the misery of the under-privileged, then there will be an orderly transition of power from the ruler to those who, in terms of the theory of social cycle, are next in line of succession. The social revolution will then represent the smooth introduction of new and radical ideas untainted by violence and social turmoil. Fortunately, the West does have precedents of peaceful change, such as occurred in the Glorious Revolution in England, and I sincerely hope that such will be the case in the forthcoming revolution as well.

Is the revolution I speak of inevitable? The answer is yes; and in so saying I am not oblivious to the fact that such Marxian prophecies have been thus far disproved by history. In the days of Marx, the acquisitive era was still in its infancy; capitalism was then much more exploitative of the masses than it is today. Child labor, the abuse of women workers, unsanitary and inhuman working conditions, incredibly long working hours were very common. In view of this grinding oppression, Marx thought that capitalism could not survive long. Had he realized that each system must reach a peak before its end, he would not have predicted an impending collapse of the capitalist order. To me the fact that capitalism has flourished and thriven so long is not at all surprising. It had to be this way, because it could not die before acquiring adolescence, youth, and maturity.

The same kind of evolution had accompanied feudalism, which at its genesis around 900 was more repressive of the serfs than when it attained its zenith in the thirteenth century. Then also the general standard of living had risen above the level of the preceding intellectual age, but that could not prevent its eventual breakdown. The question in my mind is not whether the revolution is inevitable, but whether it will be tranquil or marked by convulsions. The past record of revolutions points to bloodshed and horror, but then the West has by now discovered avenues of peaceful change. Hopefully, sanity will continue to prevail over brute force.

FUTURE WESTERN SOCIETY: THE NEW WARRIOR AGE

The end of capitalism does not mean the end of the Western world and culture, but only the end of one link in the long chain of Western civilization. Following the revolution, a new warrior era will be established with leadership passing into the hands of the rebellious warriors. Whether the new leaders will emerge from the military or from skilled blue-collar workers is a question that cannot now be answered. Past human experience points to the military officers, but quite often the outer shell of the ruling class differs markedly from that of its predecessors, although the ruler's underlying mentality in a particular era of different social cycles remains the same. Feudalism and capitalism, for instance, reveal monumental differences in appearance, but in both cases the dominating aristocracy displays an acquisitive disposition.

But even though I am not sure where the future leaders will come from, some characteristics of the forthcoming Western society can be safely foreseen from Sarkar's theory of social cycle. The present decentralized system will definitely give way to a centralized political and administrative order. Constitutions of various capitalist democracies will perhaps remain in force, but the executive will be the most powerful branch among the three branches of government. Elections might still take place, but candidates will come out of the warrior class. In spite of a high degree of governmental centralization, the fundamental human rights of all people, not just the rich, will be respected. This is because in the early stage of a warrior era the ruler provides a benevolent administration. This happened with most civilizations in the past, over the last 6,000 years and there is no reason why it should not happen in the future.

Those who stand to gain the most from this change are women and the laborers. Both these groups today are victims of economic and social discrimination, but they both have a great future; both will be accorded the esteem they have long deserved in society. Laborers deserve our respect because they do the hard work considered dirty by others. Similarly, women deserve not only equality with men in social, economic and political spheres, but also privileges superior to those that men have. This is because whereas both men and women cooperate in the perpetuation of society, women carry a much heavier burden. True, it is a biological necessity, but the truth remains that woman, not man, becomes pregnant and bears the load of a baby for nine months along with all the inconvenience that goes with it.

Therefore, while both men and women, when given equal opportunities, have equal capacities to make contributions to society, women's burden is much greater, and for this they ought to be duly compensated. Thus woman's stature in society, especially that of a mother, ought to be higher than of man not only in theory but also in practice. I am not sure whether men will ever agree with what I say, but in the coming era, Western women will get better opportunities for self-expression than they now have. In fact the current assertiveness among women reflected in the form of the women's liberation movement is a harbinger of the respect that awaits them in the not-too-distant future.

In the new era, while the entire Western society, emancipated from the clutches of super-materialism, will resume its forward march up the evolutionary ladder, in America, Canada and Australia will dawn a Golden Age. This is because these nations are mere saplings of an old tree that we call Western civilization.

In all past civilizations, the Golden Age flourished mostly in warrior eras. Whether it was in Egypt, India, or the West, the golden era appeared when men and women of martial qualities held the reins. America, Canada, and Australia are infant nations that have yet to witness the glory of a warrior era, and for this reason, I think, they will progress as never before.

In contrast with the current malaise caused by the greed of the capitalist class, the new age will be an embodiment of vivacity and adventure. As with the fifteenth-century warrior era in Europe, the state will participate in the discovery of new habitable lands; only this time the discoveries will be made among the planets and the stars, and human beings will begin migrating to the "New Earth." In fact, seeds of the future interplanetary migration have already been sown by the historic voyage of American men to the moon, much as attempts to discover alternative oceanic routes to India had begun in Europe some time before the advent of its warrior age.

The economic setup of the new warrior era may be called the cooperative economic system, as it will involve the cooperative management of factories by skilled workers. The unlimited property rights of capitalists will no longer be recognized; instead, corporations will be collectively owned and administered by employees. This system will guarantee full employment without inflation, as well as an equitable distribution of income, for profits will now be distributed among workers. Within such a framework inflation is unlikely, because quite often it results from the high wage demands of labor unions attempting to preserve their real income position that is threatened by prices raised by producers. Therefore, in the modern capitalist order inflation tends to feed on itself. But in a cooperative economic system, labor unions are unnecessary, so that the cost-push type of inflation is unlikely to occur. Once inflation is under control, full employment can be easily maintained through a proper mix of monetary and fiscal policies.

In the new era, not only will the West be delivered from its three-pronged ills—inflation, unemployment, and concentration of wealth and income—but also from other afflictions besetting it today. Crime will recede, pornography will recede, and so will all the commercialism. In short, the new era in the West will bring with it another Golden Age.

REFERENCES

[1] Beard, C. A. and M. R., *The Rise of American Civilization*, Vol. I (New York: The MacMillan Co., 1927).

[2] Fite, G. C. and J. E. Reese, *An Economic History of the United States* (Boston: Houghton Mifflin Co., 1973).

[3] Friedman, Milton, *Capitalism and Freedom* (Chicago: University of Chicago Press, 1962).

[4] Friedman, Milton and Anna Schwartz, *A Monetary History of the United States, 1867–1960* (Princeton University Press, 1963).

[5] Heilbroner, R. L., *Business Civilization in Decline* (New York: W. W. Norton, 1976).
[6] Hunt, E. K. and H. J. Sherman, *Economics: An Introduction to Traditional and Radical Views* (New York: Harper & Row, 1975).
[7] Samuelson, P. A., *The Collected Scientific Papers*, Vol. İI, ed. J. E. Stiglitz (Cambridge: M.I.T. Press, 1966) Ch. 115.

9

Spiritual Renaissance

The foregoing pages have given us an account of Sarkar's theory of social cycle, of its innate strength to explain the evolution of various civilizations, of its predictive ability and content, of its vision and generality. It is now time for a summation—for an overall view of what I have said thus far, of its submission, and the message it conveys to my fellow world-citizens and to future generations.

If there is one central theme that runs through veins of this work, it is that human nature is everywhere the same; that surface disparities of language, customs, religion, and skin color are too tenuous to mask the underlying unity of human behavior in different parts of our planet. This absolute truth, recognized by prophets since ancient times, has been distorted by vested interests again and again, but today, with the world shrunk into a family of interdependent nations, it is more apparent than ever before. Many in the past have suggested the contrary; to my mind, they stress the forms but overlook the substance.

If human culture is basically the same everywhere, so must be human evolution. That is why Sarkar's law of social cycle, which is rooted in the Evolutionary Principle, must be valid everywhere—for all civilizations. In the foregoing, only three civilizations were analyzed, but each portrayed a different picture altogether; each had a unique origin, a unique expression, a unique destiny. However, despite surface disparities, all of them turned out to have evolved in tune with the law of social cycle. It is my belief that all other civilizations, upon closer examination, will be found to be following the same rhythmic evolution: to my mind, Sarkar's masterly work has universal validity.

Today historical determinism is in disrepute, and for good reason. Time and again, scholars have sought to unravel the mystique of history, to see an invisible hand weaving uneven historical threads into a smooth fabric, to make sense out of the unruly trends of the human past—in short, to tame history into meek, interpretable hypotheses. But critics have surgically examined their evidence, dissected their dogmas, and eventually torn their message to pieces. The champions of historical determinism spent their lifetimes detecting historical patterns, but their peers had an easy time spotting flaws in their views. Sarkar's contribution, however, is of a different variety. It will no doubt generate a good deal of controversy, a good deal of ferment among intellectual circles, but it will not present as easy a target for attack as other deterministic views that are now generally considered seriously deficient.

The main line of defense of the Sarkarian hypothesis is that, unlike the theories now in disrepute, it does not emphasize one particular point to the exclusion of all others: it is based on the sum total of human experience—the totality of human nature.

Whenever a single factor, however important or fundamental, is called upon to illuminate the entire past and by implication the entire future, it simply invites disbelief and, after closer scrutiny, rejection. Marx committed that folly, and, to some extent, so did Toynbee. They both offered an easy prey to critics, and the result is that today historical determinism is regarded by most scholars as an idea so bankrupt that it can never be solvent again. Perhaps, perhaps not! Sarkar's novel theory, I think, will generate a new storm in settled waters, if only because it is an attempt to revive the very idea that today would lull the historian into sleep. But Sarkar's message is universal, and as in the preceding chapters which affirmed its validity to various civilizations, it will survive the test of questions raised by the reader and celebrated historians.

While Sarkar's thought is universal, its underlying theme is very simple. It recognizes the fact that every civilized society is basically composed of four groups, each comprising people with a distinct frame of mind: some by temperament are warriors, some intellectuals; some abound in acquisitive instincts and some are physical workers. Now the theory of social cycle simply says that the first three groups take turns in holding the reins of society, while the fourth group, of which the other three usually take advantage, seldom comes to prominence.

Sarkar characterizes his law as infallible, something applicable without reservation to all civilizations—dead or alive, ancient or modern, oriental or occidental. In the present volume, I have attempted to evaluate this claim in terms of three civilizations—Western, Russian, and Hindu—and found that they all evolved in tune with the law of social cycle. In fact, the corroborative evidence is so overwhelming that it is surprising the historical patterns attuned to Sarkar's theory have not been discovered by scholars before; especially is it surprising in view of my finding that all these civilizations have, or had in the past, undergone the social cycle more than once.

The Hindu civilization has passed through four such cycles, and is now languishing through the declining phase of its acquisitive age, which is soon going to face the avalanche of revolution. Western society, beginning with the Roman Empire, is now in the final phase of its second social cycle, and here too the ruling class is now preparing the soil for the impending revolution. Russian society, by contrast, is the youngest of the three examined in this volume: it is now lingering through the first phase of its second social cycle, has been doing so for the last four centuries, and is now ripe for moving into another era dominated by intellectuals. I am not sure whether the impending Russian evolution will be peaceful or marked by bloodshed and violence; but come it will.

This, in short, is an account of the conclusions I have reached thus far. All in all, I have expounded Sarkar's doctrine of social cycle, compared it with the well-known views of Marx and Toynbee, subjected it to the test of four different civilizations, and finally utilized it to predict the future course of the Hindu, Western, and Russian societies. The stage is now set for my submission; for a panoramic view of the global social landscape—whither it is heading, its direction, its needs, its destiny.

Sarkar's contribution appears on the world horizon at a time when a powerful wave of materialism is moving through all nations. Whether we look at the acquisitor-dominated societies, such as India and the Western world, or the warrior-dominated societies, such as the Communist block, much of the underdeveloped region, and major oil-exporting nations, materialism permeates the flesh and bone of them all. That the acquisitive instinct sways acquisitive societies is not all surprising, but warrior societies too are today afflicted by this sickness, because most of them are now passing through the downward phase of their warrior eras. This situation is quite unprecedented. Seldom before has the entire world chafed under the torrent of ultra-selfish materialism, by which I mean not the healthy international concern for the economic health of underdeveloped nations, but the fact that most countries today are ruled by people steeped thoroughly in their own interests. And if we look deeper, it is this self-centered behavior of ruling classes all over the globe which is at the root of world poverty and other problems facing humanity at large today.

Actually problems have always been there; challenges have always existed. There is nothing new in the fact that the world today is beset by dilemmas—population explosion, wealth and income inequalities within, and among, all nations, the energy crisis, the possibility of nuclear holocaust, and the whole host of other tumors. What the world is woefully lacking today is that moral fiber which can meet the challenges head on. In Toynbee's terminology, its response is poor and inadequate. Its leaders are parasites who all have their own axes to grind. Their acquisitive instinct has infected their subjects to the point that portents of impending international catastrophe are appearing in all directions. The problems of the world, in short, seem so onerous, because it now moans under the wave of materialism that has sapped its spirit of response.

It is in the cradle of such waves that mighty spiritual currents are born and nurtured. It is when the human spirit gets stifled by a failure of nerve that spiritual leaders emerge to guide it towards a new path, a new destiny: the history of all nations is a mute witness to this phenomenon. And the soil of the world is now fertile for the birth of a new spiritual movement—a new ideology that will steer it through the storms which are now, and have been for some time, in the making. The new movement will help the forces of selflessness triumph over materialism, of moralism over lethargy, pornography, and alcoholic addiction, of humanitarianism over insensitivity. It will exalt the virtues now forgotten, and its leaders will provide guidance to the groping world by leading exemplary lives, by practicing the high principles they will preach.

Not only will the new ideology touch on individual behavior, but also on all the vexing national and international problems. It will not be inimical to economic growth and science; nor will it undervalue a habitable environment. It will discard all religious dogmas and other narrow ideas that impede the essential unity of humankind. It will preach the cosmic sentiment of international brotherhood, of the one world government. In short, it, and it alone, will be able to deliver the world from the impending disaster.

If we peer deep into the acquisitive behavior of world leaders, in it we will find the cause of all international problems. I have said it before in Chapter 3, and, for emphasis, I will now say it again. Every human being is an embodiment of pure consciousness, of the knowledge of self-existence; this consciousness knows no dimensions, and, therefore, its reach is infinite, its propensity for self-expression unlimited. Every human body has limits, but not the conscious human being. Some may mistake this for religion or philosophy, but to me it is an empirical fact of which every person is subconsciously aware. It is because the human consciousness lacks dimensions that the human thirst for happiness is infinite, unlimited, cosmic. It is because of this thirst for the infinite that the human mind becomes bored with what it has, and runs after what it does not have. The attainment of more and more material objects, however, is not the answer to this thirst, for the material objects themselves are finite. Something which is finite cannot be the source of infinite joy; only the awareness of oneself as a dimensionless conscious entity can.

This fundamental point has been true since time immemorial, and will be true for all time to come. Even the mastery over the entire universe, which too is finite, will not bring the infinitude which each and every one of us seeks. Therefore to attain what we subconsciously crave, we have to turn to the realm of morality, of selfless and humanitarian action.

A self-centered action moves a person towards the realm of finiteness, because that action, by limiting his attention to himself, produces smallness and eventually debasement. The pursuit of self-interest alone is ultimately the cause of misery and disillusion, for it runs against the fundamental truth that, because of our dimensionless consciousness, we all yearn for limitless joy and beatitude. If the unchecked expression of self-interest ultimately makes one miserable, we can only imagine what the pursuit of self-interest by all, under the contagion of their leaders' lust for power and money, can do to a nation, and ultimately to our global fraternity of nations. If "every man for himself" becomes the motto of the day, then crime, addiction to drugs and alcohol, and other social tumors cannot stay far behind. For then the mind, after making merry in the realm of finiteness, has to suppress its innate urge for infinitude through wine, whisky and drugs.

This, however, is a primrose path to nothing else but individual and social disaster, which ultimately plants the seeds of spiritual rebirth. The law of systaltic motion, enunciated earlier in Chapter 2, implies that the uplifting force in society develops in proportion to the preceding degenerative force. In degeneration, the world today abounds; so the new spiritual movement is bound to appear before long—within the next two decades.

In the preceding pages, I have spoken of the internal turmoil in which the societies of India, the West and Russia will be caught in the near future. All portents and calculations point toward the turn of the twenty-first century—the year 2000. The ensuing internal conflicts, either before or a little after 2000 A.D., will eventually assume international dimensions. The entire world will then seethe under international intrigue. It is quite likely that the arsenal the world is now collecting, thanks to booming gun factories in America, Russia, and Europe, will then get a chance to come into some kind of action. It is in the wake of this turmoil that the new spiritual movement will come to the surface. Humanity will then be at crossroads, on the eve of a new alignment of forces which will usher in a new epoch in World Civilization.

We are fast approaching this turning-point, a point at which the new breaks away from the past, when gospels we have long venerated become bankrupt, conventional wisdom becomes a nightmare, familiar concepts and words no longer apply, and the treatment on which we have relied for ages no longer cures. Such tumors are now in the making; they are still benign, but in the next two decades they will become cancerous, ready to be surgically cut off, so that the way is paved for a fresh start.

In the past, the birth of every new epoch was preceded and aided by the birth of a new ideology. For instance, the Renaissance movement preceded the dawn of the new warrior era in Europe, and eventually culminated in the Protestant Reformation. Actually some changes in ideology occur whenever one era is replaced by another; but when the new social cycle is about to emerge, as will be the case with India and the West at the turn of the century, the ideological change is momentous and far-reaching: it then embraces every facet of individual and social life. By the time the social revolutions eventually erupt in India and the West, revolutions of which I have already spoken in previous chapters, the new spiritual movement will have been born and established. In fact, it will likely provide ideological inspiration to these revolutions.

Who will be leaders of this movement? Stated somewhat differently, who will be the people leading the world by means of their exemplary lives? At the outset, it is notable that every epochal movement eventually spreads its umbrella over accessible areas of the region in which it originates. This has been the experience of all great movements in the past—Buddhism, Christianity, Islam, the Renaissance. Today regional boundaries extend to the entire world; therefore, eventually the new movement will spread over all nations, unifying them in its wake and laying the foundation for world government. By the same token, even in its infancy, its leaders and followers will come from different nations. They will proclaim that all narrow sentiments —racism, casteism, nationalism—are enemies of humanity; they will demonstrate the need for world unity in order to solve all its problems.

But even though the new spiritual leaders will eventually be men and women of all complexions, they will initially come from India and the Western world. This is because these are the two societies that are now destined to pass through epoch-making conflicts. These are the ones that are about to make a break from the past and enter into a new social cycle. And for spiritual leaders to emerge on a large scale, social conflict is indispensable. Those disgruntled warriors and intellectuals, of whom I have written in preceding chapters, constitute the group out of which the world spiritual leaders will be born. Character and the strength of mind cannot be built without going through difficulties and privations. Only when the mind has undergone grueling tests and churning is it transmuted into a mighty spirit, unconcerned with its own well-being but ready to sacrifice everything for the sake of others. The ensuing social turmoil will be the bane of establishments in India and the West, but those made of sterner stuff will battle hard against official exploitation, and ultimately emerge victorious to become the world's spiritual leaders.

The new movement will win over the hearts of the young, the uncommitted, the unbiased. No democratic nation will be immune to its encroachments; and even though iron curtains of communist countries will initially be able to block its advance, eventually they too will succumb to its cosmic ideas and universalism.

To underdeveloped nations, the new movement will bring the boon of prosperity. Today the ideologies of capitalism and of totalitarian communism compete for their attention. None of them has any say in international economic policies that govern their economic conditions. They are desperately trying to cope with the problems of overpopulation, poverty, and food and energy shortages, while some other countries wallow in extravagance. The world economic and political system today is inhuman; but it cannot survive long. The new spiritual movement will quickly capture the hearts of underdeveloped nations. It will bring new radiance to their glum eyes, and ultimately deliver them from poverty.

The new ideology will attempt to solve every problem by applying the principle of genuine love for humanity. Hatred and extremism will not be its forte. It will not abolish private property, nor will it condone unbridled private accumulation of wealth.

A spiritualist has sympathy and compassion for everyone, even for the exploiter and social parasites. Those with an excessive urge for acquisition have to be treated in the same way as those addicted to alcohol and drugs, because the acquisitive instinct is also a mental malady, an addiction. And for this, a greedy person deserves as much help as any other addict. Humanitarian treatment of all socioeconomic and political ills will thus be the motto of the new movement.

Many scholars will ask to see my proof for all these assertions; many will brush them aside as dreams of a visionary or as utopian ideas blind to the current world reality. To them I say, look into past human experience, peer into the historical pageant of all nations, and therein you will find support for my views. Whenever any civilization moved from one social cycle to another, or whenever its acquisitive era, after winding up in the social revolution, moved into another warrior era, this was accompanied by ideological changes that dwarfed all such changes in its recent memory. Dogmas that it had long venerated were abruptly discarded; the economic system it had long been accustomed to was surgically altered; the political setup that its ruling classes had used to their advantage was radically transformed—in short, its structure was overhauled.

Take, for instance, Buddhism. It appeared in India at a time when Hindu society was grinding under the repressive wheels of priestly and acquisitive institutions, and the movement helped bring about the decline of brahmans during the subsequent warrior age. Similarly, consider the Renaissance movement. It emerged at a time when the medieval religious order was corrupted by sloth and simony; the Church had been in the seat of power for more than a millennium; it had decayed beyond belief, had supported the exploitative feudal system, had helped everyone but the needy. There was a clamor for reforms, a desperate need for fresh thought and vigor, a leadership vacuum, and the Renaissance emerged from grassroots to fill that vacuum. But the movement went into full swing just before the time when another warrior era was born in the West; and in demolishing the acquisitive era of feudalism, the Renaissance lent a helping hand.

Similarly, the Protestant Reformation, which finally broke the back of the medieval Church, jolted Western society only a few decades after its modern warrior era had been established in the 1460s. Actually the inspiration for the Reformation had come from the teachings and sacrifices of sages who had lived during laboring times, or during the period of transition from the acquisitive era of feudalism to the new warrior age. John Huss was the founder of a movement that demanded religious reforms at the turn of the fifteenth century. It is he who was burnt at the stake in 1414, because he refused to recant his sermons against the moral turpitude of the Catholic Church. It is his martyrdom that later provided a spark for the Reformation. Thus momentous ideological changes in the past have occurred whenever a society entered into a new social cycle.

I am not suggesting that all great movements in the past have emerged around the death of an acquisitive era, or around the birth of a warrior age; only that most of them have, and my reasoning is that the acquisitor's greed and onerous exploitation of laborers generate such a degree of materialism in society that to offset this materialism a new spiritual movement has to appear. And the time is now ripe for another spiritual regeneration.

Why a spiritual movement? Why not any other kind of movement? The Renaissance, after all, was far from a spiritual resurgence. In fact, some may argue that it was just the contrary, as its emphasis was less on the world of spirit and more on the present life; some of the Renaissance writers even championed the old Roman-style paganism, its ideals, its virtues. However the important point is that each new movement emerges as a revolt against the decadence of the established order. During the second half of the Middle Ages, the decadence of the Church was an open secret; its support of the feudal order made it an accomplice in the acquisitor's exploitation of peasants and serfs. Every exploitative institution was sanctified in the name of God by his clerical emissaries. Thus the need of the day was an emphasis on individualism and secular learning, and a de-emphasis on theology and the Church's supremacy, for every repressive act was committed in God's name. The Renaissance, therefore, emerged as an answer to the collusion between the priest and feudal magnates for maintaining their hold on society.

Today conditions are just the opposite. Every exploitative act is currently committed in the name of either individual liberty or the public interest. Our society today lays stress on superficiality, on artificial mannerism, on what is apparent and pleasing to the eye. The stress is so much on personal gain that humanitarian concerns have been completely forgotten. As a result, while earthly pleasures are readily accepted by the world, moral and spiritual values have become old-fashioned. What humanity today needs most is a spiritual revival; a return to the old-fashioned values exalting selflessness and the cosmic sentiment. It does not need rituals or regionalism, or any other chauvinistic sentiment: it needs universalism.

The pressing need of the world today is a spiritual uplift; hence the new movement arising in response to this need will also be spiritual. Its emphasis will be on altruism and selfless community service, so that one can advance into the realm of spirit in addition to that of mind and matter.

Since progress in the realm of spirit is impossible without purging oneself of self-conceit and narrow ideas, the new spiritual movement will call for world unity and an egalitarian distribution of wealth among nations. It will declare that humility and self-denial are more important for mental health and tranquility than occasionally visiting temples and uttering the name of God; it will declare that the love for God is none other than love for exploited humanity, and that this love ought to be concretely reflected in not only making sacrifices for the poor and unemployed masses of the world, but also in opposing the entrenched media of exploitation; it will declare that the solution of the world's problems lies not in amassing material wealth, but in amassing spiritual wealth.

The Renaissance and its culmination, the Protestant Reformation, gave birth to a philosophy that eventually swept aside the ideological pillars of the medieval Church and the feudal order. It was an epochal movement that preceded and then accompanied the genesis of a new social cycle in the West. Today the West as well as India is ripe for moving into yet another social cycle. The new spiritual ideology that is now in the making will also eventually dilute the current stress on materialism, self-interest and individualism. But today, thanks to science, the world has considerably shrunk; speedy means of transportation and communications have made it much smaller than the medieval world. No dynamic ideology that meets exigencies of the times stays limited to its own quarters; no cosmopolitan idea that comes with the epochal message can today remain confined to just a few regions of the world, even if they try to block its advance.

Just as rays of the rising sun pierce through the darkness of night, radiance of the spiritual sentiment will eventually pierce through roadblocks thrown in its way by any nation: it will eventually pierce through the iron curtain as well. Therefore the new movement, which I may call Spiritual Renaissance, will not only exterminate the materialistic neoclassical ideology of capitalism, but will also eventually destroy the materialistic Marxian basis of totalitarian communism. Verily, then, it will be responsible for the downfall of both capitalism and communism.

Is all this my dream? Maybe! But remember that every humanitarian institution today was yesterday's dream; and today's dream reflecting the world's present needs will become tomorrow's reality.

My discussion so far raises many questions that beg for answers. Given that the eternal rhythm of the law of social cycle cannot be broken, is humanity foredoomed to undergo the agony of ups and downs, of momentary benevolence and prolonged persecution? Are we predestined to be trampled, as in the past, under grinding wheels of oppression perpetrated in turn by the three classes of warriors, intellectuals and acquisitors? My answer is a definite no.

The Evolutionary Principle is inviolable, but by no means does it confine us to the way things have evolved over aeons. While natural laws cannot be defied, we can work within their bounds to generate a better environment—a better society. Certainly, water by its nature flows downward. But does it mean that the life-giving river flowing down the mountain to the plains cannot be dammed and harnessed to our advantage? The law of social cycle only delineates the limits which society cannot exceed, but in no way does it doom us to the long, downhill phases of social repression. We have been able to go to the moon—we certainly can devise a social order in which we all get the chance to maximize our physical, mental and spiritual potential. All this, however, takes me beyond the present volume; but I intend to return with another.

10

The Turbulent 1990s and How to Prepare for Them

Breathtaking events have swept the world since 1977, when I first wrote this book. Those were the days of soaring oil prices and the resultant economic malaise in the United States and Western Europe. Capitalism was then tottering on fluttering wings of inflation and unemployment, but communism seemed healthy and invincible.

You had to be a student of the law of social cycle to see through the inner contradiction of Marxist systems and insist that they were going to collapse in a few years. At the time of this writing, January 1990, communism is in disarray, while capitalism, by contrast, is smug and effulgent. But the law of social cycle keeps you from being fooled; believe me, both systems will be gone within the next two decades.

As the 1980s came to an end, the world was startled by the sudden fall of many communist regimes. One after another, governments in Poland, East Germany, Czechoslovakia, Hungary, and Romania were toppled by democratic forces, and with such dazzling speed that politicians in the West, especially on Capitol Hill and the White House, were totally taken by surprise. However, it came as no surprise to me, because, as you have seen in foregoing pages, I had already foreseen the demise of communism over a decade ago. Such indeed is the force and brilliance of the law of social cycle.

In order to take a panoramic look at our planet in 1990, let us examine the chart that illustrates where in successive phases of the social cycle some of the prominent societies stand today. Each

292

age has two phases, a rising period and a declining period. Along the vertical axis is measured the influence of the dominant class, and along the horizontal axis, time.

In the rising phase of any era, opposition to the dominant class slowly dies and all but disappears around the peak. At this point, leaders, having been raised in luxury, become arrogant and heartless toward the public, and opposition to their rule begins to rise. Thus begins the declining phase of the age.

To determine where a society stands in any era, it is therefore essential to examine not only the societal influence of the dominant class but also the strength or weakness of forces opposing its rule. My foregoing analysis suggests that Russia and its satellites are at the bottom of the age of warriors, ready to move into the age of intellectuals. By contrast, India and the Western world are close to a social revolution, ready to slide into the age of warriors.

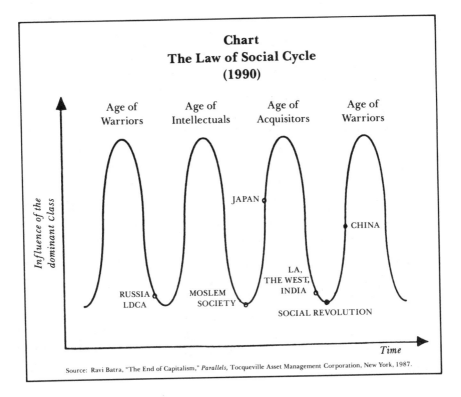

Chart
The Law of Social Cycle
(1990)

Source: Ravi Batra, "The End of Capitalism," *Parallels*, Tocqueville Asset Management Corporation, New York, 1987.

A close look at other civilizations reveals that Muslim society is now entering into the age of acquisitors or is in the early phase of the new era, whereas Japan is in the rising phase of that age. China had a social revolution in 1949 and evolved from the feudalistic age of acquisitors into an age of warriors. Latin America (referred to on chart as LA) is where India and the West are, i.e., near a social revolution, whereas the less developed countries of Africa (LDCA on chart) are at the bottom of their warrior's age, ready to march into the age of intellectuals.

Finally, most other societies, not displayed in the chart, being under the influence of Western culture, are at the bottom of their age of acquisitors and poised for various degrees of upheaval.

Thus, except for China and Japan, most societies are at the bottom of their eras, and that spells conflict between people and their dominant minorities. This is the main reason why frantic change is sweeping across the globe today. What all this means is that while the dominant class in China and Japan is not in an immediate danger, that in most other nations will be displaced by a new aristocracy. Specifically, the Soviet Union, Eastern Europe, and the less developed countries of Africa will evolve into an intellectual's democracy, whereas Western society will move into a warrior's democracy, and eventually, so will China. Muslim society will evolve into an acquisitor's democracy, whereas Japan, already moving in this system, will continue there for some time.

ACQUISITOR'S DEMOCRACY

The concepts just introduced above are new to most people. Few realize that actually three types of democracies can operate in the modern world. Until around 1700 the most common form of government on earth was monarchy, and a country's head was called a king or an emperor. The office of the monarch was more or less hereditary, as only close relatives of the king were entitled to head the kingdom. Regardless of which class dominated society, the form of government was mostly monarchical. Some rulers were powerful and absolute, and some titular and feeble, but they were all kings.

However, when Europeans began to migrate to North America, experiments began with new forms of government, with governors and legislative assemblies ruling most colonies. Similarly, in England, the parliament began to assert itself following the Glorious Revolution of 1688, and political power gravitated toward the Prime Minister. This, you may recall, heralded the West's second age of intellectuals, during which monarchy's prestige and influence declined all over Europe.

Following the First World War, monarchy all but vanished from the globe. Today Saudi Arabia is the only prominent country where a hereditary king is more than a titular ruler. The common form of government in the present-day world is republican, where not only parliaments but also heads of state are elected as prime ministers or presidents.

Thousands of years of social evolution have by now rendered monarchy obsolete. Future governments will all be republican, regardless of the character of a societal era. This does not necessarily mean that all polities will be democratic because dictatorships, as the history of communism shows, can exist even in republics.

Democracy is commonly known as a government by the people, of the people, for the people. But this is an idealistic definition which has never materialized before, and perhaps never will. This type of government is possible only if everyone is born equal in skill, vigor, and intelligence. In reality, people are born unequal, so that there will always be some kind of inequality in society. All we can hope to achieve is a social framework, where everyone is provided equal opportunities. How people utilize the opportunities will still differ; inequality will always remain, which means that one class will always be dominant over the other three even under democracies.

Essential features of a democracy are elected governments, basic freedoms, such as freedom of speech, of the press, of assembly, of location, and of religion, equality before law, and a right to have a job affording the five minimum necessities of food, clothing, shelter, education, and health care.

Since among the four classes, only three take turn to rule,

there can be three types of democracies: acquisitor's democracy, intellectual's democracy, and warrior's democracy.

The form of democracy familiar to us is an acquisitor's democracy, where money is indispensable in the electoral process. Here elected members of legislative assemblies and of the executive branch are either affluent themselves or are supported by the wealthy. Without the backing of wealth, few even dare to contest elections.

The state machinery in an acquisitor's democracy operates to further the interests of the rich; as a result the latter grow richer and richer over time at the expense of other classes. Such is the form of government prevailing today in the West, India, Japan and much of Latin America; Muslim countries, of which some are already in the age of acquisitors, will eventually evolve into this type of state.

INTELLECTUAL'S DEMOCRACY

For a democracy to exist it is not necessary that wealth play an important role or any role. People can get elected without the backing of money, as has been occurring recently in formerly Marxist dictatorships of Eastern Europe. Elections that took place in Poland and the Soviet Union in 1989 required absolutely no support from the wealthy.

A government where a majority of the elected come from the class of intellectuals, where basic freedoms are respected, and where money plays little role in the electoral process may be called an intellectual's democracy. In an acquisitor's democracy, top positions in government usually go to businessmen, bankers, merchants, and landed magnates; but in an intellectual's democracy, poets, writers, lawyers, physicians, priests, professors, scientists, economists, etc. hold the reins of government and the administration. The British parliamentary system after 1688 was an intellectual's democracy as the wealthy had no say in elections, and the legislative assembly was under the thumb of the Prime Minister.

Russia, its former satellites, and some less developed countries in Africa are soon going to evolve into intellectual's democracies.

WARRIOR'S DEMOCRACY

An elected government where money plays little role can also be a warrior's democracy. A republic, where the topmost positions of the president (or prime minister) and cabinet officers belong to the class of warriors, where human rights and freedoms are honored, and where wealth plays second fiddle to the electoral process may be called a warrior's democracy. As explained in previous chapters, the warrior mentality belongs to soldiers, policemen, firefighters, professional athletes, and skilled blue-collar workers. In a warrior's democracy, peak political influence and prestige are enjoyed by army officers, police commissioners, celebrated athletes, and accomplished workers. It is not necessary that the majority of elected legislators comes from the class of warriors; the majority may still spring from intellectuals, because the latter are mentally equipped to formulate laws, and usually do so in all eras. But the executive branch of the state is definitely in the hands of people with martial qualities.

It is interesting to note that the first president of the United States, George Washington, was an accomplished warrior. Thus American government began as a warrior's democracy, but this system was short-lived, because soon after Washington's departure, wealth began to play a dominant role in elections. Similarly, when General Dwight Eisenhower became the president in 1952, money had little significance in his election.

All this shows is that warriors can get elected in capitalist countries without any help from the wealthy, while human rights continue to be respected. What is essential for the functioning of any type of democracy is a written constitution, a free press, and an educated public conscious of its rights as well as duties. The mentality or class of the elected matters little in this regard.

The Western world, India, and most Latin American nations will soon become warrior's democracies. Note that acquisitive eras are not necessarily democratic, although most of them have decentralized governments. Similarly, not all warrior eras are dictatorial, although most have relatively centralized governments.

Future warrior eras in the West and other societies will still be centralized relative to their current acquisitive age and subsequent eras. But the centralization will be in the form of a strong executive presence. Thus the president of the United States will have much more authority than he has today, and U.S. Congress will lose some of its power. Of course, the lobbying groups patronized by the affluent will forfeit all their influence.

When money is shorn of its political power, then the age of acquisitors, and with it capitalism, will automatically die. Extensive prestige and privileges of the wealthy will also then disappear.

Is it possible for countries currently in the decadent phase of their acquisitive era to lapse into a dictatorial age of warriors? No. This is because human consciousness has evolved so much that monarchy and dictatorship have or will become mostly obsolete. The law of social cycle has the flexibility to adapt to any form of government, because the law is expressed in the form of a dominant mentality rather than dominant institutions. Within two decades we will see that the Chinese state is the only authoritarian government on earth. But by 2010, China will also evolve from a totalitarian state into a warrior's democracy, and communism will crumble there as well.

COMMUNISM'S LAST STAND

In Chapter 2, I examined Sarkar's concept of systaltic motion, which states that nothing moves in a straight line. I have earlier illustrated this concept, without actually referring to it, in Chapter 9 of my other book, *The Great Depression of 1990*. Because of systaltic motion, everything moves in an up-and-down fashion. In the rising phase of any entity, the movement is in terms of a cycle even though the trend is upward. Similarly in the declining phase also, motion is cyclical even though the trend is negative.

Since nothing moves in a straight line, the downfall of communism, already begun in the Soviet bloc, will not occur in a linear fashion. Communism in Russia is likely to recover to make one last stand before it disappears. The Soviet Union is a vast amalgam of many principalities and ethnic groups that have been held together by brute force. The current Soviet president and party secretary, Mikhail Gorbachev, an intellectual, has since 1987, followed a policy of glasnost, or openness and tolerance, which is mainly responsible for the fall of communism in Eastern Europe. He is the first Soviet head of state to encourage an open discussion of massive economic and social ills facing Russia for some time. And for his unprecedented and courageous efforts, *Time* magazine honored him as Man of the Decade for the 1980s.

But Gorbachev's policy of openness has the potential to unleash a pandora's box of ethnic minorities that have long been restive under dictatorial rule. They are beginning to simmer and some of them such as Armenia and Azerbaijan are on the verge of revolt. However, Gorbachev, as with President Abraham Lincoln in the United States in 1861, does not want to see a disintegration of the state. In the end, he may be left with no choice except to suppress assertive nationalities with military force.

Another possibility is that Soviet hard-liners, party elites, and army officers who have lost out in the recent realignment of power, could take advantage of growing unrest and economic stagnation and overthrow Gorbachev in a military coup. Communism could then return with a new totalitarian face, producing the old Soviet-style bloodshed and violence.

Thus there is a strong possibility that one of these scenarios will take place in the near future. But this will only temporarily arrest the demise of Marxism. Even when communism recovers to make a last stand, it will prove to be a rearguard action, delaying but not stopping the inevitable. The downfall of communism has already begun, and the system will breathe its last at the turn of the century. Few will mourn it when it dies.

CAN CAPITALISM BE SAVED?

Let us now turn to the question of capitalism, its current state of health and what is in store for it in the 1990s. Can capitalism be saved, and should it be saved?

Capitalism and communism are creeds that have globally competed for the heart and soul of people ever since Marx wrote his *Das Capital* in 1867. The two systems have had a checkered career. During the 1930s, capitalism was on the verge of collapse because of the Great Depression, while communism offered hope to the starving masses. Today communism is crumbling, while the sun of capitalism by contrast seems to be brighter than ever before. Isn't this the finest hour for the West?

The answer is a definite no. The collapse of the Marxist regimes, which are turning to democracy and free enterprise, creates few immediate opportunities to other nations. True, it is a triumph of Western ideas and institutions. But with the Soviet bloc economies in a shambles, the crumbling state of communism, in desperate need of aid itself, can offer no help to capitalism, which has plenty of skeletons in its own closet. Capitalist ills are internal, not external.

Modern capitalist economies display three important features that we should explore at this point. One is competitive capitalism, which prevails when there is a large number of producers and/or sellers in a majority of industries. Capitalism becomes monopolistic when most industries have few operating firms or sellers. This is the second feature. The third feature is that capitalist societies are dominated by acquisitors, whose life-styles plant the virus of materialism in the entire society.

Among the three features, competitive capitalism is the only one conforming with free enterprise. Among various acquisitive societies, Japan is one country that comes closest to a free-enterprise nation; others are characterized by monopolistic capitalism. Take, for instance, Japan's auto industry, which has at least ten firms in operation. By contrast, the much larger U.S. automobile industry had only four major producers until 1980 and has only three domestic companies at this time. Thus, contrary to long-standing propaganda of acquisitors, America does not have free enterprise; instead, it has a monopolistic enterprise. To be sure, some U.S. industries are indeed competitive. They include agriculture, some services, and retailing, but a large majority of firms are monopolistic.

To the question of should capitalism be saved? The answer is, yes and no. That part of capitalism pertaining to free enterprise can and ought to be saved. But the other two facets, acquisitiveness and monopoly, cannot and ought not be saved. This is because the last two features have always been exploitative of laborers, and soon they will produce misery for every class except the acquisitors. Salvaging free enterprise, of course, is a worthy cause, because it leads to efficiency and lowers inequality. But free enterprise, as I have argued in *Surviving the Great Depression of 1990* cannot coexist with extreme concentration of wealth prevailing in the West today.

Since free enterprise comprises a small fraction of Western economies, modern capitalism or the present-day acquisitive age cannot be rescued. This is simply the dictate of the law of social cycle. In order to salvage whatever little free enterprise remains, the influence of money has to be eliminated from politics.

History tells us that when leaders turn ultra-acquisitive and insensitive to the plight of the poor, economic conditions become so bad that revolution is the ultimate result. This happened recently in the Soviet bloc and will happen wherever tyranny reigns.

Consider, for instance, the behavior of U.S. Congress since 1977 regarding its salary increase. Since then, in the name of attracting high talent to the government, legislators have been periodically awarding themselves raises amounting to thousands of dollars a year. Parliamentary procedures have been so manipulated that no lawmaker is usually required to vote on the proposed income hike.

In 1987, the legislators voted to deny themselves a pay raise, but a day after the raise had already become law. Now this is duplicity and real chicanery. In January 1989, they sought to reward themselves with a raise of as much as 50%, again without casting a vote on the proposal. This time they failed, because the whole country was up in arms against such an open insult to people's intelligence.

However, you have to give high marks to the lower House for persistence. In November 1989, the House members voted to grant themselves a salary increase of 40% spread over two years, although the Senate accepted only a 10% hike.

What is particularly galling about the Congressional sleight of hand in pay raise is that it has been done again and again. Each time this happens, there is a public outcry, some columnists denounce the lawmakers in their columns, comedians make fun of the legislators, and then everything is forgiven and forgotten. Is this democracy in action? What all this shows is that Congress, drunk with power, has absolutely no fear of voters. Either that, or the legislators think they can fool all people all the time. So far, indeed they have succeeded.

Yet Congress, which raised its salary along with other perks many times during the 1980s, could not bring itself to increase the minimum wage in the entire decade. The lowest-paid workers, some five million of them, lost 40% in purchasing power owing to price hikes in the same period, while top income earners wallowed in luxury, and Congressmen themselves basked in affluence. A lawyer in Houston earned $400 million in 1989, while Michael Milken set an all-time record by earning $550 million in 1987, a year in which the number of the homeless also set a record.

Is this free enterprise or madness? No, this is monopolistic capitalism or the decadent phase of the age of acquisitors. Is this system worth saving? For an answer, talk to the six million families living below the official poverty line, or the two million homeless shivering in the arctic cold, or the 35 million Americans with no health insurance at all.

Another instance of the government's perfidy comes from the Social Security tax which has been raised fifteen times in the past twenty-seven years. Everyone knows that the burden of this tax is the heaviest on the poor and the middle class. The maximum Social Security tax on an individual was $374 in 1970 and soared to $3,924 by 1990, a whopping jump of 950%.

The steepest climb in the Social Security tax occurred during the 1980s, a decade in which the Reagan-Bush administration twice awarded boondoggles to the rich by cutting top income tax rates in 1981 and 1986. As a result those earning over $200,000 are now taxed at a rate of 28%, whereas a couple with a taxable income of $72,000 pays a 33% rate. All this was done in the name of tax reform. Never before in American history has there occurred such a massive transfer of the tax burden from the affluent to the poor.

But this is not all. With such heavy tax rates, the Social Security program is earning a growing surplus, which is now completely used up in financing the federal budget deficit that was initially caused by the income-tax cuts of 1981. The outrage of this all is evident to most Americans and columnists. So what did Congress do at the end of 1989 to reduce the budget deficit? It raised the maximum Social Security tax for 1990 by $69 on top of the rise of $250 that had been legislated in 1983.

In spite of the growing public outcry against the state welfare for the rich, President George Bush proposed to cut the capital gains tax, which is paid mostly by the affluent. This is heaping outrage upon outrage.

There is thus a gaping chasm between the words and actions of the politicians. While their hearts bleed for the poor, their pockets overflow with money. While the rest of society toils hard to make both ends meet, they shrink not from extorting one perquisite after another. Why? Are they blind to their constituencies, to their conscience, to the widespread public resentment to their self-serving actions? No. But they are helpless before their avarice. They are simply masters of double-talk, hypocrisy, and deception.

Now you tell me. When the so-called leaders become insensitive and heartless to the needs of the poor, the handicapped, the downtrodden, how long can their system survive? The extreme concentration of political power in the Soviet bloc courted the downfall of communism; similarly, the extreme concentration of wealth in the West will invite the downfall of capitalism.

Will capitalism make a last stand much like communism? No, because, as I predicted in *The Great Depression of 1990*, capitalism has already made its last stand in the 1980s. The decline of capitalism actually began in the 1970s as a result of sharp increases in the price of oil, but, in view of the law of systaltic motion, it recovered to have a last hurrah in the following decade. From now on, the system will go nowhere but downhill until it vanishes at the turn of the century.

There is, however, one way in which my views have changed. When I wrote this book in 1977, I was uncertain about the possibility of peaceful upheaval in the West. Having seen firsthand how momentous change occurred in 1989 without gore in most Soviet bloc countries, which have a history of terrible violence against their citizens, I am now optimistic that social revolution in the West will be nonviolent. Class conflict will be there, but hopefully it will not accompany bloodshed.

PREPARING FOR THE 1990s

The 1990s will go down in history as a time of chaos, confusion, and trouble. In 1980, I had predicted that after a decade of boom, speculation, and euphoria in the 1980s, the world would be afflicted by a massive depression beginning in 1990. Each depression starts as a recession, which, in the presence of vast debt, turns into a financial nightmare. Therefore, 1990 will be a year of recession, which will then turn into a depression by the end of 1991.

However, the 1990s will be more than just a decade of economic catastrophe; troubles will afflict many facets of life. This will be a decade of social, economic, and political turmoil. Riots, looting, hunger, demonstrations, crime, drugs, environmental disasters will bedevil almost the whole world except China and Japan. This is because except for these two countries, almost every other society is now at the bottom of its particular era, ready to move into a new age (see chart). Change does not come without a fight. Most nations are thus poised for conflict and a major overhaul of their systems.

It is then imperative that you prepare yourself physically, mentally, and spiritually for a variety of cataclysms. Trouble is unavoidable because ultra-selfish leaders world-wide have already done their job. They have generated such inequities and exploitation in post-war years that looming catastrophes can be averted only if they abdicate their power. This they will never do; so you have to take defensive measures now and in coming years.

FINANCIAL PREPARATION

Taking defensive financial action now could save you much pain in the near future, this is a part of what may be called physical preparation. I have already given extensive financial advice in my previous books, *The Great Depression of 1990*, and *Surviving the Great Depression of 1990*. Most of that advice is still good.

All I can add here is: be as liquid as possible; avoid all stocks, bonds, and other financial instruments in 1990, and spread your money in a number of banks on my list available in *Surviving the Great Depression of 1990*. Don't take any risk until the dust settles.

The world is on the verge of chaos at this time, and utmost caution is advisable in your finances. If I knew when and exactly where trouble will strike in 1990, I could pinpoint the place and the month in which to take action. But I don't. All I feel is that trouble is not too far off. That is why you have to be extremely careful now.

If you can afford it, buy some gold. It's selling at a reasonable price of around $400 per ounce. You may allocate as much as 5% of your wealth to this precious metal at this time. If the price of gold falls, then buy even more.

Be extra careful about your health, which is always precious, but more now than ever before. You cannot afford to be ill, or be laid off because of sickness. Too much is riding on your vigor and sanity.

If you smoke, drink, or take drugs, this is the best time for you to quit these habits, and put all the money so saved in your bank. You must avoid these poisons and go on a program of regular exercise. Health is always important, but never so important as at this time.

MENTAL PREPARATION

Physical preparation will take you only so far. To face pressures coming up soon, you will also have to be mentally tough and strong. You perhaps have heard about the power of positive thinking but never really experimented with it. Believe me it really works especially when you need it most.

Your mind can be either your friend or an enemy; it all depends on how you use it or control it. Ordinarily, when things are going well, the mind tends to be euphoric; it wants to brag about its success and gloat before others. But the real test comes when things go wrong, because the same euphoric mind can turn into your enemy.

It is one thing to be upset by adversity, and quite another to be depressed by it. A strong mind fights negative thoughts that produce mental depression. Negative thinking can compound what may be just simple troubles of daily life. Life has both roses and thorns; nothing in this world lasts forever. The concept of systaltic motion suggests that good is followed by bad, and bad by good. But it is human nature to be euphoric, arrogant, and vain in good times, thinking that the excitement will last forever.

Similarly, in bad times people tend to believe that sunny days will never appear again. While arrogance and vanity should be avoided, so should negative thinking that troubles will endure for good.

Troubles are looming in the near future, and they will last a few years. No matter how hopeless your situation, you should not lose hope; because nothing in this world is ever lasting. Bertrand Russell, a famous British mathematician and philosopher, used to say that one should never entertain negative thoughts even if one is struck by lightning. As long as you live to tell your experience, there should be optimism. Be grateful that you lived.

Suppose someone cheats you, or you become a victim of a heinous crime. You should tell yourself that the sun will still rise; the world will still go on; the moon will still circle the earth. Tell yourself that it is not the end of the world; that you are just a tiny speck in the vast panorama of the universe, which is still there. What you have lost, you can recover in time. This is what Bertrand Russell taught his students and it is great therapy in adversity.

Negative thoughts, which sap our energy, should always be countered by positive thoughts, which reinvigorate us and strengthen our resolve. Whenever troubles loom and you tend to be depressed, you should tell yourself, "It is bad enough that I have suffered a loss, why should I further hurt myself by getting depressed." Believe me, worry never solves any problem. Only action and positive thinking do.

This brings me to another aspect of the mental preparation, namely action. If you want to achieve something great, then be relentlessly engaged in action, which will not only give you the satisfaction of facing your problems head on, it will also keep you away from negative thoughts. In this universe, each and every action has an equal and opposite reaction. No action is ever useless; it may not yield fruit right away, but it must produce dividends some day. This is the ironclad law of nature, which operates to produce a balance among entities. Thus, the fruit must appear one day to balance out the atmospheric ripple created by each action.

Therefore, you should be always engaged in action without worrying about the reward. In fact, you should not even think about the reward, because such thinking retards your speed and energy to make an effort. Often even constant action over long periods yields no fruit; still you should not give up. Because the fruit must come, and when it does, it will surpass your expectations.

I say all this from personal experience. I wrote *The Great Depression of 1990* in 1983, and sent the manuscript to 50 publishers. When they all turned it down, I went ahead and published it myself. True, I had to break my back in the process, but I kept working despite all odds against me. The final result was that my book became a number-one *New York Times* bestseller, and remained on that list for 53 weeks. Such is indeed the cumulative force of incessant action.

Remember that I wrote the present book in 1977, and its reward is coming in 1990. People ignored this book and laughed at its title, because communism appeared unshakable to them at the time. No one is laughing now, as the Berlin Wall has already crumbled. You never know when your efforts may be fruitful.

Thus, be constantly engaged in action especially in hard times. Even when failure is certain, you should still make efforts, because you never know when the fruit may materialize. Moreover, the reward is not in our hand, but action certainly is. So do what is under your control, and the reward will one day come automatically. Never fear failure.

In short, mental preparation for coming troubles requires positive thinking and constant pursuit of action, which will keep you out of psychic depression.

SPIRITUAL PREPARATION

Positive thinking and unrelenting efforts require an enormous amount of mental energy. Countering the negative flow of mind, especially when one is under prolonged stress, is like swimming upstream in a river. Mental preparation of the type I have suggested is easier said than done. True, it is a foolproof path to success and achievement, yet it is perhaps the hardest path to cross. Limitless effort requires limitless mental energy, which comes only from practical spirituality.

What is practical spirituality? I have mentioned earlier in Chapter 3 that human thirst for happiness is unquenchable; everyone is after unlimited happiness, but the irony is that in pursuit of this goal most people ceaselessly run after material objects, which are all limited. We seek infinite joy, yet constantly pursue money, which, being finite, can never fulfill our longing.

It is this chasm between longing and materialist actions that creates misery in everyone's life. Infinite happiness springs only from a pursuit of the infinite entity, whom we commonly call God. The word "God" is actually an acronym for generator (G), operator (O), and destroyer (D). Practical spirituality means performing those actions that please God, our creator.

Modern intellectuals have literally banished God from their thinking and vocabulary. Having seen how the priesthood and religious leaders have exploited humanity all through history in the name of God, the intelligentsia have decided that God simply does not exist, or that He is not worth pursuing.

How can this be true? How can this vast universe, with countless currents crisscrossing in all directions, operate in an orderly fashion without the guidance of a supreme intellect? The cosmos is stable, because a supreme being runs it. Otherwise there would be utter confusion and chaos, and life would never come into existence. A city needs a mayor to maintain order; a state needs a governor, a country needs a head. Doesn't the universe need a chief to remain orderly? It is as simple as that. God is the sovereign of this vast universe; He must exist, otherwise we will not.

That God exists cannot be disputed logically. The question is whether He is worth pursuing and contemplating. It is true that religion in the past, and even today, has shed torrents of innocent blood. Quite often the priesthood instigated sanguinary wars of religion in which millions lost their lives. I am well aware of the fierce clerical face that tried to spread the divine mercy of God with fire and sword, and I have pinpointed numerous instances of such tyranny in previous chapters. Yet banishing God from our lives is to turn away from the truth. This is not the right way to deal with priestly perfidy.

If the intellectuals and the press will have nothing to do with God, then who would investigate the clergy and hold it accountable for its actions that victimize the gullible? Don't forget the recent debauchery, sex scandals, and money demands of Jim Bakker and Jimmy Swaggart and thousands like them in the past. No institution with a vast influence on people should be exempt from public scrutiny. It is the media's job to probe the priesthood as assiduously as secular organizations.

In any case, spirituality is not the same thing as the popular conception of religion, which is a compilation of narrow ideas and rituals designed to perpetuate the hegemony of clerics in society. Religion divides people, spirituality unites them; religion inflicts wounds on the gullible and the innocent, spirituality applies a healing balm.

The message of spirituality is simply this. God, being our creator, is our Father (or Mother), and He loves us all as His children. In age, He is even older than the universe, and we, being much younger in age and intellect, are like His newborn babies. Therefore our relationship with God should be similar to that between a baby and its parents.

Parents know what the baby needs and, even though

unasked, they offer it loving care. In fact, the baby has no idea of what is good or bad for itself. The parents automatically protect it from troubles. That is exactly how God feels about us. Having created us, He loves us tenderly and will take care of all our needs, provided we behave like babies toward Him, and perform our actions with a view to pleasing Him.

A baby loves its parents dearly; all its attention is focused on them; without them it cries, but feels safe and assured in their presence. That is exactly the way we should feel toward God, our true Father.

No father is happy when his children fight, or if some of his children wallow in luxury while others hunger. The same way God is also unhappy with man-made wars, inequities and cruelties. Therefore to please our Father, we should not only focus our attention on Him like a baby, but also oppose social oppression and tyranny of the dominant class. We should not let others exploit us in His name.

Remember that we are babies only before our divine Father; not before others, with whom we have to behave in a practical and proper way. Dependence on the Father does not mean parasitic dependence on others, but, of course, love for God signifies love and service for all His children.

Why does God permit wars and social oppression? Why doesn't He intervene and spare us from all the miseries? The reason is that He is totally impartial, and lets us learn from our errors. He intervenes in our life only if we genuinely promise to behave like true babies toward Him.

This is the simple message of practical spirituality. There is no divisiveness, narrowness, and bigotry in it. In short, practical spirituality signifies that we should love God like a baby loves its parents, behave practically and properly towards others, and oppose social injustices to create a better life for all His children.

A true spiritualist always addresses God as his Father. To him, God is not a stranger, nor the lord of the universe, but his very own, his true friend and well-wisher. The spiritualist feels that God is his beloved, the very essence of his life, his closest relative. He lives, breathes, and joyfully sings devotional songs with his divine Father. Never does he ask any favors from God, nor does he praise Him for His magnificent creations. Does a baby request favors from its parents? Or does it try to please them with flattery or praise? You do that to strangers, not to your own father.

As you can see, spirituality is different from religion as we know it. In my childhood, a priest in India taught me how to pray to God and worship Him. The priest instructed me to tell God that He is the Lord of the universe, that He has created a vast number of wonderful things and given us a comfortable life; that He is omnipotent, omnipresent and omniscient. The priest ended by saying that I should thank God for all the gifts I had received from Him. This is popular religion. Not once did the priest suggest that I should love God as my own parent.

Suppose your dad visits you from out of town, and you start telling him "O Dad, how great you are, you are a millionaire with a big account in your bank, you have given me so much money and always taken care of my needs, and I heartily thank you for these." How formal and ridiculous does it sound. Your dad will be suspicious and think that you want something from Him. He will say, "Why are you talking like a stranger? So what if I did all these things for you; I was just doing my nature."

But chances are that when your dad pays you a visit after a long time, you will be excited; you will hug him and say, "Dad, I miss you; Daddy, I love you." Such is the relationship between a true devotee and his God.

Once I was very sick in my childhood. My family priest offered to pray to God for my recovery and health. My parents accepted his offer and paid him his customary fee. He sat on my bed, closed his eyes in an earnest way, raised his face toward the sky and began to speak loudly. For about five minutes, he requested God to reduce my fever and help me recover from my pneumonia.

After he left, I vomited profusely and my fever actually went up. A month passed before I fully recovered, using proper medicine. That priest did me a great disservice, because he shook my faith in God. I said to myself, if God did not listen to this noble priest and my fever actually rose, what chance do I have to speak to Him? Later, I decided that the priest was a phony. He himself had told me that God knows everything; yet his prayer for my recovery implied that in my case God had made a mistake and that I should get a quick cure whether or not I deserved it.

My dear friends, this is religion, and it offers no help to anyone, for our Father, Who loves us all so intensely, doesn't like to be told He has made mistakes. Would you like it if you were all-knowing? God is not won by flattery, but by love for Him and service to others. Those who pray to Him for favors either for themselves or for others do not serve Him; they actually want service from Him. And how can God oblige them when they behave like strangers and not like His babies? This is simple common sense.

What does spirituality do for us? I have talked earlier about virtues of positive thinking that most psychologists and doctors applaud. Why do they think so highly of it? This is because human mind tends to acquire the qualities of what it regularly contemplates. If a person mostly thinks he is weak, unable to tackle his problems, is afraid of failure expected from any project, then he will remain weak throughout his life. On the other hand, if he constantly counters his negative thoughts by suggesting to himself that he is strong and vigorous, is capable of achieving great things, has superb health, and will never rest until he has accomplished something, then he will gradually grow strong and successful. Thinking can make a person great or insignificant.

When a person falls in love with his true Father, he regularly thinks about the infinite, and begins to tap a vast reservoir of energy hidden inside him. Contemplation of the limitless not only gives him a taste of unlimited joy, but also limitless energy to do good to himself and others. In time, as he gets immersed in thoughts of the Divine, he literally becomes a powerhouse.

Since mind tends to become what it largely contemplates, the spiritualist's mental framework also begins to expand. A true devotee of God has no narrowness, fanaticism, and bigotry in his heart, as his mind tends to attain tender and saintly qualities. Spirituality can thus free us from all our complexes such as fear, greed, temper, pride, vanity, and feelings of inferiority or superiority toward others. Once freed from these complexes, the devotee never gets depressed, no matter how huge is his loss.

Spirituality brings deep internal beatitude. Once a person's minimum needs are satisfied, his happiness depends totally on his thinking, or on his own outlook. Mind can be our friend or enemy. But for most people, it is an enemy. Often, some of those who have AIDS, cancer, drug or alcohol addiction, did it to themselves. They hurt from self-inflicted wounds.

Most people suffer because their mind bugs them; it won't let them be content with what they have. Spirituality satisfies the limitless thirst of the human heart, and the mind of the devotee bugs him no more.

Spirituality and its techniques are the priceless treasure of humanity. Our divine Father is our most precious possession. His fragrance can illuminate every heart. Yet people today have forfeited their birth right to be with their eternal beloved. They feel embarrassed to talk about their maker. Secular intellectuals scoff at the very mention of God, whereas priests prey upon the gullible in His name.

In the absence of spirituality, society worldwide is going to the dogs, decadence and degeneration abound, and crime rules the streets. Some parents are killing their children, and some children their parents. Torture and mayhem are the order of the day; drugs, prostitution and pornography are pervasive, and soon there will be a carnage of poverty around the globe. What a price humanity is paying for the loss of true spirituality.

Is there any scope for prayer in spirituality? Yes, there is. Devotion is not easy to achieve. Believing in God is one thing, falling in love with Him is another. For most, it is even hard to conceive this concept, let alone comprehend it. Devotion comes only after you intensely pray to God for it. This is the proper way to pray: "O my Father, grant me pure devotion for your lotus feet. O my Father, help me fall in love with you. O my Father, help me get infatuated with you. I seek nothing else but guidance from you."

One should repeat this prayer hundreds of times a day. This is the beginning of spirituality, which also has some other powerful techniques; but this is a good starting point. Whoever prays in this way is able to face all his troubles without falling apart. He is then truly happy. This, to my mind, is the best preparation for coming cataclysms. You will have to draw on every ounce of your energy and inner strength to live through the '90s. But then will follow a wonderful socioeconomic system unmatched before in compassion, tranquility and prosperity—a system free from the evils and horrors of today.

A GRASS-ROOTS MOVEMENT

I made a statement in the introductory chapter that I wrote this book to stir the public conscience against the excesses and cruelties of capitalism and communism. If you want to help me fight injustice, then I invite you to join a grass-roots movement I started in 1987. The name of this movement is SAD or Stop Another Depression. For more information, send a self-addressed stamped envelope to:

> SAD, c/o Ravi Batra
> Post Office Box 741806
> Dallas, Texas 75374
>
> Phone: (214) 699-3838

I am also working with an educational organization called Proutist Universal, which publishes a quarterly magazine *Prout Journal,* to which I regularly contribute articles. If you have any questions about this book, or about my financial, mental, and spiritual advice given here and elsewhere, you can write to:

> Proutist Universal
> 1354 Montague Street, N.W.
> Washington, DC 20011
>
> Phone: (202) 829-2278

I will try to answer your questions in my articles appearing in the *Prout Journal.*

My recent books have all dealt with the writings of P.R. Sarkar. His works are also available from the address in Washington DC.

Sarkar, Toynbee, and Marx

In attempting to unravel the mysteries of history, in imputing order to the seemingly disorderly currents in the human past, in reaching out to the future, Sarkar has joined the august company of Toynbee, Marx, Hegel, Spengler, Wells, among many others; and in erudition and breadth of vision, he is not excelled by any. Quite a few scholars have endeavored to detect in the chaos of history a certain rhythm, an imperceptible harmony that complies with certain natural laws, but their peers, suspicious of anything conferring rigor on past trends, have criticized and scoffed at them. Sarkar's contribution, however, belongs to a different genus. It is immune at least to those strictures to which other theories of historical determinism have been subjected.

It is important to see where the law of social cycle stands in relation to well-known explanations of history. For the sake of comparison with Sarkar's thought, I briefly appraise the views of Marx and Toynbee—two intellectual giants who, in terms of learning and catholicity of thinking, stand in a luminous class of their own. Both men attempted to solve the riddle of history—Marx through deductive reasoning, Toynbee through "scientific" empiricism. Their contributions, it turns out, are two separate pieces that fit, somewhat loosely, into Sarkar's conception of history.

THE MARXIAN VISION OF HISTORY

Karl Marx is regarded as one of the most influential historians and economists of all times. Today, through his materialistic conception of humanity, he commands from his followers a reverence that human beings usually reserve for sages—those who transcend all matter. Marx himself was contemptuous of religion; today his following adores him with a devotion that smacks ironically of fanatic religious ardor.

In order to grasp the Marxian dynamics of society, it is necessary to proceed in steps, which, though seemingly disjointed, are all interwoven in a masterly work of economics and history. Marx sought to explain the historical process through a logical argument, through dialectic, a method of inquiry that he borrowed from Hegel. However, unlike Hegel, who regarded humans as sensuous beings, Marx believed in the materialistic existence of men and women. To Hegel sense-perception was the basis of all social activity, whereas to Marx the social change was rooted in material forces, in the essentials of survival which must preempt every other human concern. "Men," said Marx, "must be able to live in order to 'make history'" [3, p. 419]. Therefore, the way individuals make a living, the means and techniques of production must be the main catalyst of social dynamics; productive and hence economic activity, more than anything else, must be the prime mover of society.

Material forces, however, affix their stamp on history in a certain rhythm. Change occurs in society because of contradictions in prevailing ideology, in its social, economic, and political order; the contradictions arise inevitably from antagonism among social classes which themselves are determined by material elements—property relations. Specifically, class divisions in society are based on who holds the property and who does not, who is the proprietor and who must be the servitor.

The ideology acceptable to the dominant class is called "thesis," that of the humbler and opposing class "antithesis." The inexorable clash between these two gives rise to another system called "synthesis." This is the so-called doctrine of "dialectical materialism"—"dialectical" because it rests on logical deduction, "materialism" because the change is alleged to stem from material forces.

Thus to Marx, economic activity or "mode of production" forms the social "structure," upon which rests the "superstructure" representing the non-economic elements such as religion, law, political institutions and so on. Not that the economic element is the only factor that propels the engine of society; nor that the edifice resting on an economic footing cannot initiate any movement of its own. But the structure exerts a vastly greater influence than the superstructure. And indeed any momentous event in society, a major overhaul of its institutions, can spring only from a crack in its underlying foundation.

Such, to Marx, is the potency of the mode of production which comprises "forces" as well as "social relations" of production. Among forces of production are included technical knowledge concerned with the advancement of capital resources—such as machinery—as well as other productive factors, such as land and labor. Social relations, by comparison, involve the institutions of property, exchange, income distribution and the consumption of goods. The superstructure includes the rest—art, religion, ethics, ideology, family, government.

Marx also details the process that initiates, feeds and regulates social dynamics. First, some powerful change occurs in the forces of production, which, as a result of changes in population, inventions and education among others, are subject to a state of perpetual motion. Second, this change gives rise to fissures in the social relations of production. Finally, the slipping foundations of the economic structure eventually shake up the superstructure, and then the whole legal, philosophical and political environment gets a new face. A new social order, with a structure and superstructure of its own, is thus born.

Social change, however, will never occur if society were not divided between hostile groups with irreconcilable interests and aspirations; but the conflicting social divisions are themselves the product of economic conditions, namely property relations among human beings. As mentioned before, Marx defines social classes in terms of those who own property and those who do not. Therefore as long as groups can be identified on the basis of their possessions, class conflict, sometimes smoldering and covert but more often overt and violent, is inevitable; and so is the transformation in society. Thus the eternal clash between socioeconomic groups occasionally leads to convulsions in the economic structure and superstructure, and in this way a new society, a synthesis, comes into being.

It is only after the institution of private property is annihilated, and society becomes classless, that humanity can enjoy a reprieve from incessant social strife. Such a society can evolve only under communism where all property is jointly owned by workers. There the community reaches its pinnacle from which there is no demeaning fall.

This, from start to finish, is the Marxian theory of historical change. It is ingrained, as stated before, in the exigencies of physical survival, which to human beings must take precedence over every other affair. It seeks to expound the entire historical process in terms of this simple, and perhaps naïve, materialistic notion.

This vision of social dynamics was utilized by Marx to explain historical change in pre-capitalist as well as capitalist societies. Prior to capitalism, the economic environment had the characteristics, in Marx's words, of "free petty landownership and of communal landed property," [2 p. 67]. In this system, which perhaps first evolved as the Oriental Commune in Asia, land was privately as well as communally owned. The people toiled on earth mainly for subsistence, for bare existence of the self and the family. Evidently Marx is here referring to Sarkar's early warrior society of the Neolithic age (as described in preceding chapters) where human beings, after abandoning cave and nomadic life, had taken up agriculture as well as tribal living under the stewardship of warriors.

In the Asian tribal organization, land was owned by the whole community, and for all practical purposes there was no private property. Part of individual labor or the surplus product was retained for family survival, whereas the other part was set apart for rites and various communal activities. This very surplus, according to Marx, gave rise to the power of landlords; and thus was born the institution of serfdom as well as the two hostile camps in the community.

The second form of pre-capitalist society, the state owner-ship system, was organized on lines similar to the first except that the central authority now exercised more power. This system, which at times was somewhat more democratic and at others more autocratic than the first, was founded on kinship as well as con-quest. It displayed greater unity and discipline. As population increased and political authority became centralized, various cit-ies emerged as nuclei of political power. The economic basis also then shifted from the land to the city, especially when external trade came into being.

At the same time, private property came into vogue, as was the case with the Romans and Greeks; no longer was the individ-ual a co-owner of land. However, since the state rested on the foundation of conquest, those who were defeated had to accept slavery. Therefore the impetus to maintain a communal order remained, and it sprang from the need to obtain allegiance from the slaves who were made to toil on the state-owned lands. Thus in the state ownership system communal property coexisted with private property, and there emerged internal schisms and class conflicts of all sorts—between towns and villages, between land-lords and merchants, between citizens and slaves.

The third type of pre-capitalistic community was the feudal estate ownership wherein vast tracts of property were owned chiefly, as in medieval Europe, by private landlords. Here land was the principal source or "force" of production, the "social rela-tion" of significance was naturally one that existed between own-ers of land (the feudal lords and barons) and farmworker (serfs). The social superstructure corresponding to such economic struc-ture was the feudal state. Production was carried on by the serfs, but the fruit of their labor was enjoyed by their masters. Here again communal and private ownership coexisted, but the commu-nal landholding had lost much of its earlier importance. No longer did it form the basis of state power.

These then are the main economic systems that preceded capitalism. Though arising at different points in time, the pre-capitalist societies had some features in common. First, their economic base rested on land and agricultural production which was carried out mainly for subsistence and not for exchange in a market; second, labor was not a commodity, as the worker did not sell it in any market for money. However, capitalism, the analysis of which engaged the bulk of Marx's copious intellect, is distinguished precisely by institutions that were nonexistent before. But even though the institutions are new, the class conflict is not. In fact, to Marx the same class warfare that tore the earlier systems apart will one day destroy capitalism as well. "The history of all hitherto existing society," proclaimed Marx in an oft-quoted line, "is the history of class struggles" [4, p. 13].

How do class divisions arise under capitalism even though it has little in common with earlier systems? Put another way, what are the contradictions of capitalism? Marx went to great length to answer these questions which had not yet been raised by his peers, the so-called classical economists. But Marx, with his vast mental horizon, foresaw what his contemporaries were unable, or unwilling, to comprehend.

Despite contradictions of its own, the Marxian contribution to the understanding of how capitalism works is phenomenal. His critique of the capitalist system is pungent and at times misleading, but he generated many provocative ideas which Keynes later used, quite ironically, to rescue the very system that according to Marx would one day end up in smoke. Keynes today, despite contradictions of his own, is regarded by many as the most prominent economist of the present century, but it is to Marx's credit that he anticipated Keynes in many ways.

There are various strands in the Marxian prognosis of capitalism, all intertwined with each other. Its basic ingredients are the two hostile classes: capitalists or bourgeoisie who own the means of production and financial capital, and workers who in exchange for money wages sell their labor to capital-owners. Both groups are interested in maximizing their incomes, but in this endless pursuit the property-owners have a decided advantage over the laborers or the proletariat, for the latter are totally dependent on the former for employment.

Labor is worth nothing if it is not in demand by the capitalist, who, of course, hires a worker only if some profit can be made. Furthermore, it is in the interest of the manufacturer to set as low a wage as possible, approximating to subsistence level, enough to ensure a steady supply of labor, and no more. Thus the working class has a precarious existence on two counts. First, the livelihood of each worker depends not only on individual labor but also on the unreliable capitalist who can sacrifice him like a pawn in the game of chess, provided the profit conditions so dictate. Second, the level of the wage rate is also at the mercy of the manufacturer whose interest, by nature, is inimical to that of the worker. Herein lies the inexorable source of social conflict.

During the days of Marx, capitalism was still in its infancy. It was characterized by what economists commonly call perfect competition, wherein so many manufacturers compete with each other for the sales of a product that none can control its price. Under such conditions not much profit can be made—provided capital is regarded as a contributor to production—and the entrepreneur's own behavior leads to maximum productive efficiency as well as the highest possible wage rate. This is the consensus among economists today. Marx perhaps had some inkling of this argument, but he wanted to show that the working class is exploited under all forms of capitalism—competitive or otherwise. He maintained that the contribution of capital as a factor of production is zero. In justification he provided an elaborate argument, but in so doing was trapped in his own labyrinth.

Marx, a champion of the labor theory of value, asserted that labor is the only source of production. Not that he was the first to make this claim; before him such eminent economists as Adam Smith and David Ricardo had argued in the same vein. Marx believed that the value of a commodity is determined by the labor time needed in its production. To value he assigned many concepts. "Use Value" denotes the quality or capacity of a commodity satisfying human wants; "exchange value" is the rate at which the commodity, possessing use value, exchanges for money, and so on. However, the relationship between the abstract Marxian value (or values) and the more visible concept of market prices is at best unclear, and at worse inconsistent.

Marx ruled out all other factors in the creation of value. Although natural resources could be brushed aside easily, for after all without the helping human hand they can make no contribution to production, capital, being a produced good, proved to be more troublesome. Marx argued that a machine incorporates past or "dead" labor, so that its value is determined by the past labor time embodied in it. In other words, capital itself contributes nothing, for the only source of all production is labor— past and present.

One major difficulty with this view is that capital goods may command prices that, being dependent on demand and supply conditions in capital markets, will generally differ from the past labor time going into their production. Moreover, current machines were produced not only from labor but also from past capital goods, which themselves embodied some labor time. How can one be sure that the value of the current capital stock corresponds to a whole series of past labor time that once entered into its production?

Actually the labor theory of value is not crucial in the demonstration of capitalistic exploitation of labor, provided goods are produced under conditions of pure monopoly, oligopoly or imperfect competition. And the irony of it all is that Marx had correctly predicted the transformation of capitalism from a purely competitive system of his day to its present form of a constrained, monopolistic system. This by itself is no mean accomplishment. Under monopoly conditions, part of labor's contribution to the total product is expropriated by the entrepreneur in terms of monopoly profit, and there is exploitation in this sense. Thus Marx really did not have to tread the circuitous route of labor theory of value to establish that capitalism engenders exploitation of the working class.

None the less, if the labor theory of value is accepted, then it follows that capitalism can be nothing but exploitative. Any profit or "surplus value," as Marx called it, can exist only if labor is denied its full share. But how can capitalism endure without surplus value?

What then is the value of labor or its wage rate? Marx treated labor under capitalism as a commodity, and its value too could not deviate far from the labor time necessary to produce it, i.e., from the level of consumption on which a worker can barely survive. Thus under capitalism a worker labors partly to earn a bare subsistence wage, and partly for the manufacturer's surplus value.

Under competitive conditions where the wage rate is governed by forces of demand and supply for labor, how is the subsistence wage to prevail? In order to ensure this, Marx introduced his concept of a reserve army of unemployed labor. Without unemployment the competition among entrepreneurs for scarce labor would raise the wage rate to a level where surplus value could all but disappear. However, well before this point is reached capitalists resort to labor-saving inventions that result in a decline in demand for labor, in unemployment, and hence in the move back towards the subsistence wage.

After all this is said, where is the element of contradiction in capitalism? Evidently the clash between the two camps has to become progressively bitter, until the workers, sick of their wretched conditions, rise in revolt and seize power in their own hands. Indeed, this is precisely the scenario laid out by Marx.

The capitalist is interested not only in maximizing surplus value from his investments, but also in exalting his sociopolitical status, which to him depends only on his affluence. Moreover, he must be frugal, must save money to grow, to stay in competition with others, to invest in new inventions, lest other capitalists devour him and take over his enterprise. Thus the system itself goads him to accumulate capital rather than spend all or most of his income for the consumption of goods.

Such economic behavior can backfire. Excessive frugality of capitalists can lead to a shortfall in the aggregate demand for commodities which must be sold if the surplus value is to be realized. If all savings find outlets in investment, then there is no problem: the demand for investment goods, when added to that of consumption goods, will then match the aggregate supply. But the rate of investment depends crucially on the rate of profit, defined as a ratio between the surplus value and the value of the capital stock. Marx argued that the rate of profit declines with increased capital accumulation, thereby choking the inducement for investment. It is this declining tendency of the rate of profit that turns out to be the Marxian lever generating contradictions in capitalism, adding to internal strike and collisions.

Eventually, therefore, the seeds of strife are sown by the very process of capital accumulation which gives rise to two forces tending to sever the roots of capitalism. First, the rate of profit tends to decline and so does investment. Second, the labor-saving inventions resulting from accumulation tend to cancel out any positive effect that the growth-induced rise in wage rates has on consumption demand. The end-result of this process is that at some point the aggregate demand falls short of total production, thereby further stifling the rate of investment.

Once this starts, a chain-reaction sets in. Falling investment increases unemployment in the capital-goods sector; this, along with the resulting diminution in wages, causes a decline in the demand for consumption goods, creating unemployment in that sector as well; manufacturers in turn are left with more unsold goods and the rate of profit slides again, and so on.

Thus an initial spark in the capitalistic economy, through its linkage effects, may flare into a conflagration; a booming economy may move into a recession and then a depression. This malaise of capitalism Marx foresaw more than a century ago. He was the first to proclaim that violent economic oscillations bedevil nothing but the market-dominated system, not because of recurring external traumas, but because of self-generated contradictions.

Once the economy is caught in the throes of depression, all groups suffer—workers much more than capitalists. Among the latter, smaller firms fall first and are in turn gobbled up by the larger firms. It is this process—occurring many times over long periods—which ultimately diminishes the number of manufacturers to such a level that monopolies and oligopolies are born. The smaller capitalists, overwhelmed by bigger ones, also join the ranks of the unemployed, thereby exerting further downward pressure on the already abysmal wage rates. The misery of the working class then beggars description; for a while the wage rate may be pushed even below the subsistence level.

Marx, however, did not believe that a depression would endure for ever. Output tumbles faster than the wage rate, so that eventually aggregate supply falls below aggregate demand and the rate of profit is restored at some respectable level. Once this happens, investment and employment rise anew, and so does national income. To Marx, then, economy under capitalism does not grow in a straight line, but rather in cycles, in boom and bust where unemployment among workers soars to high levels.

The progressive concentration of capital in the the hands of the few spells misery for the working class, at least relatively, if not absolutely. Marx argued that economic cycles, after capitalism reached a certain stage, would become more frequent and wider in amplitude. The lot of the laborers, at least during depressions, would progressively get worse; even during happier times, working conditions would be anything but comfortable, while capitalists wallowed in ever increasing affluence. This is Marx's celebrated "doctrine of increasing misery" for laborers. It prophesies progressive poverty for workers relative to capitalists.

While the number of capitalists declines, the working class swells. As communications improve with advancement in technology, the proletariat frequently come in touch with each other, become aware of their pitiful conditions, organize into unions, and turn into a formidable force. A time would come, argued Marx, when the workers would stay calm no more; they would rise in rebellion against the capitalist order, and then usher in a new era where the means of production would be collectively owned. Private property would cease and society become classless: no private ownership, no classes.

The post-capitalistic socioeconomic organization, according to Marx, is socialism, which is to be followed by communism. Under socialism some relics of capitalism remain, because private property and its creed can be only gradually abolished; communism is simply unadulterated socialism where all vestiges of capitalism have been buried in the grave. All people then become free. No more are there any social divisions or any antagonisms. Hence there is no impetus to change, and everyone lives happily everafter, enjoying a high standard of living, which to Marx is the one wholesome bequest of capitalism to humanity.

This furnishes the Marxian circle of socioeconomic evolution. The society began with the communal land ownership of pre-capitalistic times, unmolested by any divisions caused by private property; it will end up with communism, where again all property—land, money, buildings, machinery—is jointly owned, thereby completing the full circle of evolution.

SARKARIAN AND MARXIAN THOUGHT: A COMPARISON

Despite some contradictions of its own, there is much imperishable truth and resilience in the Marxian prognosis of social change. Marx's philosophy has been subjected by critics to careful and minute dissection, but its beauty lies in the fact that, after all its weak links are severed, its fundamental point is undeniable, namely that capitalism suffers from severe contradictions, that the profit-seeking, wealth-accumulating propensities of the wealthy must shoulder blame for the recurrence of business cycles, which, quite often in the last two centuries, have shaken the very foundations of Western civilization. Even today the threat of recessions looms like a Sword of Damocles over the shaky capitalistic economies.

In comparing Marx's system with Sarkar's, one is immediately struck by their divergence as well as their similarity. However, the similarities are not many and can be disposed of quickly.

Both Marx and Sarkar use a historical method of analysis, both believe in the inevitability of historical patterns of societal evolution, though not in the repetition of events themselves, and both agree that capitalism will be brought to an end by some sort of revolution, although to Sarkar this revolution may be bloody or peaceful, whereas to Marx it will be bloody and violent. Marx calls it the revolution of the proletariat, whereas to Sarkar it is the social revolution of the laborers; but the laborers and the proletariat have much in common. They are both victims of the capitalist's unbridled rapacity, of his penchant for more and more wealth, although Sarkar's laborers are vulnerable to exploitation in every facet of civilization. One might say that, as far as the description of capitalism is concerned, Sarkar draws on Marx in some respects. In a rare reference to Marx, Sarkar looks at him in an unconventional light:

> Centering round a remark about religion by the great Karl Marx, a class of exploiters goes hysteric and raises quite a storm. It should be borne in mind that Karl Marx was never antagonistic to spiritualism, moralism and good conduct. Whatever he said was against the then religion, for he had visualized, understood and felt that the then religion had paralyzed man mentally, made him impotent and despirited by instigating him to submit to the vicious circle. [7, p. 122]

Sarkar himself, while driving a wedge between spirituality and blind faith in religious dogmas, believes that emissaries of religion have in the past exploited humanity in every civilization, and continue to do so even today.

With this, the similarities between Marxian and Sarkarian thought end. Even a cursory reading of the previous chapters suggests that Sarkar's theory is immensely more general and realistic than Marxism. The latter is simply a special case of the former, one link in Sarkar's chain of social cycle.

In the first place, the Marxian message is intensely materialistic, relegating humans to the inertness of matter, whereas Sarkar's message is intensely spiritual, relying totally on the human spirit and mental characteristics. In this respect the latter is closer to Hegel and, as we shall see subsequently, to Toynbee than to Marx. The material aspect, however, is not ignored by Sarkar; it reflects itself in the laborer and the acquisitive mind, and to some degree in all human beings. But here also one discerns the human element in his philosophy. Even in the acquisitive age, economic forces, to Sarkar, shape social destiny through the medium of acquisitive human intellect, as opposed to the Marxian contention that material forces determine human consciousness and institutions at all times.

There is an element of tautology in the Marxian assertion that human beings have to survive before historical change can occur, because if survival were the only relevant factor then society would never have changed. If survival is all that counts, then why have so many men and women in the past died for a cause, for an ideal? Why would people of gallantry prefer death in war to a comfortable life at home? Why did some spend all their life in the search for truth and enlightenment, enduring at times unbelievable sufferings?

Another difference between the two systems lies in their perception of the laboring class. To Sarkar no society can even survive without the sweat and toil of laborers, but they seldom, if ever, come to power, a view that contradicts the Marxian prophecy that under socialism the proletariat will rule. Even in Russia and China, where Marxism has now been adopted as the way of life, not the worker, but an elitist group with warrior attitudes towards military and social discipline reigns supreme. It is perhaps unfair to admonish Marx for this, because we are the beneficiary of hindsight and he was not. By contrast, Sarkar's laborer revolution is not led by the proletariat, but by a coalition of intellectuals, military officers and skilled workers, i.e., by the cooperative efforts of disgruntled warriors and intellectuals diminished, by the acquisitor's (or capitalistic) rapacity, to the laborer standard of living.

Sarkar's main concern with the human element is what imparts universality to his thesis. Thus while social evolution according to Marx is governed chiefly by economic conditions, to Sarkar this dynamics is propelled by forces varying with time and space: sometimes physical prowess and high-spiritedness, sometimes intellect applied to dogmas, and sometimes intellect applied to the accumulation of wealth determine the movement of society.

Quite clearly, the Marxian view of history is myopic in comparison with the Sarkarian vision. In terms of Sarkar's terminology, the Marxian analysis implies that the acquisitors, and hence the economic factor, have always ruled society, whereas Sarkar maintains that their turn to rule comes only after warriors and intellectuals have had their turns. Marx calls upon one single element to illuminate the entire past as well as future, whereas Sarkar does this by relying on four fundamental elements rooted in human mind: Sarkarism, therefore, derives from human evolution, Marxism from material existence.

Another fundamental difference between the two viewpoints is that according to Marx Communism is the pinnacle of society after which there is no social evolution, but in the Sarkarian view every phase of society is a passing phenomenon. Sarkar is very explicit and emphatic on this point. To him social evolution signifies a relative movement of society, one among so many other relative movements which are all interconnected. Therefore if social evolution stops, then all relative movements, interwoven as they are, must cease, and this in effect is the death of the universe. In other words, societal evolution will endure as long as the universe does: there is no final synthesis; there cannot be one.

Furthermore, Sarkar's theory tosses Communism out of the realm of possibility. To him, since there are four basic types of mental attitude in human beings, there are four types of era through which every civilization has to pass. Thus one mental tendency will always be preponderant in society; not that one class will always exploit the others, only that its mores, preferences and idiosyncracies will fashion the behavior of the other three. Hence the classless society that Marx envisioned simply cannot exist. It is a utopia, and not a desirable one either, for its attainment amounts to society's dissolution.

It is not my intention to be over-critical and chastise Marx—as others have done—for minor points such as the failure of some of his prophecies. That his foresight could not completely pierce through the obscurity of the future does not diminish his analysis one bit. Some of his predictions have in fact been affirmed. What matters is the acumen with which he knitted together the discordant pieces from history, sociology and economics into a cohesion that distinguishes him as one of the most gifted writers of all time. My contention that the law of social cycle is more general is not meant to disparage Marxian contributions to humanity, but merely to underline the merits of Sarkar's thought.

TOYNBEE'S VIEW OF HISTORY

Among the current hypotheses concerning the rise and fall of civilizations, among those with which the world is well familiar, Toynbee's views appear to be the most general and cosmopolitan in scope [9]. He stands before us as perhaps the most awe-inspiring figure among historians; his work commands universal respect, his erudition a world-wide esteem. However, Sarkar's contribution, though drawing upon Toynbee's thought in some ways, turns out to be even more general. As with Marxism, Toynbee's system will also be shown to be a special case of Sarkar's.

Toynbee is among the first historians to escape the narrow confines of parochialism, and venture into universalism. He is contemptuous of nationalism in any form; civilizations to him are the only acceptable units of study, not states, nor nations.

In Toynbee's view there have been twenty-one civilizations, including the present-day survivors.[1] Of these, fifteen are affiliated to certain predecessors in the sense that the new civilization is born out of the ruins of its parent, which towards its end is established as a "Universal State." The Universal State, specifically, is an immense empire into which the previous civilization near its end had been organized; from this empire, the succeeding society inherits a "Universal Church" which represents a new religion with roots in the "internal proletariat," a body of people exploited by the dominant minority mentioned in Chapter 2.

By the internal proletariat Toynbee means not the Marxian laboring class but the common masses who are on the fringes of society, and who feel left out of the inner core of civilization. The fall of the Universal State is brought about by assaults from the neighboring barbarians (Toynbee's *Völkerwanderung*) who had been living on the borders of its territory.

Thus the relationship between the new and the old civilization resembles the parent-child affinity, because through this child's veins runs the ideology of the Universal Church, which later is going to nourish it into adolescence and maturity. Of the twenty-one civilizations, fifteen are affiliated to the original six, which had no parents and which generated themselves by vigorously meeting the obstacles created by the natural environment.

Of the six pristine or unaffiliated civilizations, two—the Egyptian and the Andean—left few traces, whereas the other four—Sinic, Minoan, Sumerian, Mayan—are still pulsating through their progeny. Four more, Hittite, Syriac, Indic, Hellenic, had remote familial ties—not characterized by the presence of Universal Churches—while three, Babylonian, Yucatec, Mexican, had much closer (or "supra-affiliated") ties with their parents. There are six more which are simply affiliates—Western, Orthodox Christian, Far Eastern, Iranic, Arabic, Hindu—while another two are distinct offshoots, the Russian belonging to the Orthodox Christian society and the Japanese-Korean to the Far Eastern society. This completes the list of twenty-one civilizations.

How were the parent civilizations born? According to Toynbee, when primitive societies successfully respond to challenges posed by adversity and hardship, civilizations come into being. It is not the salubrious soil, nor the benign climate, nor the racial element, but the spirited and triumphant battle with mighty obstacles that ought to get the accolade.

The salutary environment to Toynbee may have some influence, but it cannot be the important factor. The important factor is the "Challenge" which, however, should not be too severe, otherwise any "Response" from the struggling people will be relatively weak and inadequate to overcome the formidable obstacles. Therefore Toynbee speaks in terms of a balance, a golden mean, wherein the Challenge is harsh but not too harsh to smother the Response.

The challenge itself has been different from place to place. It may be an abrupt climatic change, or a soil turning into a barren land, or the menace of alien nations. The important point is that it is not the bountiful environment but its severity that has been the cradle of civilizations.

While a civilization springs from the increasing mastery of society over the environment, its growth depends on the rise of some creative persons or a "creative minority," which is emulated by the uncreative majority. Growth occurs when the challenge increases in severity and is met successfully by an even more resolute response from some gifted beings. Thus if the adversity grows strong, but the resolve to overcome it grows stronger, victory and hence the rapid development of society are assured.

In other words, a civilization once born need not continue to exist on a high pedestal; if it fails to meet new challenges, it will fail to blossom. This to Toynbee explains why some societies—such as the Eskimos, the Nomads, the Polynesians—were born but were prematurely "arrested." In other words, there is nothing automatic in the growth of an infant civilization. It needs nourishment, fresh stimuli and the helping genius of creative personalities.

Unfortunately, the creative persons are always in limited supply, and their continued emergence over long periods is rare. This is the basic cause of a civilization's breakdown of which so many have been the victims. Not that all civilizations have to meet this fate. Toynbee is quite emphatic on this matter. Seeking to differentiate himself from Spengler (that champion of an iron-clad law assuring the demise of every system) he makes it clear that civilizations are not like physical organisms, that if they decline then some internal "schism" is to blame, not any inexorable law of senescence.

The schisms appear in the form of social "mimesis" whereby the majority follows the minority in a blind, mechanical way; in the form of parasitic institutions embodying everything that is narrow and parochial—religious rites, rituals, caste systems; and in the form of excessive militarism that eventually succeeds in transforming the polity into a behemoth—the Universal State. All these fissures are internal. Occasionally external traumas may add fuel to the fire, but the initial disruptive spark flares from within.

The initial breakdown gradually turns into a rout. The creative minority degenerates into a dominant minority, which becomes increasingly oppressive of the masses, who in turn come into conflict with the powers-that-be and welcome any new redeeming philosophy. This is how a Universal Church comes into being. It meets open hostility from the ruling minority but a warm reception from the internal proletariat. In due course the church rises to primacy, order is restored, but the society now emerges with a new visage, bearing little resemblance to the old. Thus nations may be old, the past territorial limits may remain unchanged, but the civilization of which the nations are part is now different. This is how an offspring becomes "affiliated" to its parent civilization.

Here then is a bare skeleton of Toynbee's voluminous work which encompasses the entire history of humankind—all those millennia, beginning with the Neolithic period, of which we have knowledge.

COMPARISON BETWEEN TOYNBEE AND SARKAR

Toynbee and Sarkar seem to have an affinity in many of their views, but differences of a real and subtle character also exist. To both the historical process is rooted in the human spirit; material forces do count, but only in being the adversary over which human fortitude must prevail if a primitive society is ever to evolve into a civilization. However, in this respect Sarkar goes further by pinpointing the type of mentality which can overcome the challenges posed by the environment. To him only the warrior mind, with the active assistance of the laborers, can initially vanquish the mighty and hostile forces of nature. Perhaps the difference is only semantic; Sarkar is nevertheless more specific on this point.

A difference of deeper significance lies in the fact that Sarkar's prognosis does not rule out the salutary effects of favorable soil and climatic conditions that may lend a helping hand in the development of civilizations. For his total disregard of these factors, Toynbee has been severely taken to task by his critics. But in Sarkar's system, the growth of civilizations depends not so much on the severity of the environment and the mettlesome response that it invokes, but on the rise of the high-spirited warrior mind.

Even if no challenge appears, a civilization may emerge if the primitive society is led by a warrior mind, for this type of mind does not rest until total mastery over matter is achieved; and I do not have to labor the point that human mastery over nature even today is far from complete. Thus regardless of whether the environment is friendly or hostile, the vivacity of the warrior mind creates challenges of its own, and endeavors to meet them fearlessly and with dignity. This would explain the genesis of some civilizations which in their infancy encountered comparatively few misfortunes.

The difference here is more real than apparent. While Toynbee's accent is on both the harshness of material surroundings and the human spirit, Sarkar emphasizes only the human element and ultimately the natural human evolution. The Challenge, in the Sarkarian view, has its place, but it may spring from the hostile environment or be self-created by the warrior mind.

In Toynbee's view there is little affinity between civilizations—which are dynamic societies—and primitive communities, which he regards as entities flowing at a rate of evolution so low that to all intents and purposes they can be considered as static societies. The crucial distinction, therefore, lies in the rate of growth in a society's evolution.

Sarkar would perhaps be uncomfortable with Toynbee's definition of a primitive society, for to him nothing is static in this universe, "thronged as it is with a plethora of relativities." He therefore defines a primitive society also in terms of mental characteristics, i.e. in terms of the early laborer community. Again this difference is perhaps semantic. However, Toynbee's taste for total differentiation between primitive and civilized societies finds full expression in his somewhat arbitrary distinction between civilizations—between parent and "affiliated" societies. True, his Universal States and Universal Churches are reminiscent of some of Sarkar's warrior and intellectual eras; but to Sarkar they both belong to the same society, as two arms of the same social cycle, whereas for Toynbee the Universal Church provides the line of demarcation between the old and the new civilization.

Sarkar regards civilizations as entities that have evolved from primitive societies just as civilized humanity evolved from the primitive human being. To him the intimate anthropological kinship between the primitive and the civilized also extends to civilizations, a view that sharply contrasts with Toynbee's. Furthermore, Toynbee does not adequately explain why the Universal Church emerges toward the end of the parent civilization. Why religion, why not any mundane philosophy? Why not any other military power? To Sarkar the transition from the warrior to the intellectual era, or from Toynbee's Universal State to the Universal Church, is just an integral part of the evolutionary social cycle, something ingrained in the process of human evolution. For the subtler intellect of the intellectuals evolved on our planet much later than the high-spiritedness of the warriors. But upon its arrival, it had little difficulty in winning over the warrior mind.

It is hard to concur with Toynbee and pretend that civilizations have emerged abruptly out of primitive societies, especially when many historians believe that perhaps agriculture, more than anything else, procreated and nurtured all civilizations. In this view, the prerequisite for the dynamic movement of every society is the availability of an economic surplus, something that frees some people from toiling just for subsistence; consequently a part of society's energies can be devoted to subtle and creative avocations—architecture, music, art, literature. If the presence of economic surplus is the precondition for social progress, then civilizations must have sprouted from the primitive, Neolithic culture of which the most distinctive features are agriculture and the domestication of animals.

Sarkar believes in the unity and continuity of civilizations, whereas Toynbee, as stated before, first divides them into parents and their affiliates, and then distinguishes them by the presence of Universal States and Universal Churches.[2] These two institutions are implicit in Sarkar's warrior and intellectual eras. For example, the period of the Universal State into which the Roman Empire had been organized at the dawn of the first century is identical to Sarkar's warrior era of Western civilization. Similarly, the primacy of the Catholic Church following the collapse of the Roman State coincides with Sarkar's intellectual era of the same civilization, but to Toynbee, of course, it is now a new society.

Moreover, Sarkar, unlike Toynbee, does not stop with these two institutions but goes on to introduce his acquisitive era that follows upon the decline of the intellectuals, who were ruling through the Church. All these eras are identified with the mentality of the dominant social class, whereas in Toynbee's system particular periods of history are associated with the institutions that for a long time endured in various civilizations. Therefore if these institutions vanish from the face of the earth or lose their vitality, which they all do at one time or another, then to Toynbee a civilization is either dissolved or affiliated to its offspring. But since Sarkar speaks in terms of the lasting features of the human mind, his theory is flexible, is capable of assimilating novel organizations, mores and customs. That is why his eras may appear time and again during the course of history, of the past and of the future, even though human institutions, rules and laws, because of natural evolution, must go through numerous alterations.

Toynbee's admission of only two long-lasting and worldwide organizations—the Universal States and Churches—in a way compels him to be unusually gloomy about the prospects of Western civilization, which he thinks has been declining ever since the sixteenth century when the Universal Church in Europe was weakened by the rise of autocratic monarchs and by the Wars of Religion. He is particularly emphatic about the paralytic consequences of the religious wars of Germany, France and Spain—especially the loss of faith. There is plenty of arbitrariness here, a point noted by other historians, especially by Geyl [1], but it need not be our concern. For some reasons, real or imagined, Toynbee views the declining influence of religion as disastrous for Western society, whose breakdown to him actually began, believe it or not, four centuries ago. And he insists that once the breakdown begins, it is irretrievable; euthanasia cannot then be averted, no matter how solid the subsequent achievements of some of its individual members may be. Thus in his view, the West is now lingering through the period of disintegration, with no known timetable.

To my mind it is the paucity of "universal" institutions in his system that makes Toynbee so pessimistic about the prospects of the Western world; once the Universal Church collapses, what is left? Dissolution of course, or merger into a new civilization! However, Sarkar's framework is more sanguine; his hypothesis is resilient enough to accommodate all changes. It suggests that the West is now in the decadent phase of the acquisitive era, which, since no age can endure for ever, should eventually be replaced by a new warrior era. Thus one arm of the organic social cycle will be replaced by another, but Western civilization will survive, and perhaps emerge with greater effulgence. Of course, the new warrior era will not be dominated by monarchs and tyrannical dictators. This is simply unthinkable. But a group that displays martial qualities will be supreme. He does not say all this in so many words, but it is implicit in his discourse.

All the critics who have taken Toynbee to task for numerous errors of omission and commission are single-minded in acclaiming his work for its singular contribution not, ironically, to history but to literature—even to fiction. Some have characterized Toynbee's system as a figment of his bountiful imagination, while others have called it an outright fraud. His critics stand in awe before his monumental and voluminous work, but they do not concede its veracity. Volumes have been written as critiques of Toynbee's thought and it is not my intention to add much to them (see Stromberg [8] for a summation). Nor am I among his critics, who certainly have some valid points of their own. I think Toynbee went a bit too far. If only he had scaled down his claims, if only he had not attempted to expound almost every historical episode in terms of a perceptible cause, his following today would be much larger than it is. In any case, there is much in Toynbee's message that will endure for ever.

It is upon these enduring pillars that Sarkar constructs his thesis. Toynbee's work is a start, and Sarkar adds the finishing touch, plus much more. But in so doing he avoids many of Toynbee's errors. Thus Sarkar simply outlines a broad pattern of historical evolution, but is not so specific about a society's laws of growth and decay, because he realizes that such laws cannot be explained in terms of a single cause.[3] In his own way he recognizes Toynbee's Universal States and Churches, but, in concurrence with the latter's critics, he does not believe that the Universal

Church provides a dividing line between the old and the new civilization. Thus a civilization may endure for ever, although its distinctive institutions may come and go. It is in this way that Sarkar builds where Toynbee, and also Marx, have left off.

NOTES

1. In a later revision, Toynbee's civilizations swelled to as many as thirty.

2. Sarkar's conception of the unity of history is, of course, totally different from the obsolete European version, which exalted the West to the exclusion of every other social organism. To Sarkar, the unity of history is rooted in the fact that all civilizations have to evolve along the tracks of the law of social cycle.

3. In another volume [6], Sarkar does delineate in some detail the basic elements that propel the engine of social change, but there again he speaks in terms of broad generalization, rather than slip into the pitfall of specificity. Also see Raghunath [5] in this connection.

REFERENCES

[1] Geyl, Peter, *Debates With Historians* (Cleveland: World Publishing Co., 1962).

[2] Marx, Karl, *Pre-Capitalistic Economic Formations* (London: Lawrence & Wishart, 1964).

[3] ———, *Writings of the Young Marx on Philosophy and Society* (New York: Doubleday, 1967).

[4] ———, and F. Engels, "The Communist Manifesto," in *Essential Works of Marxism*, ed., A. P. Mendel (New York: Bantam, 1965).

[5] Raghunath, Acharya, *A New Interpretation of History* (Denver: Ananda Marga Press, 1972).

[6] Sarkar, P. R., *Idea and Ideology* (Denver: Ananda Marga Press, 1959).

[7] ———, *Human Society:* Part II (Denver: Ananda Marga Press, 1967).

[8] Stromberg, R. N., *Arnold J. Toynbee: Historian for an Age in Crisis* (Carbondale: Southern Illinois University Press, 1972).

[9] Toynbee, A. J., *A Study of History,* Vols I–X (London: Oxford University Press, 1961).

Index